Jesus Tried and True

Jesus Tried and True

Why the Four Canonical Gospels Provide
the Best Picture of Jesus

H. H. Drake Williams III

WIPF & STOCK · Eugene, Oregon

JESUS TRIED AND TRUE
Why the Four Canonical Gospels Provide the Best Picture of Jesus

Copyright © 2013 H. H. Drake Williams III. All rights reserved. Except for brief quotations in critical publications or reviews, no part of this book may be reproduced in any manner without prior written permission from the publisher. Write: Permissions, Wipf and Stock Publishers, 199 W. 8th Ave., Suite 3, Eugene, OR 97401.

Wipf & Stock
An Imprint of Wipf and Stock Publishers
199 W. 8th Ave., Suite 3
Eugene, OR 97401
www.wipfandstock.com

ISBN 13: 978-1-61097-526-1

Manufactured in the U.S.A.

Scripture quotations marked ESV are from the *Holy Bible, English Standard Version*® (ESV®). Copyright© 2001 by Crossway, a publishing ministry of Good News Publishers. Used by permission. All rights reserved.

Scripture quotations marked NIV are taken from the *Holy Bible, New International Version*® (NIV®). Copyright© 1973, 1978, 1984 by Biblica, Inc.™ Used by permission of Zondervan. All rights reserved worldwide.

All Scripture texts are taken from the ESV unless otherwise stated.

To my mother Sandra (Sandy) S. Williams,
who first taught me to "consider the source"

Contents

Acknowledgments ix
List of Abbreviations xi
Introduction xv

Chapter One   Gospel Dating / 1

Chapter Two   Eyewitness Testimony / 29

Chapter Three   Gospel Reception in Early Church History / 66

Chapter Four   Other Gospels / 100

Chapter Five   Conclusion / 132

Appendix 1— Secret Gospel of Mark / 139
Appendix 2—Early Christian Creeds / 142
Bibliography / 145
Index of Scripture, Ancient Texts, and Ancient Authors / 155

Acknowledgments

I WOULD LIKE TO thank Jordan Scheetz, Tom Marinello, Henry Baldwin, David McKinley, Dirk Jongkind, Dave Luz, Laura Thomas, and Dory Hofstra for their encouragement for this work. Gregory C. Benoit helped greatly as a copy editor. Christian Amondson and Tina Campbell Owens also helped greatly with the production of this manuscript. It was a blessing to access resources from Tyndale House in Cambridge, England and the Vrije Universiteit in Amsterdam, the Netherlands. Students, staff, and the faculty at Tyndale Theological Seminary in Badhoevedorp, the Netherlands, and church members at the Central Schwenkfelder Church in Worcester, PA sharpened my thinking considerably. A grant from the Schwenkfelder General Conference Board of Publication as well as an anonymous donor helped significantly in this publication. Conversations with my children, Henry, Abigail, and Sam have stimulated my thinking considerably. Most of all I thank my loving wife Andrea Williams for her patience and support.

List of Abbreviations

AB	Anchor Bible
ABD	Freedman, D. N., et al. *The Anchor Bible Dictionary*. 6 Volumes. New York: Doubleday, 1992.
AHR	American Historical Review
AnBib	Analecta biblica
ANF	*The Ante-Nicene Fathers: Translations of the writings of the Fathers down to AD 325*. 10 Volumes. Edited by Roberts A. and J. Donaldson. Grand Rapids: Eerdmans, 1969.
AThR	Anglican Theological Review
BA	Biblical Archaeologist
BECNT	Baker Exegetical Commentary on the New Testament
BETL	Bibliotheca ephemeridum theologicarum lovaniensium
CBQ	*Catholic Biblical Quarterly*
CGTC	Cambridge Greek Testament Commentary
CUP	Cambridge University Press
DJG	Green, J. B. and S. McKnight, editors. *Dictionary of Jesus and the Gospels*. Downers Grove: IVP, 1992.
ECNT	Evangelical Commentary of the New Testament
EKKNT	Evangelisch-katholisher Kommentar zum Neuen Testament
ETL	*Ephemerides theologicae lovanienses*
ExpTim	*Expository Times*
FF	Foundations and Facets
HeyJ	*Heythrop Journal*
HTKNT	Herders theologischer Kommentar zum Neuen Testament

List of Abbreviations

HTR	*Harvard Theological Review*
HTS	Harvard Theological Studies
ICC	International Critical Commentary
IEJ	*Israel Exploration Journal*
IVP	Inter-Varsity Press
JBL	*Journal of Biblical Literature*
JECS	*Journal of Early Christian Studies*
JETS	*Journal of the Evangelical Theological Society*
JJS	*Journal of Jewish Studies*
JSNTSup	Supplements to the Journal for the Study of the New Testament
JSOT	Journal for the Study of the Old Testament
JTS	*Journal of Theological Studies*
LCL	Loeb Classical Library
LNTS	Library of New Testament Studies
NCB	New Century Bible
NICNT	New International Commentary on the New Testament
NIGTC	New International Greek Testament Commentary
NovT	*Novum Testamentum*
NovTSup	Supplements to *Novum Testamentum*
NPNF2	*The Nicene and Post-Nicene Fathers*. 14 Volumes. Edited by P. Schaff and H. Wace. Grand Rapids: Eerdmans, 1975.
NTL	New Testament Library
NTS	*New Testament Studies*
NTTS	New Testament Tools and Studies
OTM	Oxford Theological Monograph
OUP	Oxford University Press
PETSE	Papers of the Estonian Theological Society in Exile
PNTC	Pillar New Testament Commentary
SCJ	Studies in Christianity and Judaism

List of Abbreviations

SCM	Student Christian Movement
SNT	Studien zum Neuen Testament
SPCK	Society for Promoting Christian Knowledge
TENT	Texts and Editions for New Testament Study
TNTC	Tyndale New Testament Commentaries
VC	*Vigiliae christianae*
VCSup	Supplements to *Vigiliae christianae*
WBC	Word Biblical Commentary
WUNT	Wissenschaftliche Untersuchungen zum Neuen Testament
ZNW	*Zeitschrift für die neutestamentliche Wissenshaft und die Kunde der älteren Kirche*

All abbreviations of biblical and extra biblical literature are from the Society of Biblical Literature style guide. See P. H. Alexander, *The SBL Handbook of Style: For Ancient Near Eastern, Biblical, and Early Christian Studies*. Peabody: Hendrickson, 1999.

Introduction

THE CHURCH HAS TAUGHT throughout the ages that Jesus is both fully God and fully man. This viewpoint is found in Matthew, Mark, Luke, and John, the four gospels of the New Testament. It is also found from the times of the early Christian creeds, such as the Nicene Creed and the Apostles' Creed.[1]

Recently, however, there have been novel viewpoints about Jesus that are getting attention. A significant source for these doubts has been the heightened awareness of non-canonical gospels. These gospels are not a part of the New Testament and have largely been out of the public eye. Many would call them apocryphal, meaning heretical or unorthodox. In the past, they were considered to be of questionable value and authority, but recently many are taking fresh interest in non-canonical gospels.[2]

The most noteworthy of these is the *Gospel of Thomas*. This *Gospel* does not include any miracles, stories, or anything about the crucifixion. Instead, it contains 114 secret teachings of Jesus which claim to be recorded by Didymus Judas Thomas. Some of these sayings appear to resemble the New Testament gospels, while others are clearly different from anything in the Bible. These present a secret knowledge imparted from Jesus about the world, and offer a mystical and elitist version of Christian living focused on self-denial, secret interpretations, and higher realities. Anyone who understands these, the text claims, will have eternal life.

The *Gospel of Thomas* was found in the desert of Egypt in a place just outside of Nag Hammadi in 1945. Besides *Thomas*, there were other gospels that were found there that are also attracting attention. The *Gospel of Philip*, the *Gospel of Truth*, and the *Gospel of the Egyptians* were also

1. For these creeds, see Appendix 1.
2. While the term *apocryphal* has been used for many years to describe these books, it does have negative associations. This volume will use the terms *canonical* and *non-canonical* for distinguishing gospels. The canonical gospels are the ones in the New Testament: Matthew, Mark, Luke, and John. All other gospels will be considered non-canonical. Further discussion of the term apocryphal will occur in the conclusion in chapter 5.

Introduction

found in the same location. Like the *Gospel of Thomas*, these promote the search for hidden truth, deny worldly existence, and encourage elitism. They are generally known to be Gnostic gospels.

There are other non-canonical gospels that provide information about parts of Jesus' life that are not found in the New Testament. For example, the *Gospel of Peter* recounts what happened between Jesus' death and his resurrection appearances to his disciples. The *Infancy Gospel of Thomas* provides entertaining reports of Jesus' early life. The *Protevangelium of James* recounts the birth, young life, and betrothal of Mary, and then Jesus' own birth. In *Papyrus Egerton 2*, there are several confrontations that Jesus had with Jewish leaders, and then a few additional miracles in addition to those that are found in the New Testament.

There are several Jewish-Christian gospels. Jesus' life and earliest following was in the context of Judaism. These share a Jewish background but support Jesus of Nazareth as the chosen Messiah. While there is no full length manuscript preserved from these *Gospels*, there are fragments available. Their titles are known through the works of early Christian writers and include the *Gospel of the Hebrews*, the *Gospel of the Nazareans*, and the *Gospel of the Ebionites*.

One final category of non-canonical gospels includes those books that involve dialogues and secret revelations. There is the *Gospel of Mary*, the only gospel which claims to be written by a woman. It presents a secret vision granted to Mary Magdalene by Jesus, which she now relates to the apostles. The *Gospel of Judas* is the latest to be discovered. It contains a dialogue between Jesus and Judas three days before Jesus' last Passover and completely recasts the church's understanding of Judas as the betrayer. It paints Judas as a hero rather than as a villain. These are just brief descriptions of some of the other gospels.[3]

Problems arise, however, when these other gospels are being used unfairly to challenge the historic viewpoint of Jesus and the way that the church has represented him for centuries. This took place most notoriously when Dan Brown released his novel and film, *The Da Vinci Code*. These presented the church as arbitrarily choosing certain gospels and leaving others out. According to Brown, the Roman Emperor Constantine appeared to choose only four gospels, the ones that he wanted to have, while neglecting approximately eighty others. This, as the novel

---

3. See further chapter 4.

says, took place at the Council of Nicaea in AD 325. According to Brown, it was uncertain whether Jesus was divine or human until this Council, nearly 300 years after the life of Christ.[4] Brown's book and movie caught the interest of millions.

Following the release of the *Da Vinci Code*, the discovery of the *Gospel of Judas* was used to challenge the church's viewpoint about Jesus. The British newspaper *The Daily Mail* ran an initial story with the headline, "The Gospel of Judas Iscariot: World Exclusive 'Greatest Archaeological Discovery of all Time' Threat to 2000 years of Christian teaching."[5] Many scholars were not willing to go so far, but some stated that the *Gospel of Judas* will change our opinion of who Jesus is. Implying that it would turn Christianity on its head, Bart Ehrman wrote concerning the *Gospel of Judas*, "It will open up new vistas for understanding Jesus and the religious movement he founded."[6]

There are many books that are being circulated which are challenging the historic viewpoint of Jesus as is found in the canonical New Testament Gospels. In an English bookshop in Amsterdam near where I live and work, the religion section is filled with books about other gospels with titles that provocatively cast doubt upon the way Jesus has been historically portrayed. The titles of a few of these works relating to these other gospels express the doubts clearly: *The Five Gospels: What Did Jesus Really Say? The Search for the Authentic Words of Jesus*,[7] *The Gnostic Gospels of Jesus: The Definitive Collection of Mystical Gospels and Secret Books about Jesus of Nazareth*,[8] and *Lost Christianities: The Battles for Scripture and the Faiths we never knew*.[9]

Some of these books unashamedly cast doubt on Jesus as presented in the church's tradition. For example, in the New York Times Bestseller *Jesus, Interrupted: Revealing the Hidden Contradictions in the Bible (and Why We Don't Know about Them)*, Bart Ehrman presents a "wild diversity" in the early church. He writes:

---

4. Brown, *The Da Vinci Code*, 231–33.
5. "Greatest Archaeological Discovery," *The Mail*.
6. Ehrman, "Christianity Turned on its Head," 80.
7. See Funk, *Five Gospels*.
8. See Meyer, *Gnostic Gospels of Jesus*.
9. See Ehrman, *Lost Christianities*.

Introduction

> You might think that from the beginning, Christianity was always basically one thing: a religion descended from Jesus, as interpreted by Paul, leading to the church of the Middle Ages on down to the present. But things were not that simple. About a hundred fifty years after Jesus' death we find a wide range of different Christian groups claiming to represent the views of Jesus and his disciples but having completely divergent perspectives, far more divergent than anything even that made it into the New Testament.[10]

Later in this book, Ehrman claims that one group of Christians emerged victorious in the conflict between divergent groups. He calls this winning side the "proto-orthodox" group, the spiritual ancestors of the church's traditional viewpoint of Jesus. This group includes early Christians such as Justin Martyr, Irenaeus, Tertullian, Hippolytus, Clement of Alexandria, Origen, and others. They then labeled all of the competing viewpoints as heretical (unfairly according to Ehrman).[11]

While some are not promoting a conspiracy theory for censorship, others are trying to draw attention away to other ideas about Jesus found in hidden, non-canonical gospels. In a New York Times Bestseller, *Beyond Belief: The Secret Gospel of Thomas,* Elaine Pagels encourages people to see Jesus beyond the description of the church and the New Testament.[12] Following a sincere reflection on the loss of her young son, Pagels explains how her search for strength during this crisis led her to find the *Gospel of Thomas.*

As part of her presentation, she draws attention to a diversity of Christian expression in the early centuries. She writes:

> Numerous gospels circulated among various Christian groups, ranging from those of the New Testament, Matthew, Mark, Luke, and John, to such writings as the *Gospel of Thomas* and the *Gospel of Truth*, as well as many other secret teachings, myths and poems attributed to Jesus or his disciples.[13]

These expressions of Christian faith, according to Pagels, became unfairly excluded and suppressed. As a result, most modern forms of Christianity emphasize right belief of propositions rather than the faith to recognize

---

10. Ehrman, *Jesus, Interrupted*, 191.
11. Ehrman, *Jesus, Interrupted*, 197–98. See also Ehrman, *Lost Christianities*.
12. Pagels, *Beyond Belief*.
13. Pagels, *Gnostic Gospels*, xxiii.

the light within each person.[14] This is unfair, in her opinion, but can be recovered if one looks beyond the gospels of the New Testament and reads the *Gospel of Thomas*.

Besides these popular presentations, there are some within academic quarters who are also promoting the value of non-canonical gospels over those of canonical gospels. A group known as "the Jesus Seminar" has been promoting a reexamination of the picture of Jesus as he has been told through the New Testament and the church. This group of academics, which was founded in 1985, has been critical of the gospels of Matthew, Mark, Luke, and John from its inception. They have been promoting other gospels that develop the picture of Jesus beyond what Robert Funk, the founder of the Seminar calls the "holy four."[15]

The Jesus Seminar is recognized to be a radical group which challenges historic viewpoints. For example, Richard Hays, a well-known New Testament scholar, said that the Jesus Seminar has "a set of unconventional views about Jesus and the gospels . . . Their attempt to present these views as the 'assured results of critical scholarship' is—one must say it—reprehensible deception."[16]

Despite objections such as this, the members of the Jesus Seminar have been promoting the value of other gospels for many years. They have their own publishing company called Polebridge Press, and they conduct lecture series and workshops in the United States. As New Testament scholar Ben Witherington has stated, their publisher continues to print volumes on the *Gospel of Thomas* and Q "to place the material in *Thomas* on equal footing with what we find in the Synoptic Gospels."[17] They continue to produce books and seminars for academic and popular audiences.[18] Their writings and opinions are being increasingly quoted in popular media.

These efforts from the Jesus Seminar and others are appealing to a popular audience that is becoming increasingly skeptical of the church and of the way history has been told. While the person of Jesus still

---

14. Such ideas are then propagated by various other writers, such as Krosney, *Lost Gospel*, 183.

15. Miller, *Complete Gospels*, 3.

16. Hays, "Corrected Jesus," 44.

17. Witherington, *Jesus Quest*, 48.

18. See the Jesus Seminar's website for further information: *http://www.westarinstitute.org*.

Introduction

remains revered, many within the broader populace seem interested in something different. Historian Philip Jenkins has noticed this trend and has commented upon it in his book *Hidden Gospels: How the Search for Jesus Lost Its Way*. He claims that the non-canonical gospels tell us less about the beginnings of Christianity than about "the interest groups who seek to use them today; about the mass media, and how religion is packaged as popular culture; and . . . more generally, about the changing directions of contemporary American religion."[19] People seem interested in something else just because it is different.

Before accepting novel views about Jesus, it is important to consider the history that declared the canonical gospels superior to the others. It is the purpose of this book to summarize the latest discussion for educated readers and draw conclusions. Rather than concentrating on specific non-canonical gospels like the *Gospel of Thomas* or *Judas* as many works do, it will focus broadly on why the canonical gospels are superior to the non-canonical ones. It will offer a summary of the main issues involved and then bring some of the latest research to bear.[20]

Jesus Tried and True is organized around three categories: date, authorship, and reception. The first chapter will consider the dates of different gospels. Those closest to Jesus' life should have an advantage over those of later date. The second chapter will consider the source of the canonical gospels. Those written from the perspective of eyewitnesses of Jesus have priority over those where source is uncertain. It will compare claims about this from the canonical gospels in comparison to the non-canonical ones. The third chapter will examine the reception of the four canonical gospels in early Christian literature in comparison to the other gospels. The early writings from church history are often ignored. These writings from the second and third century do provide early history's commentary on the relative value of the canonical gospels over non-canonical ones.[21]

The final chapter provides an overview of the most significant non-canonical gospels. While many have appealed to the value of other

---

19. Jenkins, *Hidden Gospels*, 5.

20. Witherington, *Gospel Code* and Bock, *Breaking the Da Vinci Code* were specifically addressed to the questions raised by Brown's *Da Vinci Code*. Porter and Heath, *Lost Gospel of Judas* and N. T. Wright, *Judas and the Gospel of Judas*, addressed the relationship between recent discoveries and the Bible.

21. The hermeneutical proximity is valuable. Cf. Casey, *Sacred Reading*, 105.

Introduction

gospels, the actual contents are at times not considered. This chapter will provide representative samples of these works and draw conclusions about the presentation about Jesus as well as their relationship with the canonical gospels.

Jesus is significant. Former president of the American Historical Association and author of over eighty books, Kenneth Latourette understood this. He had this to say when he spoke at the Presidential address for this society. He said, "As the centuries pass the evidence is accumulating that, measured by his effect on history, Jesus is the most influential life ever lived on this planet. That influence appears to be mounting."[22] Such ideas could be repeated by countless others throughout history.[23]

What one decides about Jesus is important. These conclusions are reached from evaluating historical sources. It is the hope that this volume will raise the value of the Gospels of Matthew, Mark, Luke, and John as the sources that define the remarkable person of Jesus.

---

22. Latourette, "Christian Understanding of History," 272.

23. E.g., Napoleon Bonaparte said, "Christ alone has succeeded in so raising the mind of man towards the unseen that it becomes insensible to the barriers of time and space. Across the chasm of eighteen hundred years Jesus Christ makes a demand which is beyond all others difficult to satisfy . . . He asks for the human heart . . . All who sincerely believe in Him experience that supernatural love towards Him. This phenomenon is unaccountable, it is altogether beyond the scope of man's creative powers. Time, the great destroyer, can neither exhaust its strength nor put a limit to its range. The quote is recorded in Ballard, *Miracles of Unbelief*, 265.

CHAPTER ONE

Gospel Dating

WHEN EVALUATING HISTORICAL SOURCES, the one closer in time to the person or the event is generally preferred. In everyday living, we recognize this to be true. For example, at reunions, families often relive the past to some degree. While reunions are a time to become reacquainted, they provide opportunities to remember past events and people. Around a dinner table, family members may tell the story about a great grandparent or an especially meaningful Christmas celebration. Naturally, in these conversations, those who lived closest in time to the person or the event have a much more valued opinion than those who remember from a distance. The recollection closer in time is generally more reliable than the one that is more distant.

So it is with opinions about Jesus. The one closer in time to when Jesus lived has more worth than the one further from when he lived. This is helpful to keep in mind as the value of different gospels is considered. Gospels that were written closer in time to the earthly life of Jesus have a greater worth than those that are dated later. With all of the interest being placed on other gospels recently, some may not realize that the Gospels of Matthew, Mark, Luke, and John have been considered to be written significantly earlier than the non-canonical gospels.

This chapter will investigate the dates of both the canonical and non-canonical gospels. First, it will consider the range of dates for canonical gospels. While a specific date for each of these gospels will not be agreed upon unanimously, the dating of the canonical gospels can be placed within a fairly agreed upon range. Second, it will consider the dates of several non-canonical gospels. It will pay special attention to two non-canonical gospels which some are claiming to be earlier, namely, the *Gospel of Thomas* and the *Gospel of Peter*. It will then compare the dates of the non-canonical gospels with the canonical ones. Finally, it will draw conclusions about the value of canonical gospels in relation to the non-canonical ones.

Dating the Canonical Gospels

As dates are being considered within early Christianity, we should start with matters where there is little doubt. Jesus lived in the early decades of the first century AD.[1] He ministered in the late 20s or early 30s and was crucified, at the latest, by AD 33.[2] Shortly thereafter, the apostle Paul was converted. Paul began to write his letters from the late 40s until the early 60s AD.[3] His death occurred between 64 and 65, and Peter's death occurred between AD 64 and 68.

Shortly after most of Paul's letters were written, most scholars believe that the canonical gospels were composed. Most date these works to the first century AD. What follows is a brief survey of dates for each of the canonical gospels.

Synoptic Gospels

Scholars recognize that the Gospels of Matthew, Mark, and Luke are similar in many aspects. The contents, vocabulary, and sentence structure are similar between the Gospels of Matthew and Luke. Mark's Gospel is also similar to the Gospels of Matthew and Luke. As a result, these three have been considered the Synoptic Gospels.[4]

When scholars compare the contents of Matthew, Mark, and Luke, they notice that there appears to be a written dependency on each other.

---

1. The date of Jesus' birth has been uncertain. For a brief delineation of major issues, see Witherington, "Birth of Jesus," 66–69.

2. For further discussion on the specific dates of Jesus' death, see Green, "Death of Jesus," 149.

3. If one believes that Paul is writing to churches in Southern Galatia, his earliest epistle would be AD 48 to the Galatians. If one believes that Paul is writing to churches in Northern Galatia, then 1 Thessalonians would be Paul's earliest letter in AD 51. For a chronology on Paul's life, see Hengel and Schwemer, *Paul between Damascus and Antioch*, xi–xiv.

4. According to Miriam Webster's Dictionary, the word synoptic means "presenting or taking the same or common view."

Gospel Dating

This can be seen by several factors. First, scholars notice the agreement in order within many sections of Matthew, Mark, and Luke. In Table 1, the agreement between the Gospel of Mark and Luke is most apparent, although there is substantial agreement with the order in the Gospel of Matthew, too. The placement of the choosing of the twelve disciples is the only difference in order between Mark and Luke. The two summary sections in Matthew are placed differently than Mark.

Table 1: Common Order of Events—Earlier Ministry of Jesus[5]

	Event	Matthew	Mark	Luke
a	Jesus' teaching in the synagogue in Capernaum		1:21–22	4:31–32
b	Jesus' healing of the demoniac in Capernaum		1:23–28	4:33–37
c	Jesus' healing of Peter's mother-in-law	8:14–15	1:29–31	4:38–39
d	Jesus' healing in the evening	8:16–17	1:32–34	4:40–41
e	Jesus leaving Capernaum		1:35–38	4:42–43
f	Jesus' preaching in Galilee: a summary	4:23	1:39	4:44
g	The miraculous catch of fish			5:1–11
h	Jesus' healing of the leper	8:1–4	1:40–45	5:12–16
i	Jesus' healing of the paralytic	9:1–8	2:1–12	5:17–26
j	The calling of Levi	9:9–13	2:13–17	5:27–32
k	Controversy over fasting	9:14–17	2:18–22	5:33–39
l	Controversy over plucking grain	12:1–8	2:23–28	6:1–5
m	Controversy over healing on the Sabbath	12:9–14	3:1–6	6:6–11
n	Healing by the sea: a summary	4:24–25 12:15–16	3:7–12	6:17–19
o	Choosing of the Twelve	10:1–4	3:13–19	6:12–16

---

5. This table and the next are taken from Stein, *Studying the Synoptic Gospels*, 35–36.

This table reveals that the Gospels of Mark and Luke agree with each other especially. Only the last two events—the healing by the sea and the choosing of the twelve—are different in order. The order agrees generally with the Gospel of Matthew, too, although the summaries appear to be in different places. The selection of the disciples occurs earlier in Matthew, also.[6] Apart from these small differences, the overlap between the stories and order is striking.

The Gospels of Matthew, Mark, and Luke also generally agree in order in the later ministry of Jesus, as seen in Table 2.

Table 2: Common Order of Events—Later Ministry of Jesus

	Event	Matthew	Mark	Luke
a	Peter's confession of Christ	16:13–20	8:27–30	9:18–21
b	First passion prediction	16:21–23	8:31–33	9:22
c	Teachings on discipleship	16:24–28	8:34–9:1	9:23–27
d	The transfiguration	17:1–9	9:2–10	9:28–36
e	Concerning the return of Elijah	17:10–13	9:11–13	
f	Jesus' healing of the demon-possessed boy	17:14–21	9:14–29	9:37–43a
g	Second passion prediction	17:22–23	9:30–32	9:43b–45
h	The temple tax	17:24–27		
i	Teachings on true greatness	18:1–5	9:33–37	9:46–48
j	Concerning the use of Jesus' name		9:38–41	9:49–50
k	Teachings on temptations	18:6–9	9:42–50	17:1–2 14:34–35
l	Parable of the lost sheep	18:10–14		15:3–7
m	Teachings on reproving a brother	18:15–18		
n	Teachings on the presence of Jesus	18:19–20		
o	Teachings on reconciliation with a brother	18:21–22		17:4

---

6. Stein, *Studying the Synoptic Gospels*, 35.

p	Parable of the unforgiving servant	18:23–35		
q	Departure to Judea	19:1–2	10:1	9:51
	Largest block of Lukan teaching material			9:51–18:14
r	Teaching on divorce	19:3–12	10:2–12	
s	Jesus blesses the children	19:13–15	10:13–16	18:15–17
t	The rich young man	19:16–22	10:17–22	18:18–23
u	Teachings on the dangers of riches	19:23–30	10:23–31	18:24–30
v	Parable of the laborers in the vineyard	20:1–16		
w	Third passion prediction	20:17–19	10:32–34	18:31–34
x	The request of the sons of Zebedee	20:20–28	10:35–45	
y	The healing of the blind man	20:29–34	10:46–52	18:35–43

Once again, there are striking overlaps between these accounts. Even when Luke inserts some of Jesus' teaching between 9:51 and 18:14, he returns to the same order in 18:15.[7] Apart from an omission of a few parables and a few sections of Jesus' teaching, the narratives follow the same order. The similarity is especially striking since there was other material about Jesus which could have been included, such as his many other healings.

With the striking overlap of wording and content, scholars have attempted to describe the literary relationship between the Synoptic Gospels. F. Schleiermacher has proposed that the gospel writers used memorabilia or written fragments. This explanation, however, does not explain the large amount of overlap in order.[8] Others, such as G. E. Lessing and J. G. Eichorn, propose that there was an original Aramaic gospel that informed the Synoptics.[9] A problem with this theory is that such a

---

7. Stein, *Studying the Synoptic Gospels*, 35–36. See also the general agreement of Mark 3:31—6:6 with Matthew 12:46—13:58 and Luke 8:19–56.

8. See further Schleiermacher, "Über die Zeugnisse des Papias," 335–68.

9. See further Lessing, *Neue Hypothese*. Also see Eichorn, *Einleitung* and Torrey, *Four Gospels*.

gospel has never been found. Furthermore, the original source of the Synoptic Gospels seems to look more like Mark than an independent gospel.

A third possibility is that there is some interdependence among Matthew, Mark, and Luke. In other words, two of the gospel writers used a part of another gospel to write their own. Scholars favor this as the way to explain the similarities among the Synoptic Gospels. The idea can be found in the writings of Augustine, and it has received nearly universal agreement currently among scholars.[10]

Besides the overlap in content, one of the strongest arguments for a common written source undergirding the Synoptic Gospels is the insertion of parenthetical expressions which appear in several places. For example, in Mark 13:14–16, where Jesus is foretelling the destruction of Jerusalem, the gospel writer records the following:

> When you see "the abomination that causes desolation" standing where it does not belong—*let the reader understand*—then let those who are in Judea flee to the mountains. Let no one on the roof of his house go down or enter the house to take anything out. Let no one in the field go back to get his cloak.[11] (*Italics added*)

The parenthetical expression inserted is "let the reader understand." It does not seem necessary for the discussion, but it has been placed within Jesus' prophecy. Luke's Gospel, which records the same ideas, does not have the phrase (Luke 21:20–22). The Gospel of Matthew, however, does include it. Matthew 24:15–18 says,

> So when you see standing in the holy place "the abomination that causes desolation," spoken of through the prophet Daniel—*let the reader understand*—then let those who are in Judea flee to the mountains. Let no one on the roof of his house go down to take anything out of the house. Let no one in the field go back to get his cloak.[12] (*Italics added*)

The insertion cannot result from oral tradition, since it refers specifically to the reader. The fact that it occurs in two separate gospels is one indication that a common written source informs the Synoptic Gospels. Other

---

10. See Augustine, *The Harmony of the Gospels*, 78.
11. Taken from the NIV.
12. Taken from the NIV.

indications of a common written source providing parenthetical expressions can also be found (e.g., Matt 9:6; Mark 2:10; Luke 5:24).[13]

A further indication of literary dependence is the similarity in which the Synoptic Gospels quote certain Old Testament Scripture texts. For example, all three Synoptic Gospels quote Isaiah 40:3, "A voice of one calling: 'In the desert prepare the way for the Lord; make straight in the wilderness a highway *for our God*'" (italics added). All three uses of the Isaiah passage in the Synoptic Gospels state, "Prepare the way for the Lord, make straight paths *for him*" (Matt 3:3; Mark 1:3; Luke 3:4; italics added). The three Synoptic Gospels agree with each other, in distinction to Isaiah.[14]

How is such dependence to be explained? In theory, there may be eighteen possible ways that the three gospels borrowed from each other.[15] The three best possibilities, however, are the following. Matthew wrote first, which was subsequently used by Mark, and then was used by Luke. Another possibility is that Matthew wrote first and was used by Luke. Mark then wrote last and shortened Matthew and Luke. The final and most likely possibility is that Mark wrote first and was then used by Matthew and Luke.

Gospel of Mark

When the agreements among the Gospels of Matthew, Mark, and Luke are further examined, the Gospel of Mark should be seen as the earliest dated gospel. Many scholars believe this for several reasons. Mark's Gospel agrees in wording with 97.2-percent of Matthew's Gospel. Mark's Gospel agrees with 88.4-percent of the wording in Luke's Gospel.[16] Mark is shorter than Matthew or Luke, and it is easier to envision that Matthew or Luke added sections (such as Jesus' birth, the Beatitudes, and the Lord's Prayer) than to think that Mark omitted them.[17]

---

13. See also Mark 5:8 and Luke 8:29; Matthew 27:18 and Mark 15:10. Stein, *Studying the Synoptic Gospels*, 40–44.

14. See also Matthew 22:37, Mark 12:30, and Luke 10:27, which agree with each other, as opposed to the quoted source of Deuteronomy 6:5.

15. See further Stein, *Studying the Synoptic Gospels*, 50–53.

16. Stein, *Studying the Synoptic Gospels*, 52.

17. Some are still arguing for Matthew as the earliest gospel. For example, see Black, *Why Four Gospels?*

There are other details which make it likely that Mark is dated first. The writing style within the Gospel of Mark is poorer than in Matthew or Luke. With the agreement among the Gospels of Matthew, Mark, and Luke, it is more likely that Matthew or Luke smoothed out the writing style than to believe that Mark introduced more difficult readings. The Gospels of Matthew and Luke also eliminate some of the Aramaic expressions that are found in Mark (cf. Mark 3:17; 5:41; 7:11, 34; 14:36; 15:22, 34). It would be more likely that Matthew and Luke would omit these, rather than to conclude that Mark introduced these if his gospel was indeed later.

Matthew and Luke contain a number of theological themes that would likely have been added to Mark's narration. For example, Matthew contains fulfillment quotations at several points where Mark does not have them (cf. Matt 1:22; 2:15; 3:15; 5:17; 8:17; 12:17; 13:35). It is more likely that Matthew added these to explain further the story of Jesus than to believe that Mark would have deleted them. Matthew also points the reader to Jesus as the Son of David. Luke, too, introduces theological themes, such as the role of the Holy Spirit and the importance of prayer. It would be more likely that Matthew and Luke added these later upon further reflection of Jesus' life, rather than to believe that Mark excluded them.[18]

Scholars have placed the dating of Mark within four different decades: the 40s, 50s, 60s, and 70s. It is, however, unlikely that the dating of Mark would be within the 40s. Paul would likely have mentioned a written gospel such as Mark in one of his letters, but he does not. It is an unlikely position also due to the strength of the data that would place Mark between AD 60–70. A date in the 70s is also unlikely. Those who propose a date in the 70s see the events of Mark 13 describing the defeat of Jerusalem in AD 70.[19] The events within Mark 13, however, appear to better fit Old Testament and Jewish imagery than specific instances within the siege of Jerusalem.[20] Therefore, it is best to consider the date of the Gospel of Mark before AD 70.

Dating Mark between AD 60 and 70 also finds broad support within recent commentaries.[21] Even a scholar like Bart Ehrman, who promotes

---

18. Stein, *Studying the Synoptic Gospels*, 49–96.

19. Kümmel, *The New Testament*, 68; Pesch, *Markusevangelium* 1.14; Gnilka, *Markus*, 1.34.

20. Reicke, "Synoptic Prophecies," 121–33.

21. Edwards dates the gospel at AD 65 (Edwards, *Gospel according to Mark*, 9). France

the value of non-canonical gospels, dates the Gospel of Mark between AD 65–70.[22]

Several reasons make a date between AD 60–70 possible. Early Christian tradition places the Gospel of Mark following the death of Peter, which took place between AD 64–68.[23] The onset of Nero's persecution in Rome in AD 65 also would agree well with Mark's insistence to follow the road of the cross (cf. Mark 8:34).[24] Furthermore, Mark 13 would reflect the situation during the Jewish revolt and right before the Roman entrance between AD 67–69.

Another possibility for Mark's date is in the 50s. Peter was in Rome in the mid-50s, which could have made it possible for him to influence Mark to write the gospel.[25] The strongest evidence for a date in the late 50s, however, comes from the Gospel of Luke's relationship with Mark. If Luke is dated in the early 60s and follows Mark, then Mark's Gospel would have to be written in the 50s rather than the 60s.[26] This is especially likely if Luke used material from Mark's account in some way to compose his gospel, as presented earlier.

Whether the Gospel of Mark is dated in the 50s or 60s, however, is less important to the overall argument of this chapter. The most significant point from this survey of scholarship is that the Gospel of Mark was written well before the last quarter of the first century AD, according to most New Testament scholars. This makes Mark substantially earlier than the non-canonical gospels. Mark clearly deserves pride of place in considering what can be learned about Jesus, as it is generally agreed to be the earliest gospel.

---

states, "not later than the early sixties of the first century" (France, *Gospel of Mark*, 38). Lane places the date between 60–70 (Lane, *Gospel of Mark*, 17). Stein places the date around the late 60s to 70 (Stein, *Mark*, 12–15).

22. See Ehrman, *New Testament*, 90.

23. Cf. Irenaeus (*Haer.* 3.1.2), who places the Gospel of Mark following Peter's death. See, however, Clement of Alexandria's views which are stated in Eusebius, *Ecclesiastical History*, 6.14.6–7. He states that Peter verified the Gospel of Mark. See also Papias' words in Eusebius, *Ecclesiastical History*, 2.15.2.

24. Cf. Cranfield, *Mark*, 8. See also Tacitus, *Annals*, 365–66. The burning of Rome, with blame placed on Christians, is found in section 15.44.

25. Early church historian Eusebius suggests that Peter was in Rome during Claudius' reign. This would have been before AD 54, as this is the date of Claudius' death. Cf. Eusebius, *Ecclesiastical History*, 2.14.6.

26. Carson and Moo, *Introduction to the New Testament*, 179–82. Cf. von Harnack, *Date of Acts*.

Gospel of Matthew

Like the Gospel of Mark, the majority of scholarship recognizes that the Gospel of Matthew is also dated significantly earlier than the end of the first century. As with the Gospel of Mark, there is a range of dates proposed. Even with this range, nearly all date the gospel before the end of the first century.

There have been some scholars, however, who have dated the Gospel of Matthew later than AD 100.[27] These all wrote during the nineteenth or early twentieth century before a considerable amount of study had been accomplished. Studies over the past century have revealed that the Gospel of Matthew is found within early second century documents, particularly the letters of Ignatius. Since Ignatius wrote in the first decade of the second century, the Gospel of Matthew must predate these letters by several years.[28] Thus, the Gospel of Matthew cannot be dated later than AD 100.

Most believe that the Gospel of Matthew is dated between AD 80 and 100.[29] Scholars hold to these dates for some or all of the following reasons generally. The Gospel of Matthew displays a separation between the church and the synagogue. This separation became more distinct historically in the latter decades of the first century. They also see passages like Matthew 22:6–7 and 24:1–29 as looking back upon the destruction of the Temple and Jerusalem, which took place in AD 70. Furthermore, they see the Gospel of Matthew as dependent upon the Gospel of Mark, which some date around AD 70. Allowing ten years between Matthew and Mark's composition would thus place the dating of the Gospel of Matthew in the last twenty years of the first century.

There are several scholars, however, who are promoting an earlier date.[30] In his recent commentary on the Gospel of Matthew, France selects a date before AD 70. He doubts that any sharp distinction is displayed in the gospel between the synagogue and the church. He also doubts that the destruction of the Temple in Matthew 22 and 24 is being recounted

---

27. Baur, *Kritische Untersuchungen*; cf. Holtzmann, *Die synoptische Evangelien*; Loisy, *Le quatrième évangile*; H. von Soden, *Schriften des Neuen Testaments*.

28. See further the allusions to the Gospel of Matthew in Gregory and Tuckett, *Reception of the New Testament*.

29. For a listing of scholars and the dates that they assign to the Gospel of Matthew, see Davies and Allison, *Matthew*, 1:127–28.

30. See also Gundry, *Matthew*, 599–609; Carson and Moo, *Introduction to the New Testament*, 152–56.

rather than foretold.[31] Furthermore, he believes that the author of Matthew would likely be active and writing in the 60s rather than in the latter part of the first century.[32]

Others like Keener are advocating a date in the mid-70s. Keener finds that the opposition against the Pharisees fits well with Matthew's polemical arguments. The Pharisees were particularly forceful during the mid-70s. Matthew's Jewish worldview would have fit more closely to the rabbinic viewpoint which was also strong in the 70s. Since Matthew used Mark's Gospel, it would have to be dated subsequent to Mark, and thus after AD 70. Finally from Keener's perspective, the trauma from the destruction of the Temple is likely found in Matthew 24.[33]

As in the case with the dating of the Gospel of Mark, the precise date of Matthew's Gospel is not the main issue for this study. As France states, "any 'publication date' can be advanced only very tentatively."[34] The general scholarly consensus, however, is that the Gospel of Matthew is dated before the end of the century and quite possibly even before AD 75, which is still significantly earlier than the non-canonical gospels.

Gospel of Luke

The Gospel of Luke is either dated in the 60s or between AD 75–85. According to scholarly consensus, this gospel presents different issues when it comes to dating because its date is closely connected to the dates of Mark and the Acts of the Apostles.

Unlike the Gospels of Matthew and Mark, Luke is the first of a two part work, and should be considered as Luke-Acts. This is evident from the way that the writer addresses Theophilus in Luke 1:3–4: "it seemed good to me also, having followed all things closely for some time past, to write an orderly account for you, most excellent Theophilus, that you may have certainty concerning the things you have been taught." He then resumes this address to Theophilus in Acts 1:1–2, mentioning his former book saying, "In the first book, O Theophilus, I have dealt with all that

---

31. Note that the Temple is still standing within the Gospel of Matthew (cf. Matt 5:23–24; 17:24–27; 23:16–22).
32. France, *Matthew*, 5–19.
33. Keener, *Matthew*, 42–43.
34. France, *Matthew*, 30.

Jesus began to do and teach, until the day when he was taken up, after he had given commands through the Holy Spirit to the apostles whom he had chosen." It is generally agreed that the former book spoken of in Acts is the Gospel of Luke.

When Luke and Acts are viewed together, the events at the end of Acts help to set an initial date for the Gospel of Luke. The Acts of the Apostles ends with Paul in Rome in Acts 28. Scholars recognize that date to be approximately AD 62.[35] As a result, the final composition of Luke-Acts could not have been written before AD 62. The Gospel of Luke can be dated no earlier than this.

There are several reasons why some scholars date the Gospel of Luke in the 60s. With its vivid reference to Paul's arrest, trials, shipwreck, and voyage to Rome which are found in Acts 27, Luke seems to have these events fresh in his mind. This would place the composition of Luke and Acts closer to AD 62 rather than further from it.

There are also a number of key events from AD 65–70 that are missing. These include the deaths of Peter, James, and Paul, Nero's persecution, and the destruction of Jerusalem—all of which are unmentioned in Luke-Acts. Acts also portrays tensions between Jews and Gentiles. This would place the contents of Luke-Acts closer to Paul's epistles than between AD 75–80. Luke-Acts also provides discussion about the law, table fellowship, and offending practices which would favor an earlier date of AD 65–70. For these and other reasons, many scholars believe that the Gospel of Luke was written in the 60s.[36]

The most commonly held viewpoint, however, is that the Gospel of Luke is dated between AD 75 and 85.[37] Scholars propose this because Luke depicts Jesus' prediction of the destruction of the Temple as more developed than what was written in Mark (cf. Mark 13:14; Luke 21:20).[38] Thus, these scholars believe that it was written after the fall of Jerusalem.

---

35. Cf. Riesner, *Paul's Early Period*.

36. Carson and Moo, *Introduction to the New Testament*, 207–10; cf. Bock, *Luke*, 18.

37. Fitzmeyer, *Luke*, 1:53–57. Brown, *Apostasy and Perseverance*, 273–74; Kümmel, *Introduction*, 151.

38. Mark 13:14 states, "But when you see the abomination of desolation standing where it ought not to be (let the reader understand), then let those who are in Judea flee to the mountains." Luke's rendering shows that Jerusalem is surrounded by Roman legions. Luke 21:20 reads, "But when you see Jerusalem surrounded by armies, then know that its desolation has come near." See also Luke 13:35a, 19:33–34 which also appear to show influence from the destruction of the Temple already having taken place.

Second, if Luke used Mark's writing and Mark was written in the 60s, Luke would then need to be dated later, between AD 75 and 85. Third, if Luke claims that many other accounts of Jesus' life have been written, then a later date between 75 and 85 would be favored over the early 60s. Finally, a later theology is found in Luke-Acts, often called an "early Catholic theology," with a down-played eschatology and a more developed church leadership. As a result, some see this influence as showing that the date of Luke is later than the early 60s.

As in the case with the dating of the Gospels of Matthew and Mark, the precise date of Luke's Gospel is not the critical issue for this study. The majority of scholarship dates the Gospel of Luke well before the end of the first century.

Gospel of John

Many used to date John's Gospel well into the second century. The late date was attributed to John's theology, which was considered to be more developed than the Synoptic Gospels. The reasoning went that, with more time, more doctrine would have permeated the writing. John's Gospel seemed considerably more developed theologically than the Synoptics. A further reason for dating the Gospel of John late was the lack of evidence of its presence within second century documents.

This conclusion was discarded following the discovery in the early part of the twentieth century of the Rylands papyrus, also known as P^{52}. This papyrus is a fragment of the Gospel of John and contains John 18:31–33. It dates from AD 130 and was discovered in Egypt. Since John's Gospel was written in Ephesus, this papyrus could not have been written much beyond the early part of the second century. With the discovery of this papyrus, it is now impossible to date the Gospel of John well into the second century.

Like the other canonical gospels, scholars have assigned a wide range of dates (AD 55–95) to John. It is best to see the Gospel of John as written after AD 70. Early church fathers, such as Irenaeus and Clement of Alexandria, state that the Gospel of John was the last of the four canonical gospels to be written. Early church historian Eusebius also believes that the Gospel of John was written following the Synoptics.[39] If this is the case,

---

39. See Irenaeus, *Against Heresies* 3.1.1 and Clement as cited in *Ecclesiastical History*

then John must be dated after AD 70, at the earliest, from this survey. While a few see John before AD 70, the gospel is most likely dated later.[40]

There are several other factors that would lead one to believe that John was written much later than AD 70. The destruction of the Temple occurred in AD 70. John would most likely have referred to this traumatic event if he were writing shortly thereafter. The Gospel of John also refers to the Sea of Galilee as the Sea of Tiberias in 6:1 and 21:1. Herod Antipas had founded the city of Tiberias by the Sea of Galilee in AD 20, but the city name was transferred to the Sea much later in the first century.[41] John also refers to Peter's martyrdom in 21:19, which suggests a date later in the first century when John would have had time to reflect on Peter's passing. The Gospel of John also lacks references to the Sadducees. This Jewish religious group was not in existence following AD 70, and its absence favors a later dating of John. A further element that would lead one to believe that John's Gospel is dated in the latter part of the first century is Thomas' confession. His declaration that Jesus is Lord and God in John 20:27–28 would contrast well with the emperor worship in Domitian's time (AD 81–96).[42]

Two possibilities seem best for the date of this gospel. Some scholars date John between 90 and 100.[43] These scholars note that the theology is more developed than the other canonical gospels, particularly in the area of Christology.[44] They also note that Jesus' deity is assumed in John's Gospel rather than argued for, as in the Synoptic Gospels.

Carson dates the Gospel of John between AD 80 and 85.[45] He believes that there is no reason for the gospel to be dated late or early within the range 85–95. He also asserts that the Gospel of John precedes the Johannine Epistles. If these Epistles date from the 90s and are refuting Gnosticism, then some time must elapse for the Gospel of John to circulate. This would make a dating of John between AD 80 and 85 more favorable.

3.24.7 and 6.14.7. Carson and Moo, *Introduction to the New Testament*, 266.

40. Morris, *Gospel according to John*, 30–35; Robinson, *Redating*, 254–85.

41. Carson, *John*, 268.

42. Köstenberger, *John*, 8.

43. Michaels, *John*, xxix; Ehrman, *New Testament*, 183; cf. Martyn, *History and Theology*, 27–34.

44. Cf. Dunn, *Christology in the Making*, 213–48.

45. Carson and Moo, *Introduction to the New Testament*, 267; Carson, *John*, 82.

As in the case of the discussions on dating of the Synoptic Gospels, the precise date of John's Gospel is not the critical issue for this study. The majority of scholarship is dating the Gospel of John before the end of the first century. Therefore, all canonical gospels are completed by the end of the first century. It is possible from this survey that all canonical gospels could be dated even before AD 90. This is a significant conclusion in comparison with the dating of the non-canonical gospels.

Dating the non-canonical Gospels

In comparison to the canonical gospels, most scholars date non-canonical gospels to the second century or later. As a result, this puts the majority of the non-canonical gospels after the Gospels of Matthew, Mark, Luke, and John. Many of these are at least a hundred years following the death of Jesus and forty years after the canonical gospels.

As with the canonical gospels, there is a range of dates acceptable within modern scholarship. The range of dates that scholars propose for the non-canonical gospels is broader, however, than the canonical gospels. This is due to several factors. There are fewer extant copies of these works. In some of the fragmentary gospels, for example, there is only one copy. Portions of the canonical gospels provide information about their date of composition. For example, in the discussion about the date of the Gospel of John, the Rylands papyrus provides evidence that John's Gospel cannot be dated in the second century. Other papyri help to confirm the date of the canonical gospels. With the non-canonical gospels, there is significantly less evidence to establish dating, and this results in a broader range given for them.

A second factor which makes the dating of the non-canonical gospels difficult is the fewer number of documents that borrow parts of the non-canonical gospels within their writing. Quoted portions of the canonical gospels help provide information for dating them. For example, in the discussion about the date of the Gospel of Matthew, the letters of Ignatius of Antioch provide an ending date for Matthew. This canonical gospel could not be written within the second century, since quotations from it were already found within the early second century. Fewer manuscripts, however, cite or allude to non-canonical gospels in early history. As a result, there is much less evidence to determine the date for many of the non-canonical gospels.

Paul Foster has written a short introduction called *The Apocryphal Gospels* and edited a collection of essays entitled *The Non-Canonical Gospels*. He assigns dates in this way:

- *Gospel of Thomas*: disputed
- *Gospel of Philip*: 150–250
- *Gospel of Truth*: 140–180
- *Gospel of Egyptians*: 100–150
- *Infancy Gospel of Thomas*: 200–300
- *Protevangelium of James*: 175–225
- *Gospel of Peter*: 150–200
- *Papyrus Oxyrhynchus*: 125–150
- *Papyrus Egerton 2*: 100–150
- *Gospel of the Hebrews*: following the Synoptic Gospels
- *Gospel of the Nazareans*: following the Synoptic Gospels
- *Gospel of the Ebionites*: 100–400
- *Gospel of Judas*: 140–200
- *Gospel of Mary*: 200–300
- *Fayum Gospel*: 200–250
- *Secret Gospel of Mark*: 200–300?[46]

Bart Ehrman, who has promoted the value of non-canonical gospels, dates these books in this way:

- *Gospel of the Nazareans*: end of first century or early second century
- *Gospel of the Ebionites*: early second century
- *Gospel of the Hebrews*: early second century
- *Gospel of Egyptians*: early second century
- *Gospel of Thomas*: early second century but portions may be earlier
- *Papyrus Egerton 2*: first half of second century

46. See further Foster, *Non-Canonical Gospels*; Foster, *Apocryphal Gospels*.

- *Gospel of Peter*: beginning of the second century
- *Gospel of Mary*: late second century
- *Gospel of Philip*: third century
- *Gospel of Truth*: before AD 180[47]
- *Gospel of the Savior*: second century
- *Infancy Gospel of Thomas*: first half of second century
- *Proto-Gospel of James*: about AD 150
- *Epistle of the Apostles*: mid-second century
- *Coptic Apocalypse of Peter*: third century
- *Second Treatise of the Great Seth*: third century
- *Secret Gospel of Mark*: ?[48]

Craig Evans, a critic of the modern fascination in non-canonical gospels, has dated these gospels in this way:

- *Gospel of the Egyptians*: 120
- *Gospel of Nazareans*: 120
- *Gospel of Ebionites*: 120
- *Gospel of Hebrews*: 140
- *Apocryphon of James*: 150
- *Fayum Gospel*: 150
- *Gospel of Mary*: 160
- *Gospel of Peter*: 170
- *Papyrus Egerton 2*: 180
- *Gospel of Thomas*: 180[49]

There are several reasons why these gospels are generally dated later than the canonical ones. Many of the non-canonical gospels have been linked with Gnosticism. In *The Nag Hammadi Scriptures: The Revised and Updated Translation of Sacred Gnostic Texts Complete in One Volume*,

---

47. Ehrman sees this as a second-century text.
48. See further Ehrman, *New Testament*, 204–23.
49. Evans, *Fabricating Jesus*, 55.

Meyer and Pagels list several non-canonical gospels as having Gnostic connections. They list the following gospels as Gnostic: *Gospel of Truth, Gospel of Thomas, Gospel of Philip, Gospel of Mary,* and *Gospel of Judas*.[50] While some can trace early Gnostic thinkers to the first century, Gnosticism flourished about AD 135. As a result, it would lead us to date these gospels much later than the canonical gospels, since Gnosticism flourished significantly after the writing of the canonical gospels.

A second reason to date non-canonical gospels later than Matthew, Mark, Luke, and John is the dependence that many scholars see upon the canonical gospels, particularly the Synoptic Gospels. This has been recognized by a variety of scholars, particularly those non-canonical gospels that come from Nag Hammadi (i.e., *Gospel of Thomas, Gospel of Truth, Gospel of Philip, Gospel of Mary,* and *Gospel of the Egyptians*).[51] One such comment has come from Oxford New Testament scholar Christopher Tuckett. Following a comparison of many of the Nag Hammadi Gospels with the Synoptics, Tuckett writes in *Nag Hammadi and the Gospel Tradition*:

> It would therefore appear that the texts of the Nag Hammadi Library (with the possible exception of *Gospel of Thomas*) will not be of any assistance in dealing with the problem of the development of synoptic tradition at a pre-redactional stage. Rather, these texts are witnesses of the post-redactional development of that tradition. There is thus no evidence here for the existence of texts earlier than probably the second century.[52]

Tuckett is not alone in his viewpoint. Most scholars see the non-canonical gospels as substantially later than, and influenced by, the canonical ones.

---

50. Meyer and Pagels, *Nag Hammadi Scriptures*.

51. Note several of the articles in Foster, *Non-Canonical Gospels*, 30–67, 139–70, which claim the dependence of non-canonical gospels upon the canonical ones. The authors of this collection state this for the following gospels: *Gospel of Peter, Gospel of Mary, Gospel of the Hebrews, Gospel of the Ebionites, Papyrus Egerton 2, The Fayum Gospel,* and *Papyrus Oxyrhynchus 840*. Others have noted the dependence of the non-canonical *Gospel of Thomas* upon the canonical Gospels. See Snodgrass, "The Gospel of Thomas," 299; Grant and Freedman, *Secret Sayings*, 136–7; Tuckett, "Thomas and the Synoptics," 132–57. See also Tuckett, who sees clear allusions to the New Testament in the *Gospel of Mary* (Tuckett, *Gospel of Mary*, 55–76). See also Ménard, who finds dependence upon the Gospel of Matthew and Paul's letters, especially in the *Gospel of Truth* (Ménard, *L' Évangelie de Vérité*, 7–8). See further discussion on this topic in chapter 4.

52. Tuckett, *Nag Hammadi*, 149.

As a result, they are distant and less likely to represent Jesus as accurately as the canonical gospels.

Third, some who are promoting the value of non-canonical gospels for understanding Jesus also agree that they are dated later than the canonical ones. For example, Bart Ehrman, who is encouraging attention to different views of Christianity through other gospels, dates many non-canonical gospels to the second century.[53] He writes:

> Most recognize clear and certain reasons for dating the New Testament Gospels to the first century. But giving yet earlier dates to non-canonical Gospels that are, in most cases, not quoted or even mentioned by early Christian writers until many, many decades later seems to be overly speculative and driven by an ultimate objective of claiming that Jesus was not an apocalypticist even though our earliest sources indicate that he was.[54]

While not everyone promoting the value of other gospels dates the non-canonical gospels so late, some do acknowledge the earlier dating for the canonical gospels. This should then favor the superior witness for the canonical gospels over the non-canonical ones.

These three reasons, then, should lead one to conclude that the majority of non-canonical gospels should be dated later than the canonical ones. As a result, the opinions from the non-canonical gospels about Jesus should not be considered to be as valuable as the canonical gospels. There are a few gospels, however, that some scholars are claiming as early—namely, the *Gospel of Thomas* and the *Gospel of Peter*. These deserve further consideration.

A Possible Early Date for Two Non-Canonical Gospels: Thomas and Peter

Portions of the *Gospel of Thomas* have been assumed by a few scholars to be early.[55] While the entirety of the *Gospel of Thomas* is dated later than Matthew, Mark, Luke, and John, there are a few scholars who are advocating an earlier date for some portions of this gospel.

---

53. Ehrman, *New Testament*, 204–23.
54. Ehrman, *New Testament*, 263.
55. Quispel, "Gospel of Thomas," 189–207; Davies, "Thomas," 9; DeConick, "*Gospel of Thomas*," 20–24.

There is a history to this approach. In 1993, Stephen Patterson encouraged scholars to think of the *Gospel of Thomas* as another school of early Christian thought. From his perspective, the Gospel of Matthew represented a viewpoint about Jesus from the first century. He felt that the *Gospel of Thomas* also represented an equivalent perspective on Jesus. The *Gospel of Thomas* should not be seen as dependent upon the canonical gospels, in Patterson's view, but rather should be seen as autonomous. According to Patterson, it had also drawn on early oral tradition of Jesus. As a result, this could make ideas within the *Gospel of Thomas* as early as the canonical gospels of Matthew, Mark, Luke, and John.[56]

Others have taken this premise further. G. J. Riley believed that the *Gospel of Thomas* was written in response to the Gospel of John. He advanced this viewpoint in *Resurrection Reconsidered: Thomas and John in Controversy*.[57] In 2003, Elaine Pagels promoted this perspective further in *Beyond Belief: the Secret Gospel of Thomas*. This volume went on to become a New York Times Bestseller.

Pagels argued that the Gospel of John promoted a different view of Jesus and of salvation from the Synoptic Gospels. In *Beyond Belief*, she identifies several examples in the Synoptic Gospels which, in her opinion, show that John's Gospel is promoting a different view of Jesus than Matthew, Mark, and Luke. She concludes by stating, "John's Gospel directly contradicts the combined testimony of the other New Testament Gospels."[58] While the Gospels of Matthew, Mark, and Luke saw Jesus as God's servant, John's Gospel portrays him as "God himself revealed in human form."[59]

After isolating the Gospel of John from the other canonical gospels, Pagels proceeds to show how the Gospel of John is at odds with the *Gospel of Thomas*. John and Thomas seem to have inside access to secret ideas from Jesus, writing of creation themes and of the kingdom of God as a present reality. Yet, despite some similarities, she finds the two gospels to be at odds with each other. The emphasis on Jesus in the Gospel of John is concerned with finding salvation in him, while the view of Jesus in the *Gospel of Thomas* is concerned about each person finding the truth

---

56. See further Patterson, *Gospel of Thomas*.
57. Riley, *Resurrection Reconsidered*. See also DeConick, *Seek to See Him*, 72–73.
58. Pagels, *Beyond Belief*, 35.
59. Pagels, *Beyond Belief*, 37.

within himself. True salvation can be found within oneself, according to the *Gospel of Thomas*, while the Gospel of John is definitive that salvation is found outside of oneself.

She particularly notes that the Gospel of John is critical of the disciple Thomas. Thomas appears frustrated with Jesus, wanting to die in John 11:16 rather than visit Mary and Martha following Lazarus' death. He does not know where Jesus is going in John 14:1–6. Thomas is missing when Jesus first appears (John 20:19–24). He then is represented in a lengthy section as a doubter of Jesus' resurrection (John 20:24–31). This then contributes to why she views the *Gospel of Thomas* to be of earlier date. It would indicate that this conflict is still fresh between John and Thomas.

With the Gospel of John distinguished, Pagels then views church history to have been unfairly written from the perspective of the Gospel of John. She believes that early church father Irenaeus took the Gospel of John and made it the "first and foremost of other gospels."[60] As a result, she believes that the church unjustly interpreted all other gospels through the Gospel of John and excluded the *Gospel of Thomas*.

Others have taken a different approach to dating the *Gospel of Thomas* early. Instead of comparing the Gospel of John with the *Gospel of Thomas*, others have attempted to date the *Gospel of Thomas* early by drawing comparisons with a writing that scholars believe to have existed, called Q. Nobody has found this document called Q, but many scholars claim that it did exist. The name Q was derived to signify material that predates the Gospels of Matthew and Luke and has influenced those gospels.

These scholars claim that Q existed by pointing to significant overlaps in the wording of Matthew and Luke. They see a similarity between some 230 verses common to Matthew and Luke but which are not found within Mark. The greatest parallels exist between passages such as Matthew 6:24 and Luke 16:13; Matthew 7:7–11 and Luke 11:9–13; Matthew 11:25–27 and Luke 10:21–22; Matthew 23:37–39 and Luke 13:34–35. Because of these agreements, the written source Q was proposed to lie behind Matthew and Luke.[61] While it is possible that Matthew and Luke wrote these sections that agree with each other by memory, many within

---

60. Pagels, *Beyond Belief*, 58.
61. For example, Kloppenberg, *Q, The Earliest Gospel*; Robinson, *The Critical Edition of Q*; Mack, *The Lost Gospel*; Borg, *Lost Gospel Q*.

the scholarly community support the Q hypothesis.[62] Thus, Q is deemed by many to be a writing that contains sayings that led to the composition of sections of the Gospels of Matthew and Luke.

Following the discovery of the *Gospel of Thomas*, a number of scholars have claimed a similarity between the *Gospel of Thomas* and Q. They believe that these two would be considered sayings gospels without narratives or passion material.[63] While it is not believed that Q and *Thomas* are identical, the similarity has stimulated discussion on the relationship between the two.[64]

This has led to implications regarding dating and the *Gospel of Thomas*. Since the supposed document of Q is similar to the *Gospel of Thomas*, some are drawing conclusions that Q and the *Gospel of Thomas* emerge from approximately the same time. Since Q could be dated between 50–75 AD, they then conclude that the *Gospel of Thomas* should be dated early, too.[65] Some even consider the *Gospel of Thomas* and Q to be the earliest gospels.[66]

There are many reasons to reject such a conclusion. First, scholars who are connecting Q and the *Gospel of Thomas* are drawing those connections from one document, namely Q, which is hypothetically a single document. While some support a Q document, not everyone believes that it is a single document; Q could be several sources. Second, there are sayings within the *Gospel of Thomas* that have much in common with Gnostic thought that derives from the second century. For example, *Gospel of Thomas* 50 reads as follows:

> Jesus said, "If they say to you, 'Where did you come from?' say to them, 'We came from the light, the place where the light came into being on its own accord and established [itself] and became

---

62. For a summation of the arguments supporting the existence of Q, see Stein, *Studying the Synoptic Gospels*, 97–123. He notes, "Whether Q was a single written source, a collection of several different fragments, a combination of written and oral traditions, various oral traditions, or even a single unified oral tradition are questions unlikely to be resolved in the immediate future" (121).

63. Note that scholars are divided as to whether Q is actually a gospel.

64. Conversation is currently taking place within the scholarly world about the relationship between these two sources. Note that there is a Q-Thomas section within the Society of Biblical Literature.

65. Robinson, "Bridging the Gulf from Q to the *Gospel of Thomas*," 127–76; Davies, *The Gospel of Thomas and Christian Wisdom*, 146.

66. For example, Crossan, *Birth of Christianity*, 239; Funk, *The Five Gospels*, 492–3.

manifest through their image.' If they say to you, 'Is it you?' say 'We are its children, and we are the elect of the living father.' If they ask you, 'What is the sign of your father in you?' say to them, 'It is movement and repose.'"

This text and others (cf. *Gos. Thom.* 77) agree with mid to late second century Gnosticism.[67] Thus, this would lead to the conclusion that the *Gospel of Thomas* is dated late. Finally, the early dating of *Thomas* is a minority opinion at best amongst scholars today without broad support. It is more often recognized to be a document influenced by Gnosticism.

Recent scholarship that has been favorable to an early date for the *Gospel of Thomas* has tried to isolate portions of the *Gospel of Thomas* as being early. In 2005, DeConick argued in *Recovering the Original Gospel of Thomas: A History of the Gospel and its Growth* that the original kernel of the *Gospel of Thomas*, rather than its entirety, can be dated earlier than the canonical gospels. She believes that the *Gospel of Thomas* evolved. It was written by a series of deletions, modifications, and revisions that took place over many years. Some written material may have been used, but much of the *Gospel of Thomas* from her perspective was written a little at a time over many years. This would explain the duplications and the contradictions within it.[68]

This viewpoint of *Thomas'* composition influences DeConick's understanding of its dating. Portions of the *Gospel* would have been written at different times. DeConick attempts to peel back the layers of the *Gospel of Thomas* to discover what the original kernel of the *Gospel* was. When she does so, she concludes that the original kernel can be dated between AD 30–50. The next layer in the *Gospel of Thomas* is between AD 50–60; the following layer can be dated to AD 60–100; and later additions to between AD 80–120.[69]

DeConick's viewpoint has not convinced many. Rather than seeing several layers that led to the formation of the *Gospel of Thomas*, some scholars see the different layers within the *Gospel of Thomas* as being ascribed to the compiler who used traditions that stem from the canonical gospels. While an independent kernel could exist, there are many places

---

67. Jenkins, *Hidden Gospels*, 70.
68. DeConick, *Recovering the Original Gospel of Thomas*, 55–63.
69. DeConick, *Recovering the Original Gospel of Thomas*. Cf. DeConick, *The Original Gospel of Thomas in Translation*.

within the *Gospel of Thomas* that should be seen to be dependent upon the canonical gospels.[70]

There are many instances where wording within the *Gospel of Thomas* appears similar to the canonical gospels. For example, the *Gospel of Thomas* contains portions like the Parable of the Sower in *Gospel of Thomas* 9.

> Jesus said, Look, the sower went out, took a handful (of seeds), and scattered (them). Some fell on the road, and the birds came and gathered them. Others fell on rock, and they didn't take root in the soil and didn't produce heads of grain. Others fell on thorns, and they choked the seeds and worms ate them. And others fell on good soil, and it produced a good crop: it yielded sixty per measure and one hundred twenty per measure.

This is not an isolated instance. The *Gospel of Thomas* also contains sections on the "hidden being disclosed," "the blind leading the blind," and the Parable of the Mustard Seed (*Gos. Thom.* 5, 20, 34) which would agree with the Synoptic Gospels.[71] The *Gospel of Thomas* shows evidence of incorporating other New Testament writings in other places.[72] The following are dependencies that some are seeing between the *Gospel of Thomas* and the canonical gospels.

Parallels between The Gospel of Matthew and the *Gospel of Thomas*

- Matthew 5:10: *Gospel of Thomas* 69a
- Matthew 5:14: *Gospel of Thomas* 32 (= P.Oxy. 1.7)
- Matthew 6:2–4: *Gospel of Thomas* 6, 14 (= P.Oxy. 654.6)
- Matthew 6:3: *Gospel of Thomas* 62
- Matthew 7:6: *Gospel of Thomas* 93
- Matthew 10:16: *Gospel of Thomas* 39

---

70. See footnote 51.

71. *Gospel of Thomas* 5 states, "Jesus said, 'Know what is in front of your face, and what is hidden from you will be disclosed to you. For there is nothing hidden that will not be revealed. [And there is nothing buried that will not be raised.]'"

Gospel of Thomas 20 reads, "The disciples said to Jesus, 'Tell us what Heaven's kingdom is like.'"

Gospel of Thomas 34 states, "He said to them, 'It's like a mustard seed, the smallest of all seeds, but when it falls on prepared soil, it produces a large plant and becomes a shelter for birds of the sky.'"

72. Evans, et al., *Nag Hammadi Texts and the Bible*, 88–144. See also Blomberg, "Tradition and Redaction in the Parables of the Gospel of Thomas," 177–205.

- Matthew 11:30: *Gospel of Thomas* 90
- Matthew 13:24–30: *Gospel of Thomas* 57
- Matthew 13:44: *Gospel of Thomas* 109
- Matthew 13:45–46: *Gospel of Thomas* 76
- Matthew 13:47–50: *Gospel of Thomas* 8
- Matthew 15:13: *Gospel of Thomas* 40
- Matthew 18:20: *Gospel of Thomas* 30 (= P.Oxy. 1.5)
- Matthew 23:13: *Gospel of Thomas* 39, 102 (= P.Oxy. 655.2)

Parallels between The Gospel of Luke and the *Gospel of Thomas*

- Luke 11:27–28 and 23:29: *Gospel of Thomas* 79
- Luke 12:13–14: *Gospel of Thomas* 72
- Luke 12:16–21: *Gospel of Thomas* 63
- Luke 12:49: *Gospel of Thomas* 10
- Luke 17:20–21: *Gospel of Thomas* 3 (= P.Oxy. 654.3), 113

Parallels between The Gospel of John and the *Gospel of Thomas*

- John 1:9: *Gospel of Thomas* 24 (= P.Oxy. 655.24)
- John 1:14: *Gospel of Thomas* 28 (= P.Oxy. 1.28)
- John 4:13–15: *Gospel of Thomas* 13
- John 7:32–36: *Gospel of Thomas* 38 (= P.Oxy. 655.38)
- John 8:12; 9:5: *Gospel of Thomas* 77[73]

There are thus many possible dependencies between the *Gospel of Thomas* and the canonical gospels.

Patterson, Pagels, and DeConick's perspectives on the *Gospel of Thomas* have also been countered by a recent study by Nicholas Perrin. While he notes that these scholars bring good observations forward for further understanding this important document, he does not find their conclusions adequate.

Perrin's argument is far too detailed to represent in this volume. It can be summarized in this way. Rather than assuming that the *Gospel of Thomas* was composed as a result of oral tradition, he proposes that the

---

73. Evans, *Fabricating Jesus*, 69.

Gospel of Thomas bears similarity to another ancient writing known as the *Diatessaron* that emerges from Syria in the latter part of the second century.[74] In the *Diatessaron*, Tatian, who composed the work, merged together the four canonical Gospels. It was the primary compilation of gospel texts in Eastern Christianity. Scholars who have considered both the *Diatessaron* and the *Gospel of Thomas* have noticed the overlap in language.[75] There is an overlap with themes, as well.[76]

If these two ancient documents can be linked together as Perrin advocates, it makes sense of several things in the composition of the *Gospel of Thomas*. It means that this non-canonical gospel was not put together with layers on top of the original kernel. Its order can be explained in agreement with this other document from Syria, the *Diatessaron*. It also means for our purposes that the *Gospel of Thomas* was a carefully constructed piece of literature dating to about the time of the *Diatessaron*, which is late second century.[77]

One other gospel that some have claimed to be dated early is the *Gospel of Peter*. John Dominic Crossan has promoted that the source which led to this gospel is much earlier than the canonical gospels. From Crossan's perspective, the disciples knew little of Jesus' death beyond the facts that the Savior died. When they composed the crucifixion and resurrection accounts, they formulated them based on a meditation upon the Hebrew Scriptures. The *Gospel of Peter*, Crossan reasons, is so different that it must have an independent version of the crucifixion and resurrection at its core. Crossan goes even further to say that the *Gospel of Peter* has incorporated something which he calls the "Cross Gospel." It is about eighty percent of the *Gospel of Peter*, according to him. While a Cross Gospel is not available presently, he believes that this was the true source, and it in turn influenced Matthew, Mark, Luke, and John, as well as the *Gospel of Peter*.[78]

---

74. Perrin, *Thomas*, 81–124.

75. Strobel, "Textgeschichtles zum Thomas-Logion 86," 211–14; Quispel, *Tatian and the Gospel of Thomas*, 174–90.

76. Perrin notes an overlap in language of composition, ascetical practices, hermeneutical reflections, and Hermeticism (Perrin, *Thomas*, 73–138).

77. Perrin, *Thomas*, 93–97.

78. Crossan, *Cross that Spoke*. See also Crossan, *Four Other Gospels* and Dillon, "The Primitive Gospel," 857–70. See others who have given indication of the *Gospel of Peter* being early, such as Koester, *Introduction to the New Testament*, 2:163; cf. Cameron, *The*

A few scholars have developed Crossan's ideas further. For example, Paul Mirecki has claimed that the *Gospel of Peter* is an older gospel and predates the Synoptic Gospels. He writes, "The *Gospel of Peter* was a narrative gospel of the synoptic type which circulated in the mid-first century under the authority of the name Peter."[79] He dates this gospel to about fifteen years following the crucifixion.

Despite a few scholars who take this position and an early date for the *Gospel of Peter*, this is a highly controversial viewpoint. Few scholars would support an independent Cross Gospel. It is not quoted or referred to at all within the early Christian writings of Ignatius, Polycarp, Clement, or Justin Martyr.[80] Furthermore, the date of the *Gospel of Peter* has been set by a number of scholars much later. Paul Foster dates the *Gospel of Peter* during the period AD 150–190.[81] Bart Ehrman places it also in the second century.

Rather than viewing the *Gospel of Peter* as dependent upon a source earlier than the canonical gospels, several scholars have found that *Gospel of Peter* is dependent either upon oral tradition from the Gospels of Matthew, Mark, Luke, and John, or from the actual written canonical gospels.[82] It is the "dominant position held by scholars . . . that of seeing the *Gospel of Peter* as dependent on one or more of the canonical accounts."[83] While the idea of a Cross Gospel is an innovative proposal, there is no documented reference for such a text.[84] It is much more likely that the *Gospel of Peter* and its contents date from the second century and hence after the canonical gospels.

Conclusion

This chapter has surveyed the dating of the canonical and non-canonical gospels. This investigation has shown that precise dates from these gospels are not fixed. There is a narrow range that can be established for the

---

Other Gospels, 78.

79. Mirecki, "Peter, Gospel of," 5:278–81.
80. Cf. Witherington, *Jesus Quest*, 267–8; Jenkins, *Hidden Gospels*, 96.
81. Foster, *Gospel of Peter*, 172.
82. Brown, "*Gospel of Peter* and Canonical Gospel Priority," 321–43; Stillman, "Gospel of Peter," 114–20.
83. Foster, *Gospel of Peter*, 37–38. Cf. Green, "The Gospel of Peter," 293–301.
84. Cf. Jenkins, *Hidden Gospels*, 96–97.

canonical gospels that places them all in the first century. Mark is the earliest gospel at 50 through late 60, and the Gospel of John is the latest between AD 80–100. As a result, these gospels are significantly earlier than when most scholars would date the non-canonical gospels.

The two exceptions might be the *Gospel of Thomas* and the *Gospel of Peter*. There are, however, only a few scholars who date the *Gospel of Peter* early, and there have been good arguments that counter this claim. While there may be a small kernel of the *Gospel of Thomas* that could be dated earlier than the canonical gospels, it is a minority opinion. Furthermore, there are scholars such as Perrin who have proposed sufficient responses to an early dating of the *Gospel of Thomas*. Perrin's conclusions have not been sufficiently countered.

As a result, it is fair to conclude that the canonical gospels are earlier than the non-canonical ones. While some are advocating for the worth of non-canonical gospels, we can concur with scholars Porter and Heath when they state, "How could documents written generations after Jesus' life be considered as authoritative as those written a few decades after Jesus' life?"[85] The canonical ones deserve pride of place. There is enough evidence to say that the canonical gospels are to be preferred because they are earliest.

---

85. Porter and Heath, *Lost Gospel of Judas*, 106.

CHAPTER TWO

Eyewitness Testimony

DATE IS NOT THE only factor that determines the value of a gospel. Reliability is also important. A source close in time to a past event is helpful if it is trustworthy. If the resource is not recognized as being trustworthy, however, it is of much lesser value. We know this to be the case when we evaluate our own family history. If we can return to the example of a family reunion, a story about someone who is no longer living is of value if it is told from a reliable source. If the one recalling the story is in poor health or suffering from memory loss, then that person is not a good source. If the one recounting a story of a deceased relative is aged but did not know the relative well, then his story will be of much lesser value than someone who did know the relative in question. If the storyteller has known biases, then that story is also much less reliable. So it is in evaluating accounts about Jesus. The ones that are most trustworthy have greater value than those that do not. This is helpful to keep in mind as the many different gospels are considered. Those that encourage us to trust them have a greater value than those that do not.

A critical feature in evaluating the trustworthiness will be that of eyewitness testimony. Richard Bauckham helpfully raises this perspective in his volume, *Jesus and the Eyewitnesses*. Bauckham rightly believes that testimony "asks to be trusted." The canonical gospels contain eyewitness testimony and ask to be trusted, in comparison with the non-canonical gospels, which do not contain verifiable eyewitness testimony.

With much interest being placed on other gospels recently, some may not realize that the Gospels of Matthew, Mark, Luke, and John claim to convey verifiable, eyewitness testimony. This chapter will present such evidence. It will consider sections within the canonical gospels that exhibit this feature. It will also examine sources outside of these gospels which support this claim that eyewitness testimony is to be found in the canonical gospels, and thus these are to be trusted.[1] It will also show how several of the non-canonical gospels are unreliable. Reliability makes the canonical gospels superior to those that are non-canonical.

Internal Evidence in the Canonical Gospels Regarding Eyewitness Testimony

Several factors within the canonical gospels indicate that these writings are composed of eyewitness testimony. This can be seen from the way that these writers present their stories about Jesus, the nature of the writers themselves, and the use of named individuals within their writing.

Citations Where Eyewitness History is Promoted: Luke

Certain canonical gospels state that they are using eyewitness testimony explicitly. The Gospel of Luke begins with such a declaration in its prologue. Since Luke was not one of the original disciples but a traveling companion of Paul's, this is an especially significant matter for his account. Luke describes what formed his gospel in Luke 1:1–4:

> Inasmuch as many have undertaken to compile a narrative of the things that have been accomplished among us, just as those who *from the beginning were eyewitnesses and ministers* (*ap' archēs autoptai kai hypēretai*) of the word *have delivered* (*paredosan*) them to us, it seemed good to me also, having followed all things closely for some time past, to write an orderly account for you, most excellent Theophilus, that you may have certainty concerning the things you have been taught.[2] (*Italics mine*)

The first part declares the sources that were used for the composition of his gospel (Luke 1:1–2). He gives the characteristics of these sources with two words: *autoptai*, the word for eyewitnesses, and *hupēretai*, the word translated as ministers. The word *autoptai* is used only here in the

---

1. Particularly helpful in this discussion is Richard Bauckham's perspective. Much of this chapter is dependent on his work, but a few of the conclusions are different. See Bauckham, *Jesus and the Eyewitnesses*. Bauckham rightly believes that testimony "asks to be trusted." See page 5.

2. Translation is from the ESV.

New Testament, although it is used to mean eyewitness in other writings contemporary with Luke.[3] While Luke will not use this specific word again within his gospel, he will relate what witnesses have seen in many other sections of his writing.[4] The witnessing theme refers often to those who are well-acquainted with Jesus' life. These witnesses could likely be the apostles.[5]

These sources for Luke's writing were not only eyewitnesses (*autoptai*) but also ministers (*hupēretai*) of the word that they have seen. The two words are linked together. From what these eyewitnesses saw, they also then became ministers. Their reports led to the writing of the Gospel of Luke.[6]

Luke relates that these eyewitnesses told of Jesus' ministerial activity from the beginning (*ap' arches*) of his ministry. Luke makes reference to Jesus' ministry having a beginning several times within the two-volume work of Luke and Acts (cf. Luke 3:23; 23:5; Acts 1:1).[7] The most noteworthy of these occurs in Acts 1:21–22. As Luke recounts the requirements for replacing Judas amongst the disciples, he states that it is important that the new apostle was present from the beginning. That point is John's baptism. The passage reads as follows:

> Therefore it is necessary to choose one of the men who have been with us the whole time the Lord Jesus went in and out among us, *beginning* (*arxamenos*) from John's baptism to the time when Jesus was taken up from us. For one of these must become a *witness* with us of his resurrection. *(Italics mine)*

Witnessing the resurrection of Jesus was of critical importance for replacing Judas, yet familiarity with the whole of Jesus' ministry was significant for being one of the apostles and being considered a witness. Later in Acts 10:36–42, Luke will once again draw attention to the beginning of Jesus' ministry, beginning from the time of John the Baptist. In this passage, Peter is summarizing all that has happened with Jesus,

---

3. Cf. Josephus, *Ant.* 18.342; 19.125; *Ag. Ap.* 1.55.
4. Cf. Luke 21:13; 24:44–48; Acts 1:8, 22; 2:32; 3:15; 4:33; 10:39, 41; 13:31.
5. Cf. Fitzmeyer, *Gospel according to Luke*, 294.
6. Ellis, *Gospel of Luke*, 58; Bock, *Luke 1:1–9:50*, 58.
7. There is every reason to believe that Luke and Acts should be seen together. Note how both documents begin with Theophilus (cf. Luke 1:3–4 and Acts 1:1–2).

and writes that it had a beginning which coincided with John the Baptist. Once again, Luke uses the word *arxamenos* to refer to the beginning.

> As for the word that he sent to Israel, preaching good news of peace through Jesus Christ (he is Lord of all), you yourselves know what happened throughout all Judea, beginning (*arxamenos*) from Galilee after the baptism that John proclaimed: how God anointed Jesus of Nazareth with the Holy Spirit and with power. He went about doing good and healing all who were oppressed by the devil, for God was with him. And we are witnesses of all that he did both in the country of the Jews and in Jerusalem. They put him to death by hanging him on a tree, but God raised him on the third day and made him to appear, not to all the people but to us who had been chosen by God as witnesses, who ate and drank with him after he rose from the dead. And he commanded us to preach to the people and to testify that he is the one appointed by God to be judge of the living and the dead. *(Italics mine)*

These eyewitnesses who saw Jesus' life from the time of John the Baptist then become the sources for Luke's writing. They are the ones who delivered this tradition.

It is significant that Luke uses a particular Greek word in Luke 1:2 which indicates the authority found within these sources. He uses the word *paradidōmi*, which is often used as a technical term for the handing down of authoritative material.[8] This word may refer to the passing along of tradition in oral or written form, but it is used within other New Testament texts for the dispensing of authoritative teaching.[9] By using the word *paradidōmi* in Luke 1:2, Luke tells us that he has composed "a narrative of the things that have been accomplished among us" from sources that had authority.

Luke 1:1–4, then, is an important declaration of the contents within the Gospel of Luke. By introducing the gospel in this manner, Luke is telling the reader that eyewitness testimony composed his gospel. These sources were present from the time of Jesus' baptism by John, and thus could provide information from the initial stages of Jesus' ministry. Luke

---

8. In Luke 1:2, the word is *paredosan* from *paradidōmi*.

9. Cf. Mark 7:13; Acts 6:14; 1 Cor 11:2, 23; 15:3; 2 Pet 2:21; Jude 3. See further Marshall, *Gospel of Luke*, 42.

states that he has thoroughly investigated the accounts (Luke 1:3–4), and these sources comprise his gospel.[10]

Citations Where Eyewitness History is Promoted: John

John's Gospel also explicitly states that it is communicating eyewitness testimony. This is evident by tracing the words used for testimony within the gospel. The Greek noun for witness (*martyria*) occurs 14 times within John, and the verb for witness (*martyreō*) occurs 33 times. In comparison, the noun and verb for witness occur only four times and two times respectively in the Synoptic Gospels. Testimony is a critical feature of John's Gospel.[11]

The Gospel of John begins by highlighting eyewitness testimony. John the Baptist is introduced in the prologue of John's Gospel as an eyewitness. John 1:7 states, "He came as a witness to testify concerning that light, so that through him all men might believe." While the Synoptic gospels record John the Baptist's activity, he is explicitly stated to be a witness in John's Gospel. The Synoptic Gospels provide details of John the Baptist's preaching ministry, but in the Gospel of John his one function is to witness to Jesus. In fact, John does not even record Jesus' baptism, but there is repeated mention of John the Baptist's witness.

The testifying function of John the Baptist is specifically mentioned in John 1:15: "John testifies concerning him. He cries out, saying, 'This was he of whom I said, 'He who comes after me has surpassed me because he was before me.'" John's declaration is unique amongst the canonical gospels. When John sees the dove alight on Jesus, the Gospel of John draws attention to John the Baptist's function as giver of testimony in John 1:32–37:

> And John bore witness: "I saw the Spirit descend from heaven like a dove, and it remained on him. I myself did not know him, but he who sent me to baptize with water said to me, 'He on whom you see the Spirit descend and remain, this is he who baptizes with the Holy Spirit.' And I have seen and have borne witness that this is the Son of God." The next day again John was standing with two

---

10. This has notable overlap to other early histories. Cf. Polybius, *Histories*, 1.3.1–5; 1.5.1; 1.12.5–7; Josephus, *Ag. Ap.* 1.47; *Vita* 1.47; *J.W.* 1.18. Bauckham, *Jesus and the Eyewitnesses*, 120–24.

11. Morris, *Gospel of John*, 89.

> of his disciples, and he looked at Jesus as he walked by and said, "Behold, the Lamb of God!" The two disciples heard him say this, and they followed Jesus.

While the baptism of Jesus is found in the other canonical gospels (Matt 3:13–17; Mark 1:9–11; Luke 3:21–22), the author specifically points out that John the Baptist is giving testimony in John 1:32.[12] The author then repeats that John the Baptist is testifying when he says in John 1:34, "And I have seen and have borne witness that this is the Son of God." These passages, along with several others, attest to John the Baptist's function as a provider of eyewitness testimony (cf. John 1:7–8, 15, 19, 32, 34; 3:26; 5:33, 36).

In his record of the crucifixion, John once again points to explicit eyewitness testimony. This can be seen from the way that John records this in John 19:34–35:

> But one of the soldiers pierced his side with a spear, and at once there came out blood and water. He who saw it has borne witness—his testimony is true, and he knows that he is telling the truth—that you also may believe.

It is likely that the one who is testifying is John, the disciple whom Jesus loved (cf. John 19:25–27), although there are several other possibilities.[13] Even if John the disciple is not the reference, it is plain that some type of eyewitness testimony is being presented.

After the resurrection appearances of Jesus to the disciples and to Thomas, the Gospel of John indicates that further eyewitness testimony is presented. This is evident from John 20:30–31:

> Now Jesus did many other signs in the presence of the disciples, which are not written in this book; but these are written so that you may believe that Jesus is the Christ, the Son of God, and that by believing you may have life in his name.

---

12. John notes that the dove identifies the significance of Jesus. This is a distinctive of John's Gospel. While the dove appears in the other canonical gospels, it specifically identifies Jesus as the Messiah in John. Carson, *Gospel according to John*, 151.

13. The possibilities for the one identified as "he" in "He knows that he tells the truth, and he testifies so that you also may believe" are: Jesus, the soldier, or John the disciple. See further discussion, see Carson, *Gospel according to John*, 625–27.

The author has made a selection of things to represent within the gospel. If John is the author of the Gospel of John, as several believe, this would then be an explicit occurrence of eyewitness testimony.[14]

A final passage that presents eyewitness testimony within the Gospel of John is John 21:24–25:[15]

> This is the disciple who is bearing witness about these things, and who has written these things, and we know that his testimony is true. Now there are also many other things that Jesus did. Were every one of them to be written, I suppose that the world itself could not contain the books that would be written.

The end of John 21 primarily focuses upon Jesus' interaction with Peter. Jesus asks Peter three times if Peter loves him. In each case, Peter responds by stating that he does love his master. Then, he describes the fate of Peter and John: Peter will glorify Jesus by his death, while the beloved disciple John will glorify him with a lengthy life (John 21:21-23). This beloved disciple is also the one who bears witness to Jesus and has written these things recorded in the Gospel of John.

John's testimony is then declared to be true in John 21:24: "We know that his testimony is true." The understanding of who "we" refers to has been questioned. The main options for interpreting the "we" are the following. The "we" refers to the elders in the church at Ephesus; is an indefinite expression meaning "as is well known;" or is an editorial *we* in which John refers to himself.[16] The latter is most likely (although the former is

---

14. For a discussion on the authorship of John, see Carson, *Gospel according to John*, 68–81. Other possibilities for authorship include: a disciple of John's also called John, an unknown Jew by the name of John, John the Elder, or a Johannine community.

15. Some scholars read these verses as a later addition to the Gospel of John with little connection with what came earlier; e.g., Brown, *Gospel According to John XIII–XXI*, 1126–27. There are good reasons to see John 21:24–25 as the original ending of the gospel. Structurally, John begins with a well-recognized prologue in John 1 that sets the stage for the gospel, and it would be reasonable to see John 21 as originally designed to function as an epilogue. As the prologue began from the time of creation, the epilogue then previews what the disciples' mission will be in the future as symbolized by the miraculous catch of fish. Jesus' words "until I come" in John 21:23 would correspond well to "in the beginning" in John 1:1. Besides appealing to the structure within the Gospel of John, John 21 contains vocabulary and grammar similar to previous places within John's Gospel. Finally, there is no textual evidence that separates John 21 from John 20. See further Bauckham, *Jesus and the Eyewitnesses*, 364; Carson, *The Gospel according to John*, 665–68.

16. See further Carson, *Gospel according to John*, 684.

a possibility) when compared with other passages in the gospel and the Johannine letters that use "we." In these other cases, the "we" includes the author along with the hearers (cf. John 1:14–16; 3:10–13; 1 John 1:1–5; 4:11–16; 3 John 9–12).[17] In none of these cases would an indefinite expression like "as is well known" be a reasonable meaning for the word "we" in John. The word "we" is also not used in these other cases for the elders, either. The author should be understood as meant by the "we" of this verse. By claiming that "we know his testimony is true," the author promotes his own testimony that he has communicated in the gospel.

Implied Eyewitness Testimony in the Canonical Gospels

Besides explicit statements of eyewitness testimony within the canonical gospels, there are several other pieces of evidence that indicate that the canonical gospels contain eyewitness testimony.

Matthew's Testimony in the Gospel of Matthew

Eyewitness testimony would be assumed throughout the Gospel of Matthew if the traditional viewpoint is accepted; namely, that the Gospel of Matthew was authored by Matthew, the former tax-collector and disciple of Jesus.[18] While a number of scholars hold to Matthew's authorship of the gospel, there are many that do not.[19] There are a number of others who believe that the Gospel of Matthew displayed evidence of Matthew the disciple of Jesus, but it was edited by others who were Matthew's disciples.[20]

Evidence for Matthew's authorship is best supported from external testimony from Papias and the inscription on the gospel, as will be seen below. Several other factors could reveal that eyewitness testimony from Jesus' disciple Matthew is also found within this gospel.

---

17. Bauckham, *Jesus and the Eyewitnesses*, 370–83.

18. Carson and Moo, *Introduction to the New Testament*, 140–50; Gundry, *Matthew*, 609–22; France, *Gospel of Mark*, 15; Bock, *Jesus according to Scripture*, 29. For example see Tasker, *Gospel according to St. Matthew*; Gundry, *Matthew*; Carson, "Matthew."

19. Cf. Luz, *Matthew*; Davies and Alison, *Saint Matthew*, 1:17–58; Ehrman, *New Testament*, 119; Meier, *Vision of Matthew*, 17–23.

20. Keener, *Gospel of Matthew*, 39–40; Hagner, *Matthew 1–13*, lxxvi–lxxvii; Hill, *Gospel of Matthew*, 55.

The disciple Matthew is distinguished more within the Gospel of Matthew than the other canonical gospels. For example in Matthew 9:9, Matthew's name is particularly mentioned. The verse reads, "As Jesus passed on from there, he saw a man called Matthew sitting at the tax booth, and he said to him, 'Follow me.' And he rose and followed him." Matthew's calling is recorded in Mark 2:13–17 and Luke 5:27–32, but they do not mention Matthew's name, calling him Levi. Later in Matthew 10:3, the disciple Matthew is mentioned again. His name and occupation is identified within the list of the twelve disciples as "Matthew the tax collector." While Matthew is recognized amongst the disciples in Mark 3:18 and Luke 6:15, his occupation is not stated as it is in Matthew 10:3. The Gospel of Matthew thus contains more about the disciple Matthew than the other gospels do, and this is a sign of his influence.

The Gospel of Matthew indicates that the author was familiar with money, as Matthew the tax collector would have been. Special interest is devoted to money in passages that do not have a parallel in other gospels. For example in Matthew 17:24–27, Peter is questioned about whether Jesus pays the temple tax. Matthew 18:23–25 provides a parable that concerns money, the parable of the unforgiving servant. The parable of the laborers in the vineyard and the wage that they are entitled to receive is also found uniquely in Matthew 20:1–16. These three sections are not represented in the other gospels. At the death of Jesus, money is present in Matthew but not in the other canonical gospels. In Matthew 27:3–10, Judas returns the thirty pieces of silver. That money is given to the guards for the purpose of keeping them quiet in Matthew 28:11–15.[21] It is likely that these betray Matthew's financial experience that was then incorporated into this gospel.[22]

Peter's Perspective in the Gospel of Mark

The author of the Gospel of Mark was not an eyewitness. Authorship traditionally has been ascribed to John Mark, a later traveling companion of Paul. Even though he was not an eyewitness to Jesus' life, this gospel contains significant eyewitness testimony from the apostle Peter. Peter's

---

21. See also the lengthy story of the Parable of the Talents in Matthew 25:14–30. Gundry, *Matthew*, 502–10.

22. Gundry, *Matthew*, 620–21.

viewpoint can be seen as a result of the prominent role that he plays within Mark, as well as the way the gospel is constructed.

There are several features that show his prominence. Peter's name appears more frequently within Mark than any other gospel. His name appears 19 times within 673 verses, which is a higher percentage than the other Synoptic Gospels. If the name Simon is added to these, Peter's name would then appear 22 times within Mark.[23]

He also is the first disciple named in Mark, as well as the last one mentioned, which draws attention to his importance. The apostle Peter is immediately introduced following the beginning of Jesus' ministry, which is announced in Mark 1:14–15. Jesus then immediately calls Peter in the following verses (Mark 1:16–17) which read in the ESV: "Passing alongside the Sea of Galilee, he saw Simon and Andrew the brother of Simon casting a net into the sea, for they were fishermen. And Jesus said to them, 'Follow me, and I will make you become fishers of men.'"[24]

Simon's name is particularly noticeable in this section. It appears two times within these short verses. Other versions, such as the NIV and the NRSV, only refer to Simon's name once in translation, but the original language is clear that Simon's name appears twice. When the same story is told in the Gospel of Matthew, Simon's name is not repeated (cf. Matt 4:18).[25] The double reference to Simon in Mark's Gospel is unique and carries emphasis. It underscores his stature within the Gospel of Mark.[26]

Mark's Gospel draws special attention at its end to Peter. None of the disciples are witnesses of the events at the trial or crucifixion in the Gospel of Mark except Peter who is the only one who appears. When the women visit Jesus' tomb, they are told to tell the disciples as a group, but especially Peter (Mark 16:7). None of the other disciples is mentioned individually. Thus, at this next-to-last verse within the gospel, Peter's

---

23. In Matthew, Peter's name appears 24 times out of 1,071 verses. In Luke, Peter's name is found 18 times out of 1,151 verses. If Simon is included, then Luke would name Simon Peter 22 times.

24. Simon and Peter are the same. Cf. Mark 3:16, where Jesus gives Simon the name Peter.

25. Matthew 4:18 reads, "While walking by the Sea of Galilee, he saw two brothers, Simon (who is called Peter) and Andrew his brother, casting a net into the sea, for they were fishermen."

26. Guelich, *Mark 1–8:26*, 50.

prominence is seen once again.[27] The effect of this is to highlight Peter's role within the gospel. He is the first disciple to see Jesus, and he is the last person distinguished in Mark. His role is specifically recognized from the very beginning to the end within the Gospel of Mark.[28]

The use of Peter's name within the entirety of the Gospel of Mark functions as an *inclusio*. This is a literary feature that draws attention to a key point by connecting what begins and ends a section or a book. Ancient historians, such as Lucian in *Alexander or the False Prophet* and Porphyry in *Life of Plotinus*, used *inclusios* to highlight key eyewitness testimony in their historical writings. In these biographies, the authors relied on the key testimony of two individuals. Lucian and Porphyry both begin their biographies with the key eyewitness and then end with the same person, thus raising their viewpoint prominently. This provides a significant parallel to the Gospel of Mark, which begins and ends with Peter, thus highlighting his influential testimony.[29]

Peter's prominence in Mark can be seen in many other passages. He acts as the opinion leader for the disciples when Jesus asks them, "Who do you say that I am?" (Mark 8:29). While the question is addressed to all the disciples, Peter is the one who says that Jesus is the Christ.[30] On the Mount of Transfiguration, Mark again distinguishes Peter in his narration of the event. James and John are present along with Peter when Jesus' glory is revealed, but Mark records only Peter speaking. He is the one who urges the building of shelters for Jesus, Moses, and Elijah (Mark 9:5). Then Mark 9:6 states, "For he did not know what to say, for they were terrified." While the disciples are frightened, Peter is the one who speaks. In the Garden of Gethsemane, Mark singles out Peter again. When Jesus returns to the disciples following his intense time of prayer, he finds all of the disciples sleeping, but he chooses first to address Peter.

These are some examples of the many places where Peter is seen to be the leading figure in Mark. He is the most fully characterized person within the narrative, and undergoes a life-transforming experience within the gospel. He is not a static character, but is active as a man of initiative and self-confidence (Mark 1:36; 8:29–32; 10:28). His voice

---

27. For further on the textual reasons why the Gospel of Mark ends at 16:8, see Lane, *Gospel of Mark*, 601–5.

28. Hengel, *Studies in the Gospel of Mark*, 61.

29. Bauckham, *Jesus and the Eyewitnesses*, 132–47.

30. Wiarda, "Peter as Peter," 32.

rises above the others repeatedly within this gospel. He makes statements concerning what he sees about Jesus and then is rebuked, such as at the Transfiguration (cf. Mark 9:1–8). He insists that he will not deny Jesus (Mark 14:27–31) and then is corrected.[31] He displays greater bravery than the other disciples in following Jesus at the time of his betrayal (Mark 14:50–54), but then he experiences great remorse at his own failure (Mark 14:66–72). His emotions of fear and remorse are seen plainly, and encourage the reader to empathize with him (cf. Mark 9:6; 14:22).[32] These instances, as well as others surveyed, indicate that Peter's perspective substantially influences Mark.

The Twelve Disciples as Eyewitnesses

There is evidence of other eyewitness testimony within the canonical gospels. One significant group is the disciples, who were authoritative eyewitnesses of Jesus' earthly ministry.

The presentation of the twelve disciples within the Synoptic Gospels implies that this group provides important testimony. Each of the Synoptic Gospels contains a listing of the twelve disciples (Matt 10:2–4; Mark 3:16–19; Luke 6:13–16). In each of these sections, the twelve are presented as a group. The first readers would have recognized parallels with the twelve tribal leaders of Israel. They would have remembered Moses' choice of twelve tribal leaders from Numbers 1:1–16. The parallels that the twelve disciples have with the twelve heads of the tribes of Israel would become even clearer later in the Synoptic Gospels, when the twelve disciples are predicted to judge the twelve tribes of Israel (Matt 19:28; Luke 18:28–30).[33] They would have been recognized by the first readers as an authoritative group (Matt 10:1; cf. Mark 6:7; Luke 9:1).[34]

They also functioned as eyewitnesses, since being with Jesus was a critical factor for being a disciple. Jesus specifically appointed them so that they would be observers of his activities. This point is specifically

---

31. Wiarda makes the point that the rest of the disciples eventually express the same thing. Peter has formed their opinion but is distinguished in his leading. Wiarda, "Peter as Peter in the Gospel of Mark," 34.

32. Bauckham, *Jesus and the Eyewitnesses*, 175.

33. France, *Matthew*, 377.

34. Gerhardsson considers them to be from the time that Jesus appoints them as "an authoritative collegium." Gerhardsson, *Reliability of the Gospel Tradition*, 74.

made in Mark 3:14: "He [Jesus] appointed twelve—designating them apostles—that (*hina*) they might be with him and that (*hina*) he might send them out to preach." The original language of the passage uses the word *hina*, which means "in order that." It indicates the purpose for why he chose the disciples. While there were others who traveled with him (cf. Luke 8:1–3), these twelve were set apart because their purpose was to be with him and to be sent out by him. Later, when the disciples are called upon to replace Judas Iscariot following the death and resurrection of Jesus, they choose someone who had been an eyewitness to Jesus' activities (Acts 1:21–22).[35] Then later in Acts, as Peter recounts the Christian message, he declares that he and the disciples were "witnesses of all that he did both in the country of the Jews and in Jerusalem" (Acts 10:39).[36]

Not only were the twelve recognized as a group of eyewitnesses, but the twelve are distinguished individually, too. The authors of the Synoptic Gospels could have referred to the twelve disciples as a group without recording their names, but each of these accounts mentions the twelve by name. This is particularly striking, since many of the disciples do not appear again within the Synoptic Gospels. Seven of the disciples listed in the Gospels of Mark and Luke are not mentioned by name again within these accounts, while six of the disciples are not mentioned by name again within the Gospel of Matthew. Each of the writers has made a specific point to record the name of each disciple.

The writers of the Synoptic Gospels have not copied these lists directly from each other, either. This serves to distinguish the twelve even further. While the lists follow a similar order, they are not identical. In each case, Peter is first as the leader of the group. Andrew, James, and John are found in the second, third, or fourth positions, but sometimes in different orders, depending upon the gospel.[37] Philip always heads the

---

35. See previous discussion in section entitled "Citations in which eyewitness history is promoted: Luke."

36. Bauckham, *Jesus and the Eyewitnesses*, 114–15. John's Gospel also emphasizes this further by stating that a key criterion for being a disciple is that they saw Jesus' activities. John 15:26–27 reads, "But when the Helper comes, whom I will send to you from the Father, the Spirit of truth, who proceeds from the Father, he will bear witness about me. And you also will bear witness, because you have been with me from the beginning." Because they have seen all that Jesus did from the beginning, they are able to testify in his name.

37. These four are first since they are prominent amongst the disciples, a trend that continues into the early church (cf. Acts 3:1–4:31; 8:14–25).

second group of disciples. That group includes Bartholomew, Thomas, and Matthew, but their order is different amongst the Synoptic Gospels. James the son of Alphaeus heads the third group, which includes Simon the Zealot and both Judases, but their order is different, as well. Judas Iscariot is always last, likely indicating his low position due to his betrayal of Jesus.

Besides the variance within the list, the disciples are also distinguished by their epithets. The two named Simon, the two named James, and the two named Judas are distinguished as Simon Peter and Simon the zealot, James the son of Zebedee and James the son of Alphaeus, and Judas the son of James and Judas Iscariot. In Mark's account, the nickname Boanerges, sons of thunder, is given to John and James. In Matthew's account, "the tax collector" is connected to Matthew. Simon is called either the Cananaean or Zealot, depending upon the gospel. Judas Iscariot is distinguished by being the traitor.[38]

The specific epithets attached to the disciples' names and the order in which they are stated serve to distinguish these men. It seems likely that the authors recorded each disciple's name in order to identify people who could confirm the truthfulness of what was written. These named twelve eyewitnesses could function as individuals as well as a group to endorse the truthfulness of what was written.

Particular Named Individuals Amidst Many Anonymous Ones

The canonical gospels refer to a surprising number of individuals who are relatively minor within their overall narratives. It is not surprising to see the canonical gospels identify public figures such as Herod, Caiaphas, Pontius Pilate, and John the Baptist. They would naturally correspond with the time period in which Jesus lived. It is also not surprising to see the canonical gospels leave out the names of a number of minor characters. People who meet Jesus once but do not become disciples are often not identified. Most of those who are healed by Jesus are also unspecified. For example, when Jesus cleanses the ten lepers, not one of them is distinguished by name (Luke 17:12–19).

---

38. Bauckham, *Jesus and the Eyewitnesses*, 102–108. Cf. Naveh, "Nameless People," 109–11. He argues from a similar list in *m. Sheqalim* 5:1 that this is a list of temple officials in a particular generation.

Several times, the canonical gospels will identify a group rather than point out an individual. A person can be part of some of the scribes or chief priests, or one of the guards. Sometimes an unnamed person might be distinguished as one from a group, such as in Luke 7:36, where "one of the Pharisees" asked to eat with Jesus.[39]

With so many anonymous individuals, it becomes noteworthy that there still are a number of relatively minor figures who are represented by name. The canonical gospels record specific names of minor characters in several places. Mark records the names of 14 minor characters. Matthew contains 15 specifically identified individuals. Luke records the names of 25 minor characters, and John recognizes 24 names. Some of the most noteworthy of these are: Jairus, Bartimaeus, Simon of Cyrene, Joseph of Arimathea, and Cleopas.

These people did not have to be identified for the gospel writers to tell the particular story, but the presence of their names highlights something significant. These minor characters are other eyewitnesses to the story of Jesus beyond the testimony of the disciples. Some of them even originated some portion of the gospels and likely were continuing to tell their story during the time that the canonical gospels were written. The story of the gospels could be checked against theirs. If there was some discrepancy in the way their story was represented, the truthfulness of the gospel could be called into question. By representing their names, the canonical gospel writers provide evidence that other testimony beyond the disciples and their own could verify the claims of their gospel.[40]

At times, the witness of these minor figures can be especially critical for the message of the overall gospel. For example, the women who were at the cross, burial, and empty tomb—critical events for the canonical gospels—are identified individually, instead of being anonymous or mentioned as a group.[41] In the Synoptic Gospels, the following women were present at these events. Some of the women, like Mary Magdalene and Mary the mother of Jesus, were present at all three events.

---

39. See others who are called "one of" a group. Cf. Mark 5:22; 12:28; Luke 11:45; 23:39; John 18:22, 26; 19:34.

40. Bauckham, *Jesus and the Eyewitnesses*, 39.

41. See further Bauckham, *Gospel Women*.

	Cross	Burial	Empty Tomb
Mark	Mary Magdalene Mary the mother of James the little and Joses Salome	Mary Magdalene Mary the mother of Joses	Mary Magdalene Mary (mother of James) Salome
Matthew	Mary Magdalene Mary (mother of James and Joseph) Mother of sons of Zebedee	Mary Magdalene The other Mary	Mary Magdalene The other Mary
Luke			Mary Magdalene Joanna Mary (mother) of James

Each of these gospels portrays these women as eyewitnesses, deliberately drawing attention to the fact that they saw these events. For example, Matthew is clear that they saw Jesus die in Matthew 27:55–56: "There were also many women there, looking on from a distance, who had followed Jesus from Galilee, ministering to him, among whom were Mary Magdalene and Mary the mother of James and Joseph and the mother of the sons of Zebedee." (cf. Mark 15:40; Luke 23:49). Later, they saw where he was laid in the tomb: "Mary Magdalene and Mary the mother of Joses saw where he was laid" (Mark 15:47; Luke 23:55). Afterwards, they went to see the tomb on the first day of the week (Matt 28:1). They also saw the stone that had been rolled away and the young man who was sitting on the right side and dressed in a white robe (Mark 16:4).[42]

The differing names between the accounts need not be concerning. Mary Magdalene and Mary the mother of James are present in all three gospels at these events. Salome appears at the cross and at the empty tomb in Mark's Gospel. Matthew's Gospel has the mother of the sons of Zebedee at the cross. In the Gospel of Luke, Joanna is found at the empty

---

42. Cf. Byrskog, *Story as History*, 75–78.

tomb. The different names likely would appeal to the readers of each of the gospels. The omission of Salome in Matthew and Luke may signify that she had drifted into obscurity at the time of the writing of these gospels. This may have led these gospel writers to omit her name and substitute another like the mother of the sons of Zebedee, who was more significant for Matthew's audience (cf. Matt 20:20), and Joanna, who was more significant for Luke's readers (cf. Luke 8:3).[43]

It is evident that care was given to the way that each of the gospel writers lists the witnesses at each event. Salome is not listed as present at Jesus' burial in Mark, but she is at the cross and the empty tomb. In Matthew, the mother of the sons of Zebedee is not added to those who were present for Jesus' burial. Luke also does not copy the list of women mentioned previously in Luke 8:2–3 (Mary Magdalene, Joanna, and Susanna) directly into the passion events. The authors could have simply repeated the list for those present at the burial and the empty tomb, but they chose not to do so, likely because they were paying attention to who was actually present at each event, critical in the origin of the Christian movement. It was likely that these women were accessible, and the gospel writers needed to be careful to represent accurately who was present at these critical events.[44]

Other significant minor characters are also named within the gospels. These include Bartimaeus, the blind man who was healed during Jesus' journey to Jerusalem; Simon of Cyrene, who carried Jesus' cross after all of the disciples had left; Joseph of Arimathea, who offered his tomb for Jesus' burial; and Cleopas, who met the resurrected Jesus on the road to Emmaus. These likely all joined the early Christian movement and were well-known in the circles where their stories were shared, as a number of scholars have proposed.[45] By representing these people by name, the canonical gospel writers support the validity of their writing by appealing to these other witnesses.

---

43. Cf. Gundry, *Matthew*, 579.

44. Bauckham, *Jesus and the Eyewitnesses*, 50–51.

45. Cf. Williams, *Other Followers of Jesus*, 153; Meier, *A Marginal Jew*, 2:687–90; Thiessen, *Gospels in Context*, 101, 176–7; Brown, *Death of the Messiah*, 913–16, 1223–24; France, *Gospel of Mark*, 641; Gundry, *Mark*, 1:267; Bauckham, *Jesus and the Eyewitnesses*, 45–55.

Evidence from the Titles on the Gospels

Thus far, this chapter has looked at explicit and implicit testimony within the canonical gospels which indicate that the sources which led to their composition came from those who witnessed the ministry, death, and resurrection of Jesus. Eyewitness testimony is evident from the ways that the canonical gospels have presented their narrative about Jesus from internal witness of their author to the testimony of the disciples, and the witness of minor characters. There is further evidence that accentuates the value of the canonical gospels from the titles that are attached to each.

It is often claimed that the Gospels of Matthew, Mark, Luke, and John are all anonymous and were meant to circulate as anonymous tradition like folklore. Certainly the canonical gospels contain nothing like the introductions that are seen with the letters of Paul and Peter, in which the author declares himself at the beginning of the letter. For example, Paul begins his letter to the Romans in the very first verse saying, "Paul, a servant of Christ Jesus, called to be an apostle and set apart for the gospel of God." Peter begins his letter in 1 Peter, "Peter, an apostle of Jesus Christ, to those who are elect exiles of the dispersion in Pontus, Galatia, Cappadocia, Asia, and Bithynia." There is nothing comparable to this type of introduction within the canonical gospels.

Each of the canonical gospels, however, does bear a title with a set format. The title precedes the writing and is known to have circulated with it. Each title begins with *euangelion*, the word for gospel, then the Greek preposition *kata*, which means "according to," and then ends with the names Matthew, Mark, Luke, or John, depending upon which gospel is concerned. These titles are found with each of the canonical gospels in early church papyri and reports by the second and third century church fathers. They are also found on the codices of the earliest New Testaments, namely Codex Siniaticus and Codex Vaticanus.

There is no evidence found of a version of the canonical gospels circulating within early Christianity without having a title.[46] It is highly likely that the canonical gospels circulated from the beginning with titles. Anonymous works were relatively rare and were given titles in ancient libraries. An anonymous work would sometimes receive multiple titles, but there is no instance of a canonical gospel receiving more than one

---

46. Hengel, *Studies in the Gospel of Mark*, 65–72.

title.⁴⁷ Within second century literature, church fathers criticized others for omitting some type of identification with a gospel. For example, the early church father Tertullian criticizes the heretic Marcion, who revised Luke's Gospel, taking away the Jewish elements within it. Tertullian writes, "a work ought not to be recognized, which holds not its head erect . . . which gives no promise of credibility from the fullness of its title and the just profession of its author."⁴⁸ There is no instance of a church father criticizing the canonical gospels for lacking a title. Instead, the canonical gospels bear a title uniformly from the time of the earliest manuscripts. These manuscripts come from diverse places within the Roman Empire, such as Alexandria, Antioch, Carthage, and Lyons.⁴⁹

Besides the witness from these early manuscripts, there was the expectation that particular texts would be identified within the worship service of early Christians. The public reading of a gospel within the church would have necessitated some introductory title. Early Christian history shows great interest in the source of a particular book. For example, there is quite a bit of dialogue regarding who wrote the Letter to the Hebrews. The letter is not attributed to a named person. This led to church fathers such as Tertullian, Clement of Alexandria, and Origen surmising who wrote it. Paul, Barnabas, Apollos, Luke and others have been suggested as authors of this epistle. No church father, however, placed his particular favorite author upon this debated letter, indicating how important it was to preserve accuracy in this area. It was not a trivial matter to attach titles and names to early Christian documents. Since the title for the canonical gospels is found early and is undisputed within early texts, there is good reason to believe that the canonical gospels had a title from the beginning, thus identifying the source.⁵⁰

This adds further support to eyewitness testimony being found within the gospels. Matthew and John were eyewitnesses of Jesus, and the likelihood that they wrote these gospels is increased by the evidence of the titles. This also raises the likelihood that Mark contains eyewitness testimony. Mark is more likely to have written the gospel that bears his name, due to the evidence of the title and the fact that Mark is recognized

---

47. Cf. Josephus, *J.W.*, viif; Hengel, *Studies in the Gospel of Mark*, 173 n. 65.
48. Tertullian, *Against Marcion*, 4.2.
49. See further Hengel, *Studies in Mark*, 64–84.
50. Hengel, *The Four Gospels*, 48–57.

to be substantially influenced by Peter. The title increases the likelihood that Peter's eyewitness testimony exerts its influence within the Gospel of Mark.[51] As soon as the canonical gospels circulated throughout the church, they had authors' names attached to them, although these names were not part of the text. These attribute the source of the canonical gospels to specific authors, several of whom were eyewitnesses—namely, Matthew and John.

External Witness to Eyewitness Testimony in the Canonical Gospels

Besides the titles and the contents of the canonical gospels, there is other evidence supporting the high quality of the sources that composed the canonical gospels. The testimony of early church father Papias supports the viewpoint advanced thus far that eyewitness testimony is the source of the canonical gospels.

Papias

Papias lived in the early half of the second century AD. He was the respected bishop of the church of Hierapolis in the region of Phrygia in Asia Minor. This church was also a prominent one within early Christianity. As a result, Papias became an important person within the early Christian movement. Because of the location of the church and Papias' office, he was also well positioned for collecting traditions about Jesus.[52]

Little is known about the life of Papias. He did write a five volume work between AD 90 to 140 entitled *Exposition of the Sayings of the Lord*. It was a report on Jesus' words and deeds and was intended to examine the authenticity of the tradition about Jesus. It would be a valuable work for

---

51. Cf. 1 Peter 5:13, where Mark is stated to be a convert of Peter's. Also see the internal evidence section *"Peter's Perspective in the Gospel of Mark"* that favors Peter's influence on Mark. While I am comfortable attributing these titles to authors Matthew, Mark, Luke, and John, Bauckham is not trying to claim that the authorship of these sources by Matthew, Mark, Luke, and John is concluded. His aim is to show that these works were not presented and received as anonymous. Cf. Bauckham, *Jesus and the Eyewitnesses*, 301.

52. Hierapolis is in modern southwest Turkey near Colossae and Laodicea (Col 4:13). See Bartlet, "Papias' Exposition," 17.

understanding the life of Jesus and early church history, but unfortunately only fragments of it remain. These are all found in Eusebius' *Ecclesiastical History* and Irenaeus' *Against Heresies*.

From Papias' writing, it is plain that he was familiar with the canonical gospels. He states that he knew the apostle John, and was a friend of Polycarp and others "who had seen the Lord" (Fragment 1, 3). He also claims that he was the scribe who copied the Gospel of John (Fragment 15, 16).[53]

Scholars have noted the significance of these fragments, grouping them with writings known as the Apostolic Fathers. This collection of writings has been recognized as a respected body of Christian literature since the latter part of the seventeenth century. The content of the Apostolic Fathers is recognized to be closely connected to the previous generation of apostles.[54] The writers even personally interacted with a number of the apostles. J. B. Lightfoot, a nineteenth century scholar of this body of literature, describes the value of the Apostolic Fathers as "the literary remains of those who flourished in the age immediately succeeding the Apostles, and who presumably therefore were their direct personal disciples."[55] What words we have from Papias would be considered then to be of high value.

Fragments of Papias

A range of dates, between AD 90–140, have been proposed for the fragments of Papias. Some date these writings to AD 130, while others prefer a date around AD 110 or slightly earlier. Those who prefer the later date refer to a statement about Papias made in the writings of

---

53. Ehrman identifies these fragments with these numbers. See Ehrman, *The Apostolic Fathers*, 2:95, 97, 117.

54. Grant, "Apostolic Fathers' First Thousand Years," 57:20. The term was only conclusively used in 1672 by Jean-Baptiste Cotelier. He published two volumes entitled *SS. Patrum qui temporibus apostolicis floruerunt, Barnabæ, Clementis, Hermae, Ignatii, Polycarpi opera edita et non edita, vera et supposita, graece et latine, cum notis*. The writings that were included in this volume were those of Barnabas, Clement of Rome, the Shepherd of Hermas, Polycarp of Smyrna, and Ignatius of Antioch. Such a collection would have been impossible to find previously, since the earlier part of that century saw the printing of *First and Second Clement* and the *Epistle of Barnabas*, the original Greek of Polycarp's epistles, and the Ignatian letters.

55. Lightfoot, "Apostolic Fathers," 1:3.

early church historian Philip of Side (*Fragments* 4.6). As a result, these scholars place Papias' fragments in the reign of Hadrian (AD 117–138) and prefer the AD 130 date.[56]

There are reasons, however, to believe that Papias' fragments were written much earlier than these scholars have suggested. The evidence found within Eusebius' *Ecclesiastical History* supports a much earlier date. Eusebius states that Papias became famous during the reign of Emperor Trajan and at the time of the martyrdom of Ignatius in AD 107.[57] Eusebius' description favors a date for Papias' writing between AD 100–110.

Eusebius' account about Papias is to be preferred over Philip of Side's for several reasons. Eusebius wrote his history more than a hundred years earlier than Philip of Side. The *Ecclesiastical History* was completed by 324, while Philip of Side wrote in 430. Eusebius is the historian closer to the time of Papias, and thus his viewpoint would be expected to be more reliable.

There are other reasons to prefer an early date for Papias' writing. Irenaeus, who lived at the end of the second century, as well as Eusebius never list Papias as an anti-Gnostic witness. Presumably if Papias had written later in the second century, Irenaeus and Eusebius would have recorded him as an opponent of Gnosticism. Both Irenaeus and Eusebius quote large numbers of early witnesses against Gnosticism. The absence of Papias' name in their lists makes the most sense if Papias wrote earlier than when Gnosticism became a problem. This factor makes an early dating during the first decade of the second century more likely for Papias' writing than a later one.

Papias' writing has also been noticed to bear similarity with earlier church writings, such as Ignatius of Antioch. Like Papias, Ignatius is concerned with stressing the words of Jesus (Ign. *Eph.* 15.1–2). He is interested in the sound knowledge of Jesus' life on earth and his ministry (Ign. *Eph.* 9.2). Ignatius mentions the commandments of Jesus Christ, the law of Jesus Christ, and the ordinances of Jesus Christ (Ign. *Eph.* 9.2; *Magn.* 2.1, 13.1).[58] Ignatius was martyred in the early part of the second century, likely in the first decade but possibly as late as AD 117. The similarity

---

56. Ehrman, *Apostolic Fathers*, 2:87. See also Drobner, *Fathers of the Church*, 55. Drobner dates these fragments to between AD 130–140.

57. Eusebius, *Hist. eccl.*, 3.36.1–2. Yarborough, "Date of Papias," 186–87.

58. For other instances, see Yarborough, "Date of Papias," 189–90.

between what is known of Papias' writings and those of Ignatius of Antioch favors an early date for Papias' fragments rather than a later one.

Irenaeus provides some perspective on the dating of Papias' fragments. He lived in the latter part of the second century and wrote between AD 175–185. He calls Papias an "ancient man" and "the hearer of the apostle John."[59] Such statements also imply an earlier dating for Papias' writing in the first decade of the second century, rather than 130.

One final reason to prefer the earlier date for Papias over the later date promoted by Philip of Side is the recognized unreliability of other portions of Philip of Side's writing. In his introduction to Papias, William Schoedel comments upon the untrustworthiness of Philip of Side. He claims that Philip of Side "is a bungler and cannot be trusted."[60] Robert Gundry notes that Philip of Side may have confused Papias' writing with that of Quadratus, an apologist of the second century.[61]

For these and other reasons, it is best to date Papias' writings at approximately AD 110. With these Fragments dated to the first decade of the second century, Papias' statements about how he valued the canonical gospels become especially important.

Papias and Eyewitness Testimony

Papias comments directly upon the sources that composed a number of the canonical gospels. These comments from Papias are recorded in Eusebius' *Ecclesiastical History*. Eusebius quotes Papias as saying:

> I will not hesitate to set down for you, along with my interpretations, everything I carefully learned from the elders and carefully remembered, guaranteeing their truth. For unlike most people I did not enjoy those who have a great deal to say, but those who teach the truth. Nor did I enjoy those who recall someone else's commandments, but those who remember the commandments given by the Lord to the faith and proceeding from the truth itself. And if by chance someone who had been a follower of the elders should come my way, I inquired about the words of the elders— what Andrew or Peter said, or Philip, or Thomas or James, or John

---

59. Irenaeus, *Haer.* 5.33.4; cf. Eusebius, *Hist. eccl.*, 3.39.1, 13. Gundry, *Mark*, 1027.
60. Schoedel, *Apostolic Fathers*, 120.
61. Bauckham, *Jesus and the Eyewitnesses*, 14; Bartlet, "Papias' Exposition," 16–17, 20–22; Schoedel, *Apostolic Fathers*, 51–52; Gundry, *Matthew*, 610–11.

or Matthew or any other of the Lord's disciples, and whatever Aristion and the elder John, the Lord's disciples, were saying. For I did not think that information from books would profit me as much as information from a living and abiding voice.[62]

These comments from Papias speak of the value that was placed upon eyewitness testimony in understanding Jesus. Rather than preferring information found in books, eyewitness testimony was valued.

Eyewitness testimony is not only treasured by Papias, however; the generation before him valued this, as well. In the fragment above, Papias states that he "set down for you, along with my interpretations, everything I carefully learned from the elders and carefully remembered, guaranteeing their truth." Eyewitness testimony was therefore of value to the elders, the generation before Papias.

If this is the case, Papias' statement becomes even more enlightening for discerning the sources of some of the canonical gospels. Rather than speaking of his opinion in the first decade of the second century, he is writing about matters that emerge from elders in the late first century. This is the precise time during which the canonical gospels were being written. Eyewitness testimony was a key criterion, a distinguishing feature, for those who evaluated written testimony about Jesus in the latter part of the first century.

As Papias explains what information he valued about Jesus, he states how much he esteems the "living and surviving voice." By this he does not mean oral tradition that was circulating about Jesus, but those who had an eyewitness perspective. Appreciation for the living voice of eyewitnesses was the common understanding of the phrase in the second century. Quintilian, Pliny, Polybius, and Seneca speak of the preference for an identifiable witness to a tradition as being superior to a book about the tradition.[63] Church father Jerome, who lived in the late fourth century and early fifth century, interpreted Papias' preference for the "living and surviving voice" in this way, too. He writes, "For books to be read are not so profitable for me as the living voice that even until the present day resounds on the lips of their authors." (*Vir. ill.*, 18).[64] He understood

---

62. Eusebius, *Hist. eccl.*, 3.39.3–4. Unless otherwise noted, the translations of Papias that are found in Eusebius are taken from Holmes, *Apostolic Fathers*, 562–95.

63. Alexander, "Living Voice," 224–25.

64. Bauckham, *Jesus and the Eyewitnesses*, 28.

Papias to prefer living witnesses when he considers the gospels. Firsthand information is what Papias esteemed.[65]

Papias on Mark

In *Exposition of the Sayings of the Lord*, Papias also writes specifically about Mark and Matthew as the authors of their specific gospels. He comments on the sources that led to the composition of both. These are represented in fragments in Eusebius' *Ecclesiastical History* 3.39.15. Scholars have disagreed about the translation of several key words. The Greek words inserted in this text will receive comments below.

> And the Elder used to say this: "Mark, having become Peter's interpreter (*hermēneutēs*), wrote down accurately everything he remembered, though not in order (*taxei*), of the things either said or done by Christ. For he neither heard the Lord nor followed him, but afterward, as I said, followed Peter, who adapted his teachings as needed (*chreiai*) but had no intention of giving an ordered account (*suntaxin*) of the Lord's sayings. Consequently Mark did nothing wrong in writing down some things as he remembered them, for he made it his one concern not to omit anything which he heard or to make any false statement in them."

As with the previous fragment from Papias, this represents tradition that Papias received from an earlier generation. Thus, the information found in this fragment tells about the perception that was current in the latter part of the first century.

This fragment from Papias is the earliest text that we have which presents Mark's Gospel as being highly influenced by Peter, a chief witness to Jesus' activities. According to Papias, Mark is Peter's interpreter (*hermēneutēs*), which likely means that Mark functioned as Peter's translator.[66] Papias states that Mark "wrote down accurately everything he remembered." He claims that he did not substantially alter Peter's words. This would fit in line also with ancient translation practice. Ancient translators believed that they were representing their sources accurately.[67] Pa-

---

65. Gamble, *Books and Readers in the Early Church*, 30–31.

66. For alternative translations of the word "interpreter" as expositor or intermediary, see Kürzinger, *Papias von Hierapolis*, 45–46. See also Gundry, *Mark*, 1035–36 for a more detailed argument.

67. Cf. Philo, *Mos.*, 2.34; Josephus *Ant.* 10.218; cf. 1.17; 6.196; 14.1; 20.260–63.

pias finds Mark's approach admirable because he was Peter's interpreter, like a translator, putting his readers directly in touch with Peter's recollections.[68] Mark is the one who translated from Peter's Aramaic into Greek, thus forming the Gospel of Mark.[69]

Papias finds Peter an accurate firsthand source for Mark. He states that Mark wrote down accurately the various anecdotes from Peter within his gospel. Papias does, however, criticize the gospel in regard to its order. Rather than devaluing the source of the Gospel of Mark, Papias' words criticize the overall composition of Mark. This interpretation agrees well with the presence of the two Greek words (*taxis* and *syntaxis*) within this fragment. These words have been noted to refer to orderly arrangement rather than the criticism of source.[70] Papias could be criticizing the lack of order within the Gospel of Mark due to his belief in Peter's memory being faulty.[71]

Papias says that Mark presented these stories from Peter in the form of *chreiai*. This word has led to the translation "who adapted his teachings as needed (*chreiai*)." Such a translation suggests that perhaps Mark adjusted these stories to fit the particular need of his audience.

Studies recently, however, have challenged this translation, noting that the word *chreiai* is a Greek rhetorical term. Rather than referring to needs, the word *chreiai* instead would mean a concise and pointed narrative. One translator has recently proposed the word "anecdote" for *chreiai*. If this translation is adopted, it would then signify that Mark is representing concise stories—in other words, anecdotes—from Peter, rather than adapting these stories to the perceived need of an audience.[72] This understanding would change the translation of the sentence to read, "who used to give his teachings in the form of concise and pointed accounts (*chreiai*)." Such a translation would lend further support to the source of the Gospel of Mark. Instead of adapting the gospel to the audience's

---

Bauckham, *Jesus and the Eyewitnesses*, 208–9.

68. Bauckham, *Jesus and the Eyewitnesses*, 205–10.

69. Peter did speak Greek from his growing up days in Bethsaida. See Bockmuehl, "Simon Peter and Bethsaida," 82. It does not mean that he would have preferred to teach in Greek at this stage of his Christian service. See further Bauckham, *Jesus and the Eyewitnesses*, 206.

70. Cf. Colson, "*Taxei* in Papias," 62–69.

71. Gundry, *Mark*, 2:1036.

72. Cf. Gundry, *Mark*, 1037; Witherington, *Gospel of Mark*, 22; Byrskog, *Story*, 272.

needs, Papias would be affirming that Peter gave concise anecdotes from Peter that were recorded by Mark in his gospel.[73]

Papias on Matthew

Immediately following his remarks about Mark, Eusebius represents Papias' comments on the Gospel of Matthew. These comments may or may not have followed so closely within Papias' writing, but Eusebius represents them as if they did. The fragment reads, "So Matthew composed the oracles in the Hebrew language and each person interpreted them as best he could."[74] This is a difficult saying that scholars have also debated. It needs some explanation as the source for the Gospel of Matthew is considered. Questions center upon whether Matthew could himself have composed the Gospel of Matthew, and then what is meant by "the Hebrew language" and "each person interpreted them as best he could."

One question about this statement concerns whether Matthew could have composed the Gospel of Matthew. The testimony of early church history supports Papias' statement that Matthew composed the Gospel of Matthew and thus contributed eyewitness testimony. Irenaeus' writing, which comes from the latter quarter of the second century, supports Papias on Matthew's authorship in *Against Heresies* 3.1.1:

> Matthew also issued a written Gospel among the Hebrews in their own dialect, while Peter and Paul were preaching at Rome, and laying the foundations of the Church. After their departure, Mark, the disciple and interpreter of Peter, did also hand down to us in writing what had been preached by Peter. Luke also, the companion of Paul, recorded in a book the gospel preached by him. Afterwards, John, the disciple of the Lord, who also had leaned upon His breast, did himself publish a Gospel during his residence at Ephesus in Asia.

Others following Irenaeus support this point of view. Tertullian and Origen, who wrote in the early third century, support Matthew's authorship of the gospel (*Hist. eccl.* 5.8.2; 6.25.4; *Marc.* 4.2).[75] In the fourth century, *Epiphanius* (*Pan.* 30.3), Eusebius (*Hist. eccl.* 5.8.2), and Jerome (*Prol.*

---

73. Bauckham, *Jesus and the Eyewitnesses*, 214–17.
74. Eusebius, *Ecclesiastical History*, 3.39.16.
75. Origen is quoted by Eusebius. The other reference is to Tertullian's writing.

in Matt.; *Praef. in Quat. Ev.*; *Vir. ill.* 3) also support Matthew's authorship of the Gospel of Matthew.[76] Thus, Papias' testimony that predates these early church leaders is supported. Matthew is the source of this gospel if external testimony is considered.[77]

The statement from Papias that Matthew composed a gospel in the Hebrew dialect needs further clarification. While this might lead some to believe that there was a Gospel of Matthew first written in Hebrew, this conclusion is unlikely when the contents of Matthew are examined. The Gospel of Matthew is known for its many Old Testament quotations. Many of these fit the pattern of the Greek Old Testament known as the Septuagint, rather than a Hebrew model. Furthermore, the many verbal connections between the Gospels of Mark and Matthew make it unlikely that Matthew was first written in Hebrew. Finally, the Gospel of Matthew does not read like Hebrew translated into Greek. Therefore, a Hebrew version of Matthew preceding the current Gospel of Matthew is unlikely. It is best to conclude that the Gospel of Matthew was written first in Greek.[78]

Scholars have attempted to explain Papias' statement about "oracles in the Hebrew language" in various ways. Some believe that Papias could be mistaken on the Hebrew origins of Matthew's Gospel, while not being mistaken on all points.[79] Others believe that Papias could be talking about the Jewish style of the gospel, which appears to be more orderly than a Greek style. While Mark followed Peter's perspective which lacked arrangement, they believe that Matthew followed a Hebrew order in comparison.[80]

Others believe that Papias is seeing the order of Matthew's Gospel altered by translation. As a result, its order is different from the order found in John's Gospel. Papias would have known John's Gospel and could have considered it to be the one in proper order. He faults Matthew's lack of

---

76. McKnight, "Matthew," 527.

77. Objections to Matthean authorship usually surface due to the significant overlap that Matthew has with the earlier Gospel of Mark. The weight of external testimony, however, is significant in considering Matthew's authorship. Cf. Keener, *Gospel of Matthew*, lxxvi–lxxvii.

78. Carson and Moo, *Introduction to the New Testament*, 143–44; France, *Matthew*, 609–22. It may be possible that some Aramaic sources influenced the composition of the Gospel of Matthew, but it did not emerge from a Hebrew version.

79. Carson and Moo, *Introduction to the New Testament*, 146.

80. Gundry, *Gospel of Matthew*, 619–20; Kürzinger, *Papias von Hierapolis*, 9–32; McKnight, "Matthew," 527.

order to what he believes to be interpretation. From this perspective, additions or interpretations may have been inserted within the text, but not in violation of the original source of Matthew, the disciple of Jesus.

Another possible interpretation of Papias' comment that "everyone translated them as he was able" may refer to other versions of the Gospel of Matthew that were circulating at that time. For example, the *Gospel of the Hebrews*, which is based on the Gospel of Matthew, may have been circulating and may have been known by Papias.[81] Other gospels could have been circulating by then, too (cf. Luke 1:1–4). The meaning of this part of Papias' statement is difficult to determine, but this last option is slightly preferable.

If this interpretation is adopted, Papias' comment would have an apologetic tone to it.[82] Papias would be endorsing Matthew as the source of the Gospel of Matthew, supporting Matthew over the other gospels that were similar.

Summary

It is helpful to see Papias' statements about the Gospels of Matthew and Mark in parallel with each other, with comments added.

Mark	Matthew
Peter, an eyewitness,	Matthew, an eyewitness,
related *logia* (*chreiaia*) about Jesus	put the *logia* about Jesus
orally	in writing
in Aramaic	in Aramaic/Hebrew
but not in literary order.	in literary order.
Mark, not an eyewitness,	Each person, not an eyewitness,
translated Peter's teachings	translated Matthew's written *logia*
and put them in writing	
accurately and omitting nothing.	as well as they were able.[83]

---

81. Cf. Gregory, "Jewish-Christian Gospels," 55.
82. Metzger, *Canon of the New Testament*, 54.
83. Bauckham, *Jesus and the Eyewitnesses*, 223.

Seen in comparison with each other, these two statements provide two stages from Papias' perspective. The activity of the eyewitness is stated first, and then the activity of those who are not eyewitnesses follows afterwards. In Mark's case, the eyewitness Peter spoke in Aramaic, and Mark translated into Greek. In Matthew's situation, Matthew wrote in Aramaic or Hebrew, and others translated into Greek.[84] While the order was not what Papias preferred, the eyewitness influence is evident within each gospel from Peter, in the case of the Gospel of Mark, or Matthew, in the case of the Gospel of Matthew.

Papias and Other Early Witnesses for John

Papias' statements also reveal his view of the Gospel of John. While there are no explicit comments about this gospel, Papias does reveal that he knows the Gospel of John and considers it as eyewitness testimony.

Papias' comments about the Gospel of Mark betray influence from the Gospel of John. Considering Papias' fragment that is found in Eusebius' *Ecclesiastical History* 3.39.3-4, it is important to note the sequence in which the elders are cited, since they reveal that Papias knew the Gospel of John.

> I will not hesitate to set down for you, along with my interpretations, everything I carefully learned from the elders and carefully remembered, guaranteeing their truth. For unlike most people I did not enjoy those who have a great deal to say, but those who teach the truth. Nor did I enjoy those who recall someone else's commandments, but those who remember the commandments given by the Lord to the faith and proceeding from the truth itself. And if by chance someone who had been a follower of the elders should come my way, I inquired about the words of the elders— what Andrew or Peter said, or Philip, or Thomas or James, or John or Matthew or any other of the Lord's disciples, and whatever Aristion and the elder John, the Lord's disciples, were saying. For I did not think that information from books would profit me as much as information from a living and abiding voice.[85]

The first six names that he provides in this passage are in their order of appearance in the Gospel of John: Andrew, Peter, Philip, Thomas,

---

84. Bauckham, *Jesus and the Eyewitnesses*, 223.
85. Eusebius, *Hist. eccl.* 39.3-4.

James, and John (John 1:40–41, 43; 11:16; 21:2). This appears to be deliberate. Papias did not list the disciples as found within the Gospels of Matthew or Mark, but he rather chose a list much more in agreement with the Gospel of John. The only omission is of Nathanael (John 1:45–49). It has already been noted that Papias supports eyewitness testimony in Mark and Matthew. By speaking about Mark and Matthew in the same section where he supports the testimony of disciples found in the Gospel of John, Papias implies that the Gospel of John carries eyewitness testimony, too.

From what source did eyewitness testimony come in the Gospel of John? Some believe that the eyewitness testimony comes from John the elder, whom they believe is a different person than the beloved disciple John. These scholars make a distinction between the first John that Papias lists and the second John who is called "the elder John" in the above quotation. They view this latter John as a disciple of the son of Zebedee who wrote John's Gospel.[86]

This understanding for the word elder, however, is not necessary. He could be describing the apostle John as elder. The arrangement of the sentence favors John being called "the elder" because he is associated with the apostles and different from Aristion. By calling John "the elder," Papias could also be picking up language from 3 John where "the elder" writes the letter. Papias has likely used the word elder to distinguish between witnesses who have died and witnesses who are still alive.[87]

There are many reasons to affirm that the beloved disciple John is the source for this gospel beyond this implication found within Papias' writing. Other early church historical evidence supports this. For example, Irenaeus supports the apostle John's influence in the writing of the Gospel of John. His words are recorded in Eusebius' *Ecclesiastical History* 5.20.5–6:

> For when I was a boy, I saw thee in lower Asia with Polycarp, moving in splendor in the royal court, and endeavoring to gain his approbation. I remember the events of that time more clearly than those of recent years. For what boys learn, growing with their mind, becomes joined with it; so that I am able to describe the very place in which the blessed Polycarp sat as he discoursed, and his goings out and his comings in, and the manner of his life, and his physical appearance, and his discourses to the people, and

---

86. Cf. Bauckham, *Jesus and the Eyewitnesses*, 420–23.
87. Carson and Moo, *An Introduction to the New Testament*, 233–35.

the accounts which he gave of his intercourse with John and with the others who had seen the Lord. And as he remembered their words, and what he heard from them concerning the Lord, and concerning his miracles and his teaching, having received them from eyewitnesses of the 'Word of life,' Polycarp related all things in harmony with the Scriptures.

Irenaeus knew Polycarp personally. Polycarp was a disciple of John, and he transmitted this information about the Gospel of John.

John as author is supported in other places by Irenaeus. "John, the disciple of our Lord, who also had leaned upon his breast, did himself publish a gospel during his residence at Ephesus in Asia" (*Haer.* 3.1.1). This identifies the author with the beloved disciple, as it says in John 13:23, "One of them, the disciple whom Jesus loved, was reclining next to him." Several other early church fathers support John's authorship (cf. Tertullian, *Marc.* 4.3; Clement of Alexandria in Eusebius *Hist. eccl.* 6.14.5–7). Clement is recorded in Eusebius' *Ecclesiastical History* in 6.14.7 as saying, "But, last of all, John, perceiving that the external facts had been made plain in the gospel, being urged by his friends, and inspired by the Spirit, composed a spiritual Gospel."

Eyewitness testimony is found within the Gospel of John when several things are considered. When citations about eyewitness testimony are considered, it is evident. This is affirmed by the implications from Papias and then confirmed by later church tradition.

A Note on Luke

Unlike the other three canonical gospels, the Gospel of Luke is not mentioned in Papias' writings that have survived. Luke was not an eyewitness of the events surrounding the life of Jesus, but rather was a compiler of eyewitness testimony (Luke 1:1–4). Thus, his absence within Papias' writing is not surprising.

Early documents do support the trustworthiness of the Gospel of Luke. Marcion identified Luke as the author from the middle of the second century. Marcion believed that it was impossible to reconcile the Old Testament with the New Testament. As a result, he proposed a canon of Scripture based on the Gospel of Luke and ten of the Pauline letters, although he edited these.[88] As a result, Luke was the first of the gospels to be distinguished from others, albeit in its revised Marcionite way.[89] The selection of his gospel along with the Pauline letters also displays the connection of his gospel with Paul from an early time, further supporting its reliability.[90] It can be deduced that the heretic Marcion felt as if this was the only gospel that could be trusted at this time, by singling it out for his collection of Scripture.

The anti-Marcionite Prologue to Luke, which is dated to the late second century, also supports the trustworthiness of Luke's Gospel:

> Luke is a Syrian of Antioch, a Syrian by race, a physician by profession. He had become a disciple of the apostles and later followed Paul until his (Paul's) martyrdom, having served the Lord continuously, unmarried, without children, filled with the Holy Spirit he died at the age of eighty-four years in Boeotia.
>
> [Since there were already other gospels, that According to Matthew written in Judea, that According to Mark (written in) Italy, he was urged by the Holy Spirit to write his whole gospel among those in the regions of Achaea, as he indicates this in the preface that there were already other writings before him . . .][91]

While this prologue does not ensure that eyewitness testimony is found in Luke (which can only be accomplished by looking within the Gospel of Luke), it does indicate that Luke was considered to be trustworthy.

Eusebius in his *Ecclesiastical History* also supports the trustworthiness of Luke's use of sources when he writes in 3.24.15:

> But as for Luke, in the beginning of his gospel, he states himself the reasons which led him to write it. He states that since many others had more rashly undertaken to compose a narrative of the events of which he had acquired perfect knowledge, he himself, feeling the necessity of freeing us from their uncertain opinions, delivered in his own Gospel an accurate account of those events in regard to which he had learned the full truth, being aided by his

---

88. For the significant ways that he changes the Gospel of Luke, see Irenaeus' comments in *Against Heresies*, 1.25.1.

89. Koester, *Ancient Christian Gospels*, 334.

90. Cf. Col 4:14.

91. See Aland, *Synopsis Quattuor Evangeliorum*, 553. The translation is from Koester, *Ancient Christian Gospels*, 335. Koester takes the second part of the prologue that is in brackets to be dated in the fourth century.

Jesus Tried and True

>intimacy and his stay with Paul and by his acquaintance with the rest of the apostles.

Eusebius supports Luke's claim in Luke 1:1–4 for writing accurate history according to the eyewitnesses. Rather than undermining Luke's claim, Eusebius underscores it.

Comparing Sources with Non-Canonical Gospels

When one examines the sources that led to the composition of the canonical gospels, there is a great difference between the canonical and non-canonical gospels. The sources for Matthew, Mark, Luke, and John are much better than those of the non-canonical gospels.

Beginning with the internal evidence for eyewitness testimony, the canonical gospels contain this to a much greater degree than the non-canonical ones. There are explicit citations regarding eyewitness testimony in the canonical gospels, such as Luke and John, which are not found within the non-canonical sources. The implied features that emphasize Peter's predominance and testimony in the Gospel of Mark are not found either in the non-canonical gospels.

Many of the non-canonical gospels do relate hidden things. A number of these non-canonical gospels concern private teaching, visions, reflections, or revelations (*Gospel of Thomas*, *Gospel of Mary*, *Gospel of Philip*, *Gospel of Truth*, *Gospel of Judas*). They do not concern events that took place over the breadth of Jesus' ministry.

Some of the non-canonical gospels do convey events that took place over greater points in time. These gospels, however, are seen to be dependent upon the canonical gospels (*Gospel of Peter*, *Infancy Gospel of Thomas*, *Protevangelium of James*). Many of their unique ideas, however, do not have other external sources to verify their claims, such as a cross that speaks in the *Gospel of Peter*, Jesus' boyhood miracles in the *Infancy Gospel of Thomas*, or the perpetual virginity of Mary in the *Protevangelium of James*.

When one considers minor characters that could confirm eyewitness testimony, the canonical gospels are much stronger. In comparing this feature with the non-canonical gospels, few of the non-canonical gospels contain names of minor figures. The *Gospel of Peter* does give the centurion a name at the grave of Jesus, calling him Petronius. The *Gospel of the*

Nazareans has the woman with the hemorrhage who is named Mariosa (cf. Matt 9:20; Mark 5:25; Luke 8:43), and a man with a withered hand is named Malchus.[92] A few disciples, namely Levi, Andrew, and Peter, are mentioned in the *Gospel of Mary*. The *Protevangelium of James* mentions Anna, Joachim, Zacharias, Elizabeth, and Salome. In comparison to the many minor characters found in the canonical gospels, these are relatively few.

Regarding the titles that were placed on the canonical gospels, the non-canonical gospels cannot claim the same evidence to support eyewitness testimony. The titles for non-canonical gospels are not uniform. Some of these non-canonical gospels place the phrase "gospel according to" within their writings. Their use of these titles has been claimed to be an imitation of the canonical ones.[93] The Gnostic gospels followed the pattern of the earlier canonical gospels using the phrase "gospel according to." They likely sought recognition in the church by using this title, although sometimes these titles were placed later in the document. For example, the *Gospel of Thomas* has this type of title at the end of the work rather than at the beginning. The original introduction to this work is found in *Gospel of Thomas* 1.1, which reads, "These are the secret teachings which the living Jesus spoke and which Didymos Judas Thomas wrote down."[94] The *Gospel of Philip* and *Gospel of Mary* also have the title at the end of the work and not at the beginning.[95]

Some non-canonical gospels did not follow the pattern of naming the individual writer. Instead of naming individual writers who could be considered to provide testimony, a number of non-canonical gospels are named after groups of people. There is the *Gospel of the Hebrews*, the *Gospel of the Nazareans*, and the *Gospel of the Ebionites*. Other non-canonical gospels, because of their fragmentary nature, are impossible to examine in this regard (e.g., *Gospel of Peter*, *Papyrus Egerton 2*). The evidence from titles for identifying the source of the gospels favors the canonical ones over the non-canonical.

Contemporary external attribution to the non-canonical gospels is much weaker in comparison with the canonical ones. Papias would

---

92. Bauckham, *Jesus and the Eyewitnesses*, 43.
93. Hengel, *Four Gospels and the One Gospel of Jesus Christ*, 59.
94. Koester, *Ancient Christian Gospels*, 20–21.
95. Hengel, *Four Gospels and the One Gospel of Jesus Christ*, 249.

not have known many of these non-canonical gospels, because most of them were later than his writing. Other writings from the second century predate the majority of the non-canonical gospels. None of these second century documents attribute eyewitness testimony to any non-canonical gospel.

At times, second- and third-century historical works also deem these non-canonical gospels to be of much lesser value. Early church historian Eusebius had made judgments on various books circulating within Christian circles by AD 303, if not before the end of the third century. In *Ecclesiastical History* 3.25, he places different Christian books within different categories. The first category designates those that are accepted and include the canonical gospels (*Hist. eccl.* 3.25.1). His second section concerns disputed books, which are recognized by some but not by others. Within this he lists the non-canonical *Gospel of the Hebrews* as a disputed book (*Hist. eccl.* 3.25.3–5).[96] His third category concerns those books which were heretical. In this list, the *Gospel of Peter*, the *Gospel of Thomas*, and other similar gospels of the apostles are considered to be heretical and completely unreliable (*Hist. eccl.* 3.25.6–7).[97] Eusebius' comments predate the Council of Nicea in AD 325, which resolved the Arian controversy. His comments also precede the Council of Carthage from AD 397, when the books of the New Testament were canonized. By AD 303, however, several non-canonical gospels were already seen as less reliable than the canonical ones by Eusebius, an early church father.

Conclusion

This chapter has surveyed the quality of sources found within the canonical and non-canonical gospels. The canonical ones relate eyewitness testimony. The Gospels of Luke and John explicitly claim to be representing this within their writing. The presentation of Peter within the Gospel of Mark indicates that Mark was using eyewitness testimony that came from the apostle. While much weaker, the large number of references to finances supports Matthew's influence within the Gospel of Matthew. Other evidence

---

96. Other disputed books from Eusebius' perspective include: James, Jude, 2 and 3 John, the *Acts of Paul*, the *Shepherd of Hermas*, the *Apocalypse of Peter*, *Barnabas*, the *Didache*, and Revelation.

97. Scheetz, "Books of the Bibles in early Christianity," 2.

Eyewitness Testimony

of eyewitness testimony within the canonical gospels is displayed by the presentation of the twelve disciples, the presence and function of minority figures, and the titles ("according to Matthew," "according to Mark," and "according to John") on the particular canonical gospel. The citations from Papias' fragments confirm that eyewitness testimony was present within the canonical gospels. This testimony inspires trust.[98]

In contrast, none of the non-canonical gospels can claim this amount of eyewitness testimony regarding the person of Jesus. These exhibit much less evidence internally and externally to elicit trust in them. While some may recall an event within Jesus' ministry, many refer to only one particular event. Many non-canonical gospels refer to secret conversations, visions, or mystical reflections that only a few would know. Many times, these non-canonical gospels depend also upon canonical works. The titles of many of these non-canonical gospels do not support eyewitness testimony like the canonical ones, since most appear to be imitating the earlier canonical gospels. Other early church historical material that comments upon the non-canonical gospels is silent at times about the testimony of non-canonical gospels, sometimes suspicious of these, and at times condemning. Eyewitness testimony concerning Jesus is not found within these documents, and thus they are inferior to the canonical gospels.

---

98. Cf. Paul Ricouer who wrote, "First, trust the word of others, then doubt if there are good reasons for doing so." Ricoeur, *Memory, History, Forgetting*, 165.

CHAPTER THREE

Gospel Reception in Early Church History

THE VALUE THAT ONE gives to a source can be measured in several ways. A report closer in time to the person or the event is generally preferred over a later one. An account with eyewitness testimony within it is also to be preferred over ones without it. One other criterion for confidence would be the support that others give it within the subsequent generation. This is particularly important if the story is many years old.

Returning to the example of family history, a story about someone who lived several generations earlier has much greater value if those who lived shortly afterwards believed it to be true, too. A story about a great grandfather has more value, for example, if one's grandmother or grandfather believed the account to be true. They have the advantage of being closer in time to the beloved relative. Their view is even more valuable if it is confirmed by great uncles or cousins who lived near the time of the distant relative. A wealth of testimony from the generation after the older relative adds credibility.

This is a significant point in the examination of canonical gospels and non-canonical gospels. There is a wealth of early church testimony that is often ignored which supports the superiority of Matthew, Mark, Luke, and John over the others. While some are unfairly promoting that the canonical gospels were unjustly chosen by a few powerful people many years ago, these are not considering the wealth of history that supports the superiority of the canonical gospels. This history is oftentimes forgotten but needs to be recovered, as several scholars are urging.[1]

---

1. Cf. Bockmuehl, *Seeing the Word*; Williams, *Retrieving the Tradition*; Webber, *Ancient-Future Faith*; Hall, *Reading Scripture with the Church Fathers*; Hall, *Learning Theology with the Church Fathers*. See also Oden, *Ancient Christian Commentary*.

It is the purpose of this chapter to display how the four canonical gospels rose to prominence. It will examine sources from the late first century up until the time of Irenaeus, who wrote at the end of the second century. Sources that will be considered are the Apostolic Fathers, Justin Martyr, the Muratorian Canon, and Irenaeus. The reception of Matthew, Mark, Luke, and John will be compared with the way in which non-canonical gospels were received.[2]

The Apostolic Fathers

The first set of Christian documents following the New Testament is a group of writings traditionally known as the Apostolic Fathers. While this set of books has been recognized to be important for the light that they shed on early Christianity, many within the church today are unfamiliar with them.

The Apostolic Fathers are a group of writings by early Christians that were closely associated with the New Testament. This collection of writings includes Ignatius of Antioch's seven letters (to the Ephesians, Magnesians, Trallians, Romans, Philadelphia, Smyrnaeans, Polycarp), *First* and *Second Clement*, *The Epistle of Barnabas*, *The Didache*, *Martyrdom of Polycarp*, *Shepherd of Hermas*, *Fragments of Papias*, and *The Epistle to Diognetus*.

There was no council that brought these books together. They were designated as Apostolic Fathers as a result of a few people within church history who noticed their close connection with the New Testament. The actual term Apostolic Fathers may have been used by someone in the early church named Severus in the sixth century. He so designated these writings as Apostolic Fathers due to the close connection that they had with the previous generation of apostles.[3] Many years later in 1672,

---

2. It should be noted that Paul received the canonical gospels in his writing in places such as: 1 Cor 7:10–11, which alludes to Mark 10:11–12; 1 Cor 9:14, which alludes to Luke 10:7; and 1 Cor 11:23–26, which alludes to Mark 14:22–25. Other Pauline parallels to the synoptic gospels include the following: Rom 12:14 and Luke 6:27; Rom 12:17 and Luke 6:29; Rom 12:18 and Mark 9:50; Rom 13:7 and Mark 12:13–17; Rom 14:10 and Luke 6:37; Rom 14:13 and Mark 9:42; Rom 14:14 and Mark 7:15; 1 Thess 5:2 and Luke 12:39; 1 Thess 5:13 and Mark 9:50; 1 Thess 5:15 and Luke 6:29. McDonald, *Biblical Canon*, 254. In contrast, non-canonical gospels are not found within Paul's letters.

3. Grant, "The Apostolic Fathers' First Thousand Years," 20.

Jean-Baptiste Cotelier published the writings together as a group, and the name Apostolic Fathers stayed with these documents ever since.[4]

The close connection with the New Testament can be seen in other important ways. For example, several of the books in the Apostolic Fathers, namely the *Didache*, the *Epistle of Barnabas*, and *1 Clement*, were included in some of the New Testament collections called codices that were travelling around the ancient world from around the fourth century. Certainly some within the ancient world thought of these documents with canonical status, even though the church eventually decided that they were not of that same caliber.

What is of great importance for this chapter is the proximity that the Apostolic Fathers have to the New Testament. They are generally dated between AD 70–135, which is at the same time as or immediately after the canonical gospels were written. They form the next stage of the Christian church. During this time, there was no apostle to rely on for authoritative answers, as the church was developing answers to problems that it was facing.

The Apostolic Fathers respected the canonical gospels. This is evident from the way that they incorporated their words and ideas into their writing. They did not reproduce lengthy sections from these gospels, but there are enough citations and allusions to show that the Apostolic Fathers respected the canonical gospels but not the other gospels.

Conclusions must be somewhat measured regarding the presence of the canonical gospels in the Apostolic Fathers. Some of the writings within the Apostolic Fathers were composed about the time that the canonical gospels were being written. Thus, when something is present that looks like a canonical gospel, it may be the gospel text itself or another source that was used to compose one of the canonical gospels. Furthermore, oral remembrances of Matthew, Mark, Luke, and John were also circulating at the writing of the Apostolic Fathers. So it may be possible that something oral was represented in the Apostolic Fathers rather than

---

4. Jean-Baptiste Cotelier published two volumes entitled *Sanctorum Patrum qui temporibus apostolicus floruerunt, Barnabae, Clementis, Hermae, Ignatii, Polycarpi, opera edita et inedita, vera et suppositicia*. The writings that were included in this volume were those of Barnabas, Clement of Rome, the Shepherd of Hermas, Polycarp of Smyrna, and Ignatius of Antioch. Such a collection would have been impossible to find prior to Cotelier's time, since the earlier part of that century saw the printing of *First and Second Clement* and the *Epistle of Barnabas*, the original Greek of Polycarp's epistles, and the Ignatian letters.

a written portion from the canonical gospels.[5] Even with these cautions, conclusions can be drawn for the respect of Matthew, Mark, Luke, and John within the Apostolic Fathers.

The Didache

A high appreciation for traditional gospels can be seen, for example, in the *Didache*, an important document from the late first century that witnesses to church ethics and order. The book is divided into two parts. The first part contains the "Two Ways," which is a list of ethical teachings. One way leads to life: the path of obedience, which consists primarily of loving God and loving one's neighbor. The other way of disobedience leads to death. These instructions comprise the first four chapters of the *Didache* and largely reflect Jesus' teaching that was given at the Sermon on the Mount.

The second half of the *Didache* is what some would consider a church order. It contains the earliest account of baptism and the Lord's Supper. There is teaching about how to fast and pray. Then there are instructions involving traveling Christian prophets and apostles. Finally, there are instructions for community life and exhortations for the election of bishops and deacons, as well as teaching on the return of the Lord. These topics have been composed with reference to a fair amount of New Testament material, particularly that of the Gospel of Matthew and the letters of the Apostle Paul.

Didache 8.2–3

While there are many references to the Synoptic Gospels, we will concern ourselves with some of the most clear.[6] In *Didache* 8.2–3, we can see that the Lord's Prayer is present. The italicized portion shows the overlap with the Gospels of Matthew and Luke.

---

5. Bauckham, "The Study of Gospel Traditions outside the Canonical Gospels," 383–86.

6. E.g., *Did.* 1.1 and Matt 7:13–14 and Luke 13:24; *Did.* 1.2 and Matt 7:12; 22:36–39 and Mark 12:28–31 and Luke 6:31; *Did.* 2.2–3 and Matt 19:18–19 and Mark 10:19 and Luke 19:20; *Did.* 3.7 and Matt 5:5; *Did.* 6.1 and Matt 24:4 and Mark 13:5; *Did.* 7.1 and Matt 28:19; *Did.* 8.1 and Matt 6:16; *Did.* 9.5 and Matt 7:6; *Did.* 11.2–4 and Matt 10:40–41. For further references, see *The New Testament in the Apostolic Fathers*, 24–36.

> Nor should you pray like the hypocrites. Instead, "pray like this," just as the Lord commanded in his Gospel: *Our Father in heaven, hallowed be your name, your kingdom come, your will be done on earth as it is in heaven. Give us today our daily bread, and forgive us our debt, as we also forgive our debtors; and do not lead us into temptation, but deliver us from the evil one; for yours is the power and the glory forever.*
>
> Pray like this three times a day.[7]

This passage is found in two places in the New Testament: Matthew 6 and Luke 11.

> Pray then like this: "*Our Father in heaven, hallowed be your name. Your kingdom come, your will be done, on earth as it is in heaven. Give us this day our daily bread, and forgive us our debts, as we also have forgiven our debtors. And lead us not into temptation, but deliver us from evil.*" (Matt 6:9–13)

> And he said to them, "When you pray, say: '*Father, hallowed be your name. Your kingdom come. Give us each day our daily bread, and forgive us our sins, for we ourselves forgive everyone who is indebted to us. And lead us not into temptation.*'" (Luke 11:2–4)

The wording in the *Didache* is closest to Matthew's Gospel (Matt 6:5, 9–13), but there is also a close resemblance to Luke's Gospel (Luke 11:2–4). Since the *Didache* states that this prayer should be prayed in contrast to the way that the hypocrites pray, it makes a resemblance with Matthew's Gospel more likely. While there are some differences between Matthew and the *Didache*, the overlaps with Matthew's version seem clear.[8]

One other factor that is intriguing about *Didache* 8.2–3 is that this is the first time that the writing has used the word "gospel."[9] There is some debate about how the *Didache* uses this word, particularly if it refers to an overall message or to a written gospel. Scholars seem divided over this. Despite this controversy, however, it is difficult to conclude anything

---

7. Michael Holmes' translation is being used for the Apostolic Fathers, unless indicated otherwise. See Holmes, *Apostolic Fathers*.

8. There are some differences. The *Didache* has a doxology at the end of the prayer, while Matthew's Gospel does not. The *Didache* speaks of forgiving our "debt" (singular), while Matthew's Gospel has the plural "debts." The *Didache* says "forgive us our debt, as we also forgive our debtors," using the present tense. Matthew uses a perfect tense: "Forgive us our debts, as we also have forgiven our debtors."

9. This word will appear in *Didache* 11.3; 15.3, 4.

other than what C. M. Tuckett has declared: "Overall, it seems hard to resist the notion that there is some relationship between the *Didache* and Matthew here."[10]

Didache 1.3

A second reference that shows Synoptic Gospel influence can be found in *Didache* 1.3–5. This passage interweaves ideas from Matthew and Luke. The italicized portion shows direct correspondence to Matthew and Luke.

> For what credit is it, *if you love those that love you? Do not even the Gentiles do the same?* But you must love those that hate you and you will not have an enemy.

There are clear parallels to Matthew 5:46–47.

> *For if you love those who love you,* what reward do you have? Do not even the tax collectors do the same? And if you greet only your brothers, what more are you doing than others? *Do not even the Gentiles do the same?*

Influence from Luke 6:32, 35 may be possible, as well.[11]

> "If *you love those who love you*, what benefit is that to you? For even sinners love those who love them . . . But love your enemies, and do good, and lend, expecting nothing in return, and your reward will be great, and you will be sons of the Most High, for he is kind to the ungrateful and the evil."

Didache 1.4

In *Didache* 1.4, there is the presence of more of the Sermon on the Mount which is likely to have emerged from Matthew.

> Abstain from physical and bodily cravings. *If someone gives you a blow on your right cheek, turn to him the other as well*, and you will be perfect. *If someone forces you to go one mile, go with him two miles*; if someone takes your cloak, give him your tunic also;

---

10. Tuckett, "*Didache*," 106. Tuckett leaves open the possibility that this came from a Matthean community which was significantly informed by the Gospel of Matthew.

11. Cf. Tuckett, "*Didache*," 121–23.

if someone takes from you what belongs to you, do not demand it back, for you cannot do so.

But I say to you, Do not resist the one who is evil. But if *anyone slaps you on the right cheek, turn to him the other also.* And if anyone would sue you and take your tunic, let him have your cloak as well. *And if anyone forces you to go one mile, go with him two miles.* (Matt 5:39–41)

Didache 1.5

Part of Matthew 5:26 appears to influence *Didache* 1.5:

Give to everyone who asks you, and do not demand it back, for the Father wants something from his own gifts to be given to everyone. Blessed is the one who gives according to the command, for such a person is innocent. Woe to the one who receives; if, on the one hand, someone who is in need receives, this person is innocent; but the one who does not have need will have to explain why and for what purpose he received, and upon being imprisoned will be interrogated about what he has done, *and will not be released from there until he has repaid every last cent.*

Truly, I say to you, *you will never get out until you have paid the last penny.* (Matt 5:26)

There is strong evidence that the Gospel of Matthew in particular was influential upon the *Didache*. In the words of one scholar who has examined the presence of the Synoptic Gospels in the *Didache*, "The wording is strikingly similar to the Synoptic Gospels."[12] The Oxford Society of Historical Theology examined the presence of the Synoptic Gospels in the *Didache* in 1905 and concluded that it was "most likely."[13] These occurrences are most likely the earliest ones where a high appreciation for the Synoptic Gospels can be seen.

---

12. Tuckett, "*Didache*," 126.
13. Lake, "*Didache*," 35.

Letters of Ignatius

Wording from the four traditional gospels can be found in Ignatius' letters. In their study of the presence of the gospels in Ignatius' letters, the Oxford Society of Historical Theology lists five passages which show a high degree of probability of use from the Gospel of Matthew: Matthew 15:13 in Ignatius' *Letter to the Trallians* 11.1 and *Letter to the Philadelphians* 3.1; Matthew 3:15 in Ignatius' *Letter to the Smyrnaeans* 1.1; Matthew 19:12 in Ignatius' *Letter to the Smyrnaeans* 6.1; Matthew 10:16 in Ignatius' *Letter to Polycarp* 2.2; and Matthew 18:19–20 in Ignatius' *Letter to the Ephesians Eph.* 5.2.[14] Ignatius was from Antioch, where the Gospel of Matthew was written, so it is likely that he was familiar with this writing.[15]

There has been speculation as to who Ignatius was. Byzantine writings identified him as the child whom Jesus displayed as an example (Matt 18:2), whereas Jerome took him to be one of the Apostle John's disciples.[16] He lived in the first century and died between AD 105 and 135. Eusebius reports the death of Ignatius between AD 107–110, during the reign of Emperor Trajan (AD 98–117). While there may be speculation on some of these matters, it is agreed that Ignatius had a close relationship with the apostles.[17]

Of the Apostolic Fathers, the seven letters of Ignatius have received the most attention. Part of this is due to the background surrounding their composition. These are letters written by Ignatius, bishop of Antioch in Syria (*Ign. Rom.* 2.2). He was the second or third bishop at Antioch following Peter.[18] He was arrested by Roman authorities in the beginning

---

14. *The New Testament in the Apostolic Fathers*, 76–77.

15. Bauckham, "The Study of Gospel Traditions outside the Canonical Gospels," 383–86.

16. Drobner, *Fathers of the Church*, 50.

17. There is some question as to how many letters Ignatius wrote. There is a longer recension of thirteen letters, twelve addressed by him and one addressed to him. There is the middle recension of seven letters. Then, there is a shorter recension which contains the shortened version of three of the letters. These letters are in order: *Letter to the Ephesians, Letter to the Magnesians, Letter to the Trallians, Letter to the Romans, Letter to the Philadelphians, Letter to the Smyrneans*, and *Letter to Polycarp*. What is generally accepted is the middle recension. The letters are listed in relation to the date in which they were likely sent.

18. For the viewpoint that Ignatius was the second bishop, see Origen, *Hom. Luc.* 6. For the viewpoint that Ignatius was the third bishop, see Eusebius, *Ecclesiastical History* 3.22.36. Eusebius says that Ignatius was second bishop after Evodius in one reference

of the second century and taken to Rome for trial and then execution. He wrote these letters en route to his martyrdom in Rome.

As he was being taken across Asia Minor, he had a brief stop in Smyrna where he met Polycarp. Representatives from other churches in Asia Minor came to meet him while he was traveling, asking for his help. In response, he wrote letters to Ephesus, Magnesia, and Tralles. These letters urge churches to seek unity, come together under the bishop, eliminate heretical teaching, and encourage prayer for the church in Antioch. Ignatius also wrote a letter to the church in Rome, urging them not to interfere with legal proceedings, as he wanted to be martyred.

When he arrived in Troas, he wrote letters to Philadelphia and Smyrna, and also to Polycarp. These letters contain gratitude for the hospitality that he received. They also request that members from these churches visit him. While these three letters contain similar ideas to his earlier ones, they also indicate that the situation in Antioch had been resolved. As a result, Ignatius also encourages the churches to rejoice with the church in Antioch.

The last letter that he wrote was to Polycarp, bishop of Smyrna. In this letter, he asks Polycarp to send letters ahead of him to churches that he might encounter on the way. This is the last that we hear from Ignatius. According to Polycarp's letter to the Philippians, Ignatius did stop off at Philippi. Polycarp also tells of Ignatius' martyrdom (Pol. *Phil.* 9).

Ignatius' Letter to the Trallians 11.1 and Letter to the Philadelphians 3.1

Below are two sample passages that exhibit ideas specifically from Matthew's Gospel, which I have indicated with italics:

> Flee, therefore, from these wicked offshoots that have deadly fruit; if anyone even tastes it, he dies on the spot. *These people are not the Father's planting (fyteia patros).* (Ignatius' Letter to the Trallians 11.1)[19]

> Keep yourselves from those evil plants which Jesus Christ does not tend, because *they are not the planting of the Father (fyteia patros).* Not that I have found any division among you, but exceeding purity. (Ignatius' Letter to the Philadelphians 3.1)

(*Hist. eccl.* 3.22.1), but second after Peter in another (*Hist. eccl.* 3.36.2).

19. All writings from the Apostolic Fathers in this section are from the *ANF* version.

He answered, "Every *plant* (*fyteia*) that my heavenly *Father* (*patēr*) has not planted will be rooted up." (Matt 15:13)

Matthew's Gospel alone describes people as "plantings" in a negative way. In Matthew 15:13, Jesus is asked by the disciples regarding the Pharisees. Jesus calls them a plant that the Father did not plant. The word translated "plant" (*fyteia*) is used exclusively in Matthew. Ignatius uses this word and idea, which makes it likely that he was influenced by Matthew 15:13.[20]

Ignatius' Letter to the Smyrnaeans 1.1b

A second example of the influence of the canonical gospels within Ignatius' writing can be found in his *Letter to the Smyrnaeans* 1:1b. In this passage, Ignatius uses Matthew 3:15 to interpret Jesus' baptism. Matthew and Ignatius' *Letter to the Smyrnaeans* 1:1b both describe Jesus' baptism, and they both provide the same interpretation of the event, that righteousness might be fulfilled.

> I glorify God, even Jesus Christ, who has given you such wisdom. For I have observed that ye are perfected in an immoveable faith, as if ye were nailed to the cross of our Lord Jesus Christ, both in the flesh and in the spirit, and are established in love through the blood of Christ, being fully persuaded with respect to our Lord, that He was truly of the seed of David according to the flesh, and the Son of God according to the will and power of God; that He was truly born of a virgin, was baptized by John, *in order that all righteousness might be fulfilled by Him.*

> But Jesus answered him, "Let it be so now, for thus it is fitting for us to *fulfill all righteousness.*" Then he consented. (Matt 3:15)

Matthew alone of the canonical gospels gives this motive for the Lord's baptism. It was to fulfill all righteousness.

---

20. In support of this are Massaux, *Influence de l' Évangile de saint Matthiew*, 88; Köhler, *Die Rezeption des Matthäusevangeliums*, 80.

Jesus Tried and True

Ignatius' Letter to the Romans 7.2

References to the Gospel of John have been noticed within Ignatius' letters.[21] While there is debate as to whether actual texts from John's Gospel are present, "Ignatius' knowledge of John can be taken as proved."[22] In Ignatius' letter to the Romans 7.2, he refers to living water which is a reference to John's Gospel.

> My love has been crucified, and there is no fire in me desiring to be fed; but there is *within me a water that liveth* and speaketh, saying to me inwardly, Come to the Father.

> Jesus answered her, "If you knew the gift of God, and who it is that is saying to you, 'Give me a drink,' you would have asked him, and he would have given you *living water*." But whoever drinks of the water that I will give him will never be thirsty forever. The water that I will give him will become in him a spring of water welling up to eternal life." (John 4:10–14)

Scholars examining Ignatius' *Letter to the Romans* 7.2 and its surroundings have also noticed the influence of John's Gospel. J. B. Lightfoot comments that "the whole passage is inspired by the Fourth Gospel."[23] W. R. Inge states, "On the whole direct literary dependence seems much the most probable hypothesis."[24]

Ignatius' Letter to the Philadelphians 7:1

A second passage that has been categorized as most likely dependent upon John's Gospel is Ignatius' *Letter to the Philadelphians* 7.1.[25] This passage uses ideas about the Holy Spirit as were found in John's Gospel.

---

21. Inge lists six others than the ones considered above. Ignatius' Letter to the *Magnesians* 7.1 and 8.2 from John 8:28–29; Ignatius' *Letter to the Ephesians* 5.2 and Ignatius' *Letter to the Romans* 7.3 from John 6:13; Ignatius' *Letter to the Ephesians* 6.1 from John 13:20; Ignatius' *Letter to the Ephesians* 17.1 from John 12:1–8; Ignatius' *Letter to the Philadelphians* 9.1 from John 10:9. Inge, "Ignatius," 81–83.

22. Hill, *The Johannine Corpus in the Early Church*, 442. See Foster, who makes too fine a distinction between "knowledge of John" and "use of John." Foster, "Epistles of Ignatius of Antioch," 183–184; Cf. Schoedel, *Ignatius of Antioch*, 206.

23. Lightfoot, *The Apostolic Fathers*, 2.2.224.

24. Inge bases this on other parallels to John 4, such as Inge, "Ignatius,"82.

25. Inge, "Ignatius," 82.

> For though some would have deceived me according to the flesh, yet the *Spirit*, as being from God, is not deceived. For it knows both *whence it comes and whither it goes*, and detects the secrets of the heart. For, when I was among you, I cried, I spoke with a loud voice: Give heed to the bishop, and to the presbytery and deacons.
>
> The wind blows where it wishes, and you hear its sound, but you do not know *where it comes from or where it goes*. So it is with everyone who is born of the *Spirit*." (John 3:8)

Besides these references, Ignatius' letters likely contain reference to other ideas from the canonical gospels. In one place in his letters, he states that there was a star present at Jesus' birth (Matt 2:2 in Ign. *Eph.* 19.1). In two other places, Ignatius refers to the word becoming flesh, which are likely references to John's Gospel (John 3:8 in Ign. *Phld.* 7.8; John 10:9 in Ign. *Phld.* 9.1).[26]

Ignatius' Letter to the Philadelphians 5.1–2

One final point of interest is the development of the authority of the gospels in Ignatius' mind in relation to other authoritative writings at that time. In several places, Ignatius refers to the gospel as having authority as the prophets, prophecies, or the Law of Moses. Thus, in Ignatius' time, the gospel is being regarded as a religious authority on par with the Old Testament and then exceeding them. The most clear of these passages is Ignatius' *Letter to the Philadelphians* 5.1–2.

> My brethren, I am greatly enlarged in loving you; and rejoicing exceedingly over you, I seek to secure your safety. Yet it is not I, but Jesus Christ, for whose sake being bound I fear the more, inasmuch as I am not yet perfect. But your prayer to God shall make me perfect, that I may attain to that portion which through mercy has been allotted me, while I flee to the *Gospel* as to the flesh of Jesus, and to the apostles as to the presbytery of the Church. And let us also love the *prophets*, because they too have proclaimed the *Gospel*, and placed their hope in Him, and waited for Him; in whom also believing, they were saved, through union to Jesus Christ, being holy men, worthy of love and admiration, having had witness borne to them by Jesus Christ, and being reckoned along with in the *Gospel* of the common hope.

---

26. Brent, "Ignatius and Polycarp," 329.

In Ignatius' mind from the early part of the second century, the word gospel is connected with the apostles. This would then distinguish any gospel with apostolic claim from other gospels without such a claim from the time of the early second century.[27]

Epistle of Barnabas

One final document from the Apostolic Fathers deserves special attention. Portions of the Synoptic Gospels can be found in the *Epistle of Barnabas*.

This work is a letter that has been ascribed to Barnabas, the Apostle Paul's traveling companion. It is agreed that it is pseudepigraphic, however, and thus was written by someone other than Barnabas.[28] There are good reasons for this conclusion. Barnabas' name does not appear in the epistle. The author also seems to place his followers and him in opposition to the Jewish people. This is the opposite of the way that Barnabas explains his support of Judaism in other early Christian literature (cf. Gal 2:13–14). Furthermore, many scholars believe that Barnabas had died before the date of composition.[29] With these factors in mind, any connection with Barnabas becomes highly doubtful.

Besides doubts about the authorship, there are other uncertainties. There are no firm conclusions regarding why the book was written. There is not certainty about its recipients, although the eastern portion of the Roman Empire is favored. Modern scholarship supports the place of writing to be Syria, Palestine, or Asia Minor, but Alexandria, Egypt is still a possibility.

While there is a fair amount of uncertainty about the book, there are some things that can be said about its content. The first part of the epistle commands faithful readers to flee from sin and practice Christian virtues. The second part encourages Christian freedom from the Mosaic Law. In this latter section, there is a great deal of allegory. The author shows how the rules of the Law should be understood as referring allegorically to

---

27. Other passages that promote one of the canonical gospels as being on par with portions of the Old Testament are: Ignatius' *Letter to the Philadelphians* 8.2; 9.1–2; Ignatius' *Letter to the Smyrnaeans* 5.1; 7.2. See Hill, "Ignatius, 'the Gospel,' and the Gospels," 271–80.

28. A pseudepigraphic letter is one which was not written by the person named, but ascribed to someone who would bolster the reputation of the letter to its readers.

29. Cf. Paget, *Epistle of Barnabas*.

Christian virtues and institutions. The *Epistle of Barnabas* concludes with the author employing the "Two Ways" which are also found in the *Didache*, although this time these ways are described as the way of light and darkness.

The letter should be dated following the destruction of the Temple, since *Epistle of Barnabas* in 16.3–4 speaks to the rebuilding of that great structure. Thus, it must be dated after AD 70, when the Temple was destroyed, and before 135, when Hadrian constructed a new Roman temple on the site. Since there is reference to conflict within the epistle, the majority favor a date between AD 96–117 when Christianity had grown hostile to its Jewish roots.

Epistle of Barnabas 4.14

The main text to consider is *Epistle of Barnabas* 4.14. In this passage, a clear reference to Synoptic Gospel material is found. It is elevated to the same standing as other Old Testament Scripture.

> And consider this also, my brethren, when you see that after such great signs and wonders were wrought in Israel they were even then finally abandoned; let us take heed lest as it was written (*gegraptai*) we be found "*many called but few chosen.*"
>
> For *many are called, but few are chosen*. (Matt 22:14)

There are several things that make this text interesting. The quotation is introduced by the word *gegraptai*, which means "it was written." This is one of the words that is used normally to introduce Old Testament citations. Instead of introducing Old Testament Scripture, it introduces what looks most like Matthew 24:14, "For many are called, but few are chosen."[30]

There are two significant implications. First, this is one of the earliest occurrences in which a New Testament gospel is recognized as having the same authority as Old Testament Scripture. Second, the first gospel recognized to be as authoritative as the Old Testament is one of the traditional gospels, namely Matthew, rather than a non-canonical gospel.

---

30. There are other proposals, such as that this text is from the Old Testament apocryphal book *4 Ezra* 8:3, which reads, "Many are created but few are saved," or from *4 Ezra* 9:15, which states, "More are of the lost than of the redeemed." The closest reading, however, is Matthew 22:14. Paget, "*Epistle of Barnabas*," 232–33.

Like other books within the Apostolic Fathers, the *Epistle of Barnabas* contains other possible references to the Synoptic Gospels. The *Epistle of Barnabas* contains the quotation about Jesus that "he came not to call the righteous but sinners" (*Barn*. 5.8–9 and Matt 9:13). It also contains the quotation, "When they shall smite their shepherd, then the sheep of the flock shall be destroyed" (*Barn*. 5.12 and Matt 26:31; Mark 14:27; or Zech 13:7). The crucifixion account in the *Epistle of Barnabas* contains details that Jesus was given gall and vinegar, like Matthew 27:34.[31] These add to the support that this early Christian document provides to the canonical gospels.

Conclusion from the Apostolic Fathers

The presence of the Synoptic Gospels and John in the *Didache*, Letters of Ignatius, and the *Epistle of Barnabas* indicates that respect for the canonical gospels was present from the generation immediately following the apostles. The Synoptic Gospels and particularly Matthew were recognized as being on par with other authoritative writings.

There are several other passages from the Apostolic Fathers that could still be mentioned with respect to reception of the canonical gospels. Their dependence upon Matthew, Mark, Luke, and John, however, is less clear. There are passages from *First Clement* that may show dependence, particularly 1 Clement 13.2 and 46.8. The canonical gospels may be present, but it is possible that oral tradition could account for these texts.[32] Polycarp's *Letter to the Philippians* also has parallels with the

---

31. For further discussion, see Paget, "*Epistle of Barnabas*," 229–251.

32. *1 Clement* 13.2 reads,
For thus He spoke: [1]Be ye merciful, that ye may obtain mercy; [2]forgive, that it may be forgiven to you; [3]as ye do, so shall it be done unto you; [4]*as ye give, so shall it be given to you*; [5]*as ye judge, so shall ye be judged*; [6]as ye are kind, so shall kindness be shown to you; [7]*with what measure ye mete, with the same it shall be measured to you*.

There are many possible texts from the canonical Gospels present. The raised number indicates the beginning of an influence within *1 Clement*. A close verbal agreement is indicated with italics. The overlaps are with [1]Matthew 5:7 and Luke 6:36, [2]Matthew 6:14 and Luke 6:37, [3]Matthew 7:12 and Luke 6:31, [4]Luke 6:38, 5 Matthew 7:2 and Luke 6:37, [6]Luke 6:35, [7]Matthew 7:2 and Luke 6:38. There is also overlap with Pol. *Phil*. 2.3.

1 Clement 46.7–8 reads:
Remember the words of Jesus our Lord how He said, [1]*Woe to that man* [by whom offenses come]! [2]*It were better for him that he had never been born*, [3]*than that he should cast a stumbling-block before one of my elect*. Yea, [4]it were better for him that a millstone

canonical gospels.[33] Scholars have also seen references to the Synoptic Gospels in *Shepherd of Hermas* and *2 Clement*.[34] While these texts may show the presence of the canonical gospels, it is less likely than the passages cited from the *Didache*, the letters of Ignatius of Antioch, and the *Epistle of Barnabas*.[35]

Justin Martyr

As one progresses into the later second century, the status of the canonical gospels becomes more identifiable and more revered. This is evident from their presence within the writings of Justin Martyr.

Justin Martyr is the most well-known Christian apologist of the second century AD. He was a well-educated Gentile who taught and defended the Christian faith in Asia Minor and Rome, and was eventually martyred in AD 165 during the reign of Marcus Aurelius. Before becoming a Christian, Justin studied in the schools of the philosophers. He came to Christ as a result of being impressed by the fearlessness of Christians in the presence of death and because of the truths found in the Old Testament. Following his conversion, he became a great persuader of the truths of Christianity in many parts of the world, particularly Ephesus and Rome.

---

should be hung about his neck, and he should be sunk in the depths of the sea, [5]than that he should cast a stumbling-block before one of my little ones.

The overlaps are with [1]Matthew 26:24, [2]Matthew 26:24 and Mark 14:21, [3]Matthew 18:6 and Mark 9:42, [4]Matthew 18:6, [5]Luke 17:2. Carlyle, "First Clement" in *The New Testament in the Apostolic Fathers*, 58–59. In *1 Clement* 15.2, Clement also quotes Isaiah 29:13, a verse that is quoted in Matthew 15:8 and Mark 7:6.

33. Matt 5:3, 10 and Luke 6:20 in Pol. *Phil.* 2.3; John 5:21, 25 and 6:44 in Pol. *Phil.* 5.2; Matt 6:12 and 11:4 in Pol. *Phil.* 6.1–2; Matt 6:13; 26:41 and Luke 11:4 in Pol. *Phil.* 7.2.

34. Herm. *Sim.* 3.3; 4.2; 5.2 and Matt 13:30, 38, 40. Herm. *Vis.* 3.6.5 and *Sim.* 9.20.1–2 and Matt 13:20–21 and Mark 4:18–19. Luke 19:10 in *2 Clem.* 2.7; Matt 10:32 and Luke 12:8 in *2 Clem.* 3.2; Matt 7:21 and Luke 6:46 in *2 Clem.* 4.2; Matt 7:23 and Luke 13:27 in *2 Clem.* 4.5; Matt 10:16, 28 and Mark 2:17 and Luke 5:32 in *2 Clem.* 2.4; Luke 10:3 and 12:4–5 in *2 Clem.* 5.2–4. For further see Verheyden, "Shepherd of Hermas," 322–29 and Gregory and Tuckett, "2 Clement," 251–92.

35. See further *The New Testament in the Apostolic Fathers*, which rates as "less likely" most of these occurrences from *First Clement*, Polycarp's *Letter to the Philippians*, *Shepherd of Hermas*, and *Second Clement*.

He wrote many treatises but, unfortunately, there are only three that we can identify clearly as being written by him.[36] We have two apologies which bear his name, and also the *Dialogue with Trypho*. These were written in the mid-second century between the years 153 and 161.

Both of Justin Martyr's apologies were written with Christian fervor. The *First Apology* contains two main parts. The first part defends against an accusation that Christians are atheists (*1 Apol.* 1–29). While Christians do not worship Roman gods, they do worship the one true God as a result of Jesus Christ, the Son of God. The second part advocates from the Old Testament that Jesus is the Messiah, the Son of God, and not a magician (*1 Apol.* 30–60). The apology concludes with a description of a baptismal service, the celebration of the Lord's Supper, and a short address to Emperor Hadrian (*1 Apol.* 61–68). Justin's *Second Apology* was written following the order of the execution of three Christians for professing the name of Christ. It was written shortly following his *First Apology*. In this work, Justin Martyr appeals to the Roman emperor to prevent further killings.

His *Dialogue with Trypho* is the oldest existing anti-Jewish apology. It is a record of a two day conversation with an educated Jewish man named Trypho. The *Dialogue* is the first detailed explanation within Christian history that Christ is the Messiah of the Old Testament. It is also the first systematic effort to show that Christianity is superior to Judaism. There are three main parts. Within the introduction (2–8), Justin gives his autobiography. He then moves to a section that explains the Old Testament from the Christian viewpoint (9–47). In the next portion, Justin defends respecting Christ as God (48–108). The final section argues that the nations believing Christ and observing his law are the new Israel, the true people of God (108–142).

Justin Martyr's writings contain many references to the canonical gospels of Matthew, Mark, and Luke in particular. The following is a survey of the most significant places where the canonical gospels are present within his writing.

---

36. Besides the two apologies and the *Dialogue with Trypho*, some have ascribed other documents to Justin, including: *An Address to the Greeks*; *A Hortatory Address to the Greeks*; *On the Sole Government of God*;. *An Epistle to Diognetus*; *Fragments from a work on the Resurrection*; and *Other Fragments*. They are written fairly early, but there is doubt as to whether they were from Justin Martyr. See Schaff, *Apostolic Fathers with Justin Martyr and Irenaeus*, 161.

First Apology 15.1, 3

In one section of the *First Apology*, Justin Martyr refers to approximately twenty short sayings from Jesus which are found in the canonical gospels (*1 Apol.* 15–17). These three chapters he has entitled "What Christ himself taught," "Concerning patience and swearing," and "Christ taught civil obedience." Immediately before he quotes these Synoptic Gospel passages, he states that these sayings of Jesus are commandments and possess the "power of God" (*1 Apol.* 14.4–5).[37] An example of what he cites is the following from *First Apology* 15.1, 3 which is taken from Matthew 5:28, 29, 32. In this and subsequent examples, the parts that are dependent upon the canonical gospels are in italics.

> Concerning chastity, He uttered such sentiments as these: "*Whosoever looketh upon a woman to lust after her, hath committed adultery with her already in his heart before God.*" And, "*If thy right eye offend thee, cut it out; for it is better for thee to enter into the kingdom of heaven with one eye, than, having two eyes, to be cast into everlasting fire.*"[38]

This is one example of many other verses from Matthew and Luke, particularly from the Sermon on the Mount, that can be found in this section from *First Apology* 15–17.[39]

First Apology 61.3

Later in the *First Apology*, Justin gives Jesus' words from a canonical gospel the same status as the Old Testament. In *First Apology* 61.3, words of Jesus from John 3:5 are placed on the same level as Isaiah 1:16–20.

> For, in the name of God, the Father and Lord of the universe, and of our Saviour Jesus Christ, and of the Holy Spirit, they then receive the washing with water. For Christ also said, "*Except ye be born again, ye shall not enter into the kingdom of heaven.*" Now, that it is impossible for those who have once been born to enter into their mothers' wombs, is manifest to all. And how those who have

---

37. Bellinzoni, *Sayings of Jesus in the Writings of Justin Martyr*, 49–100.
38. The translation of Justin Martyr that is being used is from *ANF*.
39. He cites these, as well as other passages from the gospels, with slightly different wording, e.g., Matt 5:44, 46; 6:19–20; 9:13; 16:26; 19:12; Luke 6:28, 30, 34. See *ANF*, 1:167–68.

> sinned and repent shall escape their sins, is declared by Esaias the prophet, as I wrote above; he thus speaks: "Wash you, make you clean; put away the evil of your doings from your souls; learn to do well; judge the fatherless, and plead for the widow: and come and let us reason together, saith the Lord. And though your sins be as scarlet, I will make them white like wool; and though they be as crimson, I will make them white as snow. But if ye refuse and rebel, the sword shall devour you: for the mouth of the Lord hath spoken it."

In other passages, Justin Martyr will also place words from the canonical gospels on the same level as words from the Old Testament.[40]

First Apology 66.3

Justin Martyr's writing contains an especially striking development from the Apostolic Fathers. He states that the gospels are now passed along in *written* form. In *First Apology* 66.3, he makes it clear that these teachings are written memoirs of the apostles and called "gospels." This he does in the context of worship and the Lord's Supper, referring at the same time to a canonical gospel passage from Luke 22:19.

> For not as common bread and common drink do we receive these; but in like manner as Jesus Christ our Saviour, having been made flesh by the Word of God, had both flesh and blood for our salvation, so likewise have we been taught that the food which is blessed by the prayer of His word, and from which our blood and flesh by transmutation are nourished, is the flesh and blood of that Jesus who was made flesh. For the apostles, in the memoirs composed by them, which are called Gospels, have thus delivered unto us what was enjoined upon them; that Jesus took bread, and when He had given thanks, said, "*This do ye in remembrance of Me, this is My body;*" and that, after the same manner, having taken the cup and given thanks, He said, "This is My blood;" and gave it to them alone.

---

40. For example, in the *Dialogue with Trypho*, there are several places where Justin puts Jesus' words as recorded in the canonical gospels on the same level as Isaiah. Cf. *Dial.* 17–18.1. Justin places Exodus 3:6, Matthew 11:27, and Luke 10:16 on the same authoritative level in *Dial.* 63. Stanton, "Jesus Traditions and Gospels in Justin Martyr and Irenaeus," 357. For further references, see Hill, *Justin and the New Testament Writings*, 48.

Jesus' words about the Lord's Supper are now declared to be authoritative and identified as being in gospels.[41] It is the first mention of the plural word "gospels" within early Christian writings. Justin will write in many other places that the words from Jesus are written.[42]

First Apology 67.3

Besides referring to the words of Jesus as gospels, Justin uses a noteworthy phrase in his writing: "memoirs of the apostles." He uses this expression twice in *First Apology*, then another thirteen times in his *Dialogue with Trypho*. Every time he uses this phrase, Justin means that these should be seen with the highest regard. This is best illustrated by the way that he uses the expression in *First Apology* 67.3. In this passage, Justin states that these memoirs are read each week and are of the same level of importance as the prophets.

> And on the day called Sunday, all who live in cities or in the country gather together to one place, and the memoirs of the apostles or the writings of the prophets are read, as long as time permits; then, when the reader has ceased, the president verbally instructs, and exhorts to the imitation of these good things.

Dialogue with Trypho 103.8

What Justin means by the memoirs are the four canonical gospels. When we considered *First Apology* 66.3 earlier, Justin used the phrase in relation to Luke's Gospel and the celebration of the Eucharist. In *Dialogue with Trypho* 103.8, "memoirs of the apostles" is also related to the canonical gospels. He uses this phrase with reference to a citation from Matthew 3:17 and 6:9–10.

> For this devil, when [Jesus] went up from the river Jordan, at the time when the voice spake to Him, "*Thou art my Son: this day have I begotten Thee*," is recorded in the memoirs of the apostles to have come to Him and tempted Him, even so far as to say to

---

41. Stanton, "Jesus Traditions and Gospels in Justin Martyr and Irenaeus," 356.

42. See the number of times that Justin Martyr refers to the reading of written material about Jesus: *1 Apol.* 14.1; 26.8; 42.1; 44.12, 13; 45.6; *2 Apol.* 3.6, 8; 15.3; *Dial.* 88.3. Stanton, "Jesus Traditions and Gospels in Justin Martyr and Irenaeus," 350.

Him, "Worship me;" and Christ answered him, "*Get thee behind me, Satan: thou shalt worship the Lord thy God, and Him only shalt thou serve.*"

Dialogue with Trypho 106.4

In *Dialogue with Trypho* 106.4, "memoirs of the apostles" is found in relation to Mark's Gospel.[43] This passage refers to Jesus' calling of James the son of Zebedee and John the brother of James, the sons of thunder. It reads:

> And when it is said that He changed the name of one of the apostles to Peter; and when it is written in the memoirs of Him that this so happened, as well as that He changed the names of other two brothers, the sons of Zebedee, to Boanerges, which means sons of thunder; this was an announcement of the fact that it was He by whom Jacob was called Israel, and Oshea called Jesus (Joshua), under whose name the people who survived of those that came from Egypt were conducted into the land promised to the patriarchs.

The description of James and John as "sons of thunder" appears only in Mark's Gospel (cf. Mark 3:17). Thus, Justin must be referring to Mark's Gospel as part of the "memoirs of the apostles."

John's Gospel, too, should be considered as part of the "memoirs of the apostles." Earlier, we saw Justin appear to quote from John 3:5 in *First Apology* 61.3. Other passages in Justin's writing refer to John's Gospel specifically, such as *Dialogue with Trypho* 88.

> For when John remained by the Jordan, and preached the baptism of repentance, wearing only a leathern girdle and a vesture made of camels' hair, eating nothing but locusts and wild honey, men supposed him to be Christ; but he cried to them, "I am not the Christ, but the voice of one crying; for He that is stronger than I shall come, whose shoes I am not worthy to bear."

Only John's Gospel contains John the Baptist's cry, "I am not the Christ" (John 1:20).[44] Other uses of John can be seen in the way that he refers to Jesus as the Word (*1 Apol.* 46; cf. John 1:1, 9). Later in Justin's

---

43. Abramowski, *Die Erinnerungen der Apostel bei Justin*, 334–5.
44. Hengel, *Johannine Question*, 12–13.

writing, he will refer to Jesus as the Word and connect this with his memoirs (*Dial.* 105).

Justin Martyr's writing shows a significant development in the presence and value of the canonical gospels. Unlike the Apostolic Fathers, who presented small quotations or allusions to the canonical gospels, Justin Martyr cites clearly from Matthew, Mark, and Luke. He either cites or alludes to John. These gospels are stated to be written and on the same level of authority as the Old Testament. They are used often in the worship of the early church community and compose the memoirs of the apostles. There is no evidence that he knew or used any other gospels besides these four.[45]

Tatian's Diatessaron

Justin Martyr's disciple Tatian also has something to contribute to the reception of traditional gospel material. While fewer people may know of Tatian, his significance has been stated by Arthur Vööbus in *Early Versions of the New Testament*: "In the history of the versions, as well as in the early phase of textual developments of the New Testament as a whole, there is no greater and more important name than Tatian. This is not an overstatement."[46]

We know little about Tatian. He was born in Mesopotamia or Syria. He was repulsed by the grossness and immorality of the pagans, and he then searched for truth through philosophy. Like Justin, he converted to Christianity. Following his conversion, he spent time with Justin Martyr in Rome. When Justin died, Tatian became a leader of a heresy called Encratism. This group abstained from meat and wine, and saw marriage as necessary for Christianity. This led to his expulsion from Rome and also led to him settling back in the East again.

Tatian wrote a number of works, of which only two survived.[47] The second work is the *Diatessaron*, which is of importance for this discussion. It was composed between AD 165 and 180. The *Diatessaron*, which literally means "through the four," is a harmony of the four traditional gospels. In this work, Tatian attempted to minimize all contradictions

---

45. May, "The Four Pillars," 72–75; cf. Osborn, *Justin Martyr*, 129–30.
46. Vööbus, *Early Versions of the New Testament*, 1.
47. The first is an apology for the Christian faith called *Oratio ad Graecos*.

and discrepancies and make a unified gospel. The framework for the *Diatessaron* was the Gospel of John.

Some believe that Tatian may have used other gospels in his work.[48] While there has been speculation of another source influencing Tatian's composition, this is quite uncertain.[49] There is only evidence of a possible addition to Jesus' baptism. The *Diatesseron* includes a great shining light following the baptism, which may suggest that this came from the *Gospel of the Ebionites*.[50] Yet there is another occurrence of the same idea in Justin's writing in the *Dialogue with Trypho* (*Dial.* 88). Since this is the only evidence of another gospel present in the *Diatesseron*, and since Justin Martyr's writing contains a similar idea and was Tatian's teacher, it seems more likely that Tatian's account of a great light following Jesus' baptism came from Justin rather than from another gospel outside of the four.

Furthermore, it would seem rather odd for Tatian to harmonize only four gospels if he felt that others were authoritative. How could he have produced an authoritative text unless he considered all of the texts that he felt were authoritative? The *Diatesseron* should thus be seen as *only* influenced by the four canonical gospels.[51]

The reception of Tatian's *Diatesseron* witnesses further to the widespread acceptance of a fourfold gospel. Until AD 425, Tatian's *Diatessaron* was the standard gospel text of the Syrian church. As late as the ninth century, it was being cited by Syrian commentators. Even as late as the fourteenth century, scholars were in awe of Tatian's accomplishment. Manuscripts of the *Diatessaron* spread from Syria to as far as China, England, and possibly Iceland. It was translated into Syriac, Latin, and even Armenian. As a result, as *Diatessaron* scholar W. L. Petersen states, "the *Diatessaron* is often regarded as the oldest of the Versions. Save for the canonical gospels, no monument of early Christian literature saw such broad dissemination as the *Diatessaron*."[52]

The *Diatessaron* serves as a witness to the elevation of the four traditional gospels during the second century. Furthermore, by its popularity for many subsequent centuries, it serves to elevate the four traditional

---

48. E.g., Charlesworth, "Tatian's Dependence upon Apocryphal Traditions," 5–17; Hahnemann, *The Muratorian Fragment and the Development of the Canon*, 98–99.

49. Petersen, *Tatian's Diastesseron*, 427–28.

50. Koester, *Ancient Christian Gospels*, 422–23.

51. May, "The Four Pillars," 76.

52. Petersen, *Tatian's Diatessaron*, 1–2.

Gospel Reception in Early Church History

gospels over others. The *Diatessaron* is a strong witness to the exclusivity of the four gospels by the mid- to late-second century.[53]

Muratorian Fragment

Most lists of Scriptural books are dated after the first half of the fourth century. A list called the Muratorian fragment (also called the Muratorian Canon) has been traditionally dated to the late second century or early third century. Some would wish to date this later, but there are still significant reasons to remain with the traditional dating.[54] The most important reason is the reference that the Muratorian Fragment makes to its own dating. Within the Fragment, it states that "Hermas wrote the *Shepherd of Hermas*, in our times, in the city of Rome, while bishop Pius, his brother was occupying the [episcopal] chair of the church of the city of Rome."[55] Since Pius I died in AD 157, this would affirm the traditional date and successfully overcome any attempt to conclude that the Muratorian Fragment is a later writing.[56] It is by far the earliest surviving "canon list" of New Testament documents and has been noted to be significant for determining the contents of the New Testament canon.

The Muratorian Fragment was discovered by a man named Lodovico Antonio Muratori in the Ambrosian library in Milan in 1740. It is designated "a fragment" since we only have a portion of the writing of about eighty lines. The beginning is lost, and the ending is abrupt. The author of the Muratorian fragment is unknown. The candidate most suggested is Hippolytus, who lived from AD 170–235 and was a learned man from the church in Rome.

The Muratorian fragment provides us with a type of introduction to the New Testament. It is not attempting to give a description as to how books were accepted into the New Testament canon. It does give us a

---

53. May, "The Four Pillars," 77–79.

54. It is dated to the second century due to the reference to Pope Pius and the fact that the *Shepherd of Hermas* was written very recently. Metzger, *The Canon of the New Testament*, 191. Sundberg argues for a later dating of the fourth century. Sundberg, "Canon Muratori," 1–41. This argument has now been revived by Hahneman, *The Muratorian Fragment and the Development of the Canon*. See also McDonald, *Biblical Canon*, 371–73.

55. These are taken from lines 73–76 in the Muratorian Fragment.

56. For further support of the traditional dating, see Hill, "The Debate over the Muratorian Fragment and the Development of the Canon," 437–52.

listing, however, of what books were authoritative. From the list, it appears clear that the marks of inspiration are apostolicity, antiquity, and general acceptance into the churches.

What follows is the beginning portion of the Muratorian Fragment. It begins with the last words of a sentence that refers to the Gospel of Mark. It is presumed that the brief comments of the Gospel of Matthew were not preserved.

> . . . at which nevertheless he was present, and so he placed [them in his narrative]. The third book of the gospel is that according to Luke. Luke, the well-known physician, after the ascension of Christ, when Paul had taken with him as one zealous for the law, composed it in his own name, according to [the general] belief. Yet he himself had not seen the Lord in the flesh; and therefore, as he was able to ascertain events, so indeed he begins to tell the story from the birth of John. The fourth of the gospels is that of John, [one] of the disciples. To his fellow disciples and bishops, who had been urging him [to write], he said, "Fast with me from today to three days, and what will be revealed to each one let us tell it to one another." In the same night it was revealed to Andrew, [one] of the apostles, that John should write down all things in his own name while all of them should review it. And so, though various elements may be taught in the individual books of the gospels, nevertheless this makes no difference to the faith of believers, since by the one sovereign Spirit all things have been declared in all [the gospels]: concerning the nativity, concerning the passion, concerning the resurrection, concerning life with his disciples, and concerning his twofold coming; the first in lowliness when he was despised, which has taken place, the second glorious in royal power, which is still in the future. What marvel is it then, if John so consistently mentions these particular points also in his Epistles, saying about himself, "What we have seen with our eyes and heard with our ears and our hands have handled, these things we have written to you?" For in this way he professes [himself] to be not only an eye-witness and hearer, but also a writer of all the marvelous deeds of the Lord, in their order.[57]

The list testifies to the collection of gospels which appears to be closed by the Gospel of John. Furthermore, the way that John's Gospel is represented in the Muratorian fragment makes it seem as if it carries with it the authority of the twelve apostles. John's Gospel appears to be

---

57. Metzger, *Canon of the New Testament*, 305–7.

a synthesis of the teaching of the twelve disciples, while other gospels, such as Mark and Luke, bear witness to various traditions.[58] There is no mention of any other gospels beyond Mark, Luke, John, and presumably Matthew.

Irenaeus

As stated earlier, it is likely that a four-gospel canon was becoming fixed prior to the time of Irenaeus, who wrote about AD 170–180. With Irenaeus, however, there is the clearest declaration of a four-gospel canon. Following the time of Irenaeus, the designation of certain books as Scripture becomes more pronounced.

Irenaeus of Lyons was born in Asia Minor. There he had heard church father Polycarp of Smyrna. He migrated to Gaul, which is present-day France. He traveled to Rome at one point, where he may have met Justin Martyr. Shortly after his return to Lyons, he was appointed as bishop. He died around AD 200.

Irenaeus wrote a number of works that are recorded by Eusebius, the church historian. Only two are known to be from him and available today: *Against Heresies*, which is the longest, and *Demonstration of the Apostolic Preaching*. *Against Heresies* was written to combat Gnosticism in AD 180. In this book, Irenaeus condemns Gnosticism for claiming that it possesses true knowledge, or *gnosis*. Christ had proclaimed the true and complete knowledge of faith to the apostles. This becomes Irenaeus' means of procedure in *Against Heresies*, critiquing Gnosticism and then presenting true knowledge as being found in the orthodox Christian faith.

While Irenaeus did not work with a canon of Scripture, it may be assumed that he felt it was established on the basis of his argumentation. Gnostic writings would have been excluded, such as some of the other gospels that some are promoting today. For Irenaeus, it is the task of the church to preserve its faithfulness which he found to be linked to successive faithful bishops who were successors to the apostles.

---

58. Metzger, *Canon of the New Testament*, 195.

Jesus Tried and True

Against Heresies 2.27.2

In his writing, he states explicitly that there are only four gospels. The Gospels of Matthew and John were written by named apostles. The Gospels of Mark and Luke were written by their followers (*Haer.* 3.10.1, 5; 3.11.1). These are clearly seen to be Scripture from the following passage.

> Since, therefore, the entire Scriptures, the prophets, and the Gospels, can be clearly, unambiguously, and harmoniously understood by all, although all do not believe them; and since they proclaim that one only God, to the exclusion of all others, formed all things by His word, whether visible or invisible, heavenly or earthly, in the water or under the earth, as I have shown from the very words of Scripture; and since the very system of creation to which we belong testifies, by what falls under our notice, that one Being made and governs it, those persons will seem truly foolish who blind their eyes to such a clear demonstration, and will not behold the light of the announcement [made to them]; but they put fetters upon themselves, and every one of them imagines, by means of their obscure interpretations of the parables, that he has found out a God of his own.[59]

At the end of book 2, he states that he will support his argument from divine Scripture. Book 3 is filled with many more references to the gospels than to the Old Testament.

Against Heresies 3.1.1–2.1

In *Against Heresies* 3.1.1–2, Irenaeus presents clearly the four gospels as Scripture.[60]

> We have learned from none others the plan of our salvation, than from those through *whom the Gospel has come down to us*, which they did at one time proclaim in public, and, at a later period, by the will of God, *handed down to us in the Scriptures, to be the ground and pillar of our faith*. For it is unlawful to assert that they preached before they possessed "perfect knowledge," as some do even venture to say, boasting themselves as improvers of the apostles. For, after our Lord rose from the dead, [the apostles] were invested with power from on high when the Holy Spirit came

---

59. All translations within this section are from *ANF*.
60. See also *Haer.* 1.9.4; 2.26.1–2; McDonald, *Biblical Canon*, 290.

down [upon them], were filled from all [His gifts], and had perfect knowledge: they departed to the ends of the earth, preaching the glad tidings of the good things [sent] from God to us, and proclaiming the peace of heaven to men, who indeed do all equally and individually possess the Gospel of God. *Matthew* also issued a written Gospel among the Hebrews in their own dialect, while Peter and Paul were preaching at Rome, and laying the foundations of the Church. After their departure, *Mark, the disciple and interpreter of Peter*, did also hand down to us in writing what had been preached by Peter. *Luke* also, the companion of Paul, *recorded in a book the Gospel preached by him*. Afterwards, *John*, the disciple of the Lord, who also had leaned upon His breast, *did himself publish a Gospel* during his residence at Ephesus in Asia. (*italics added*)

These have all declared to us that there is one God, Creator of heaven and earth, announced by the law and the prophets; and one Christ the Son of God. If anyone does not agree to these truths, he despises the companions of the Lord; nay more, he despises Christ Himself the Lord; yea, he despises the Father also, and stands self-condemned, resisting and opposing his own salvation, as is the case with all heretics.

Against Heresies 3.11.8

A little later on, in *Against Heresies* 3.11.8, Irenaeus states three times that there can be "no more no less" than four gospels.

> It is not possible that the Gospels can be either more or fewer in number than they are. For, since there are four zones of the world in which we live, and four principal winds, while the Church is scattered throughout all the world, and the "pillar and ground" of the Church is the Gospel and the spirit of life; it is fitting that she should have four pillars, breathing out immortality on every side, and vivifying men afresh. From which fact, it is evident that the Word, the Artificer of all, He that sitteth upon the cherubim, and contains all things, He who was manifested to men, has given us the Gospel under four aspects, but bound together by one Spirit. As also David says, when entreating His manifestation, "Thou that sittest between the cherubim, shine forth." For the cherubim, too, were four-faced, and their faces were images of the dispensation of the Son of God. For, [as the Scripture] says, "The first living creature was like a lion," symbolizing His effectual working, His

leadership, and royal power; the second [living creature] was like a calf, signifying [His] sacrificial and sacerdotal order; but "the third had, as it were, the face as of a man,"—an evident description of His advent as a human being; "the fourth was like a flying eagle," pointing out the gift of the Spirit hovering with His wings over the Church. And therefore the Gospels are in accord with these things, among which Christ Jesus is seated. For that according to John relates His original, effectual, and glorious generation from the Father, thus declaring, "In the beginning was the Word, and the Word was with God, and the Word was God." Also, "all things were made by Him, and without Him was nothing made." For this reason, too, is that Gospel full of all confidence, for such is His person ... For the living creatures are quadriform, and the Gospel is quadriform, as is also the course followed by the Lord.

The repetition of the idea "no more, no less" than four gospels is repeated in *Against Heresies* 3.11.9. It is a famous phrase for which Irenaeus is known as a church father. This phrase implies a closed canon for gospels by the end of the second century AD.[61]

Irenaeus' clear statements on the fourfold gospel canon were then followed by declarations from other church fathers about authoritative Scripture. Tertullian, the church father who wrote from Carthage in Africa, cites all four gospels (c. 160–225). Others composed lists of Scriptural books that include only four gospels, such as Eusebius (c. 260–340) and Origen (c. 185–254).[62] In AD 367, Athanasius gave his famous *Thirty-Ninth Festal Letter*. This document lists the books of both the Old and New Testaments. Only four gospels are represented. While these later church fathers clearly state the superiority of the four gospels, the process had already been in progress long before.

Non-Canonical Gospel Reception Through the Time of Irenaeus

In contrast to the reception of the canonical gospels, the non-canonical gospels were not received as positively by the end of the second century. This is not surprising, due to their later dating. Their lack of reception,

---

61. Stanton, "The Gospels in Justin and Irenaeus," 370.

62. Eusebius, *Ecclesiastical History*, 3.25.1–7. Origen's list of books can also be found from Eusebius' history. See *Ecclesiastical History*, 6.25.3–14. Cf. McDonald, *Biblical Canon*, 305–10.

however, also indicates the lesser interest for these other gospels. Some of the instances of reception of non-canonical gospels are listed below.

The earliest appearance of non-canonical gospel material may be found in *Second Clement*. While it is not a letter like *First Clement* or written by Clement of Rome, it is an early Christian writing in the second century. It is most likely dated to around AD 150. It is a sermon written by an unknown author, an unnamed presbyter (*2 Clem. 17.3*). While the New Testament contains sermons within it, such as portions of the book of Acts (e.g., Acts 3:12–26; 20:18–35) and possibly the book of Hebrews, *Second Clement* is generally recognized as the first full length sermon in Christian literature that has survived.[63] *Second Clement* is an exposition of Isaiah 54:1 and urges repentance, purity, and faithfulness in the midst of persecution. Presumably, this message was for a Gentile congregation that was struggling with Gnosticism.[64]

Some, like Bart Ehrman, have pointed to texts that resemble non-canonical gospels that are found within the letter of *Second Clement*. The one that seems most noteworthy is the parallel between *Logion* 22 in the *Gospel of Thomas* that may be found in *2 Clement* 12.2. The passage reads, "For when the Lord himself was asked by someone when his kingdom would come, he said: 'When the two shall be one, and the outside as the inside, and the male with the female [is] neither male nor female.'"[65] Ehrman also has suggested that *2 Clement* 5.2–4 comes from Jesus. He notes that it may come from the *Gospel of Peter*, but he provides no reference.

While Ehrman sees these passages as important for establishing his viewpoint that this is evidence of uncertain steps toward the canon, his viewpoint ought to be questioned. The source of this text within *2 Clement* 12.2 has been recognized to be "extremely complex."[66] It is possible that 2 *Clement* 12.2 may also be found within the writings of Clement of Alexandria (*Strom.* 3.19.32).[67] The possible reference to the *Gospel of*

---

63. For the Epistle to the Hebrews as a sermon, see Walker, "A Place for Hebrews?" 231–49.

64. Richardson, "An Anonymous Sermon," 183–202; Koester, *Introduction to the New Testament*, 233–36.

65. Ehrman, *Lost Christianities*, 236–37.

66. Gregory and Tuckett, "2 Clement," 272. See further T. Baarda, "2 Clement 12 and the Sayings of Jesus," 261–88.

67. Clement writes, "The Lord said, when you tread upon the garment of shame, and when the two become one, and when the male with the female is neither male nor

Peter within *2 Clement* 5.2–4 has also been seen to be dependent upon the canonical gospels (Matt 10:28; Luke 12:4–5).[68] While *2 Clement* does contain some sayings of Jesus that cannot be traced to a particular gospel, these may have been oral traditions that were circulating at the time. This writing does also contain several references to the Gospels of Matthew and Luke.

The *Gospel of the Ebionites* is alluded to within the writings of Irenaeus. He alludes to this gospel in his writing *Against Heresies* 1.26.2; 3.11.7. Later in his writings, he states that they deny the virgin birth and argues against their understanding (*Haer.* 3.21.3; 5.1.3). Thus, all that we know about this gospel through the time of Irenaeus is that it differs in relation to the birth of Jesus from the canonical gospels. The first traces of the *Gospel of the Ebionites* can be found later in Clement of Alexandria, Origen, and Didymus the Blind's writings.[69]

Within the writings of Irenaeus is also a reference to the *Gospel of Judas*. In his volume *Against Heresies* 1.31.1, he writes:

> Others again declare that Cain derived his being from the Power above, and acknowledge that Esau, Korah, the Sodomites, and all such persons, are related to themselves. On this account, they add, they have been assailed by the Creator, yet no one of them has suffered injury. For Sophia was in the habit of carrying off that which belonged to her from them to herself. They declare that Judas the traitor was thoroughly acquainted with these things, and that he alone, knowing the truth as no others did, accomplished the mystery of the betrayal; by him all things, both earthly and heavenly, were thus thrown into confusion. They produce a fictitious history of this kind, which they style the Gospel of Judas.

While Irenaeus refers to the *Gospel of Judas*, he is not positive towards it. The next reference to the *Gospel of Judas* would be found substantially later in Epiphanius, the fourth century monk.[70]

There is reference to the *Infancy Gospel of Thomas* within Irenaeus' writings. In a passage in which Irenaeus is critical of a group called the Marcosians in *Against Heresies* 1.20.1, he writes:

female."

---

68. Koester, "Gospels and Gospel Traditions in the Second Century," 31. Koester notes the similarity of *2 Clem.* 5.2–4 to Justin Martyr's *First Apology* 19.7.

69. Gregory, "Jewish Christian Gospels," 57.

70. DeConick, "The *Gospel of Judas*," 107.

> Besides the above [misrepresentations], they adduce an unspeakable number of apocryphal and spurious writings, which they themselves have forged, to bewilder the minds of foolish men, and of such as are ignorant of the Scriptures of truth. Among other things, they bring forward that false and wicked story which relates that our Lord, when He was a boy learning His letters, on the teacher saying to Him, as is usual, "Pronounce Alpha," replied [as He was bid], "Alpha." But when, again, the teacher bade Him say, "Beta," the Lord replied, "Do thou first tell me what Alpha is, and then I will tell thee what Beta is." This they expound as meaning that He alone knew the Unknown, which He revealed under its type Alpha.

He appears to allude to the *Infancy Gospel of Thomas* 14. As with the *Gospel of Judas*, he is not positively inclined to the work.[71]

Irenaeus also knew of something like the *Gospel of Truth*. He writes in *Against Heresies* 3.11.9:

> But those who are from Valentinus, being, on the other hand, altogether reckless, while they put forth their own compositions, boast that they possess more gospels than there really are. Indeed, they have arrived at such a pitch of audacity, as to entitle their comparatively recent writing "the Gospel of Truth," though it agrees in nothing with the gospels of the Apostles, so that they have really no Gospel which is not full of blasphemy. For if what they have published is the Gospel of truth, and yet is totally unlike those which have been handed down to us from the apostles, any who please may learn, as is shown from the Scriptures themselves, that that which has been handed down from the apostles can no longer be reckoned the Gospel of truth. But that these Gospels alone are true and reliable, and admit neither an increase nor diminution of the aforesaid number, I have proved by so many and such [arguments].

While it is possible that Irenaeus is referring to something other than the *Gospel of Truth* that we have in our possession, it is quite possible that it is identical. As with the other non-canonical gospels, he is negative towards it.

Earlier references to other non-canonical gospels are often suspect. For example, some have suggested that Justin Martyr refers to the *Gospel of Peter* in his *Dialogue with Trypho* 106.3. The text in question is:

---

71. Chartrand-Burke, "The *Infancy Gospel of Thomas*," 127.

> And when it is said that He [Jesus] changed the name of one of the apostles to Peter; and when it is written in the *memoirs of Him* that this so happened, as well as that He changed the names of other two brothers, the sons of Zebedee, to Boanerges, which means sons of thunder (*italics added*)

While some have advocated that the *Gospel of Peter* is what is meant,[72] the majority opinion is against this viewpoint.[73] While there may be some presence of non-canonical gospels within early Christian literature, their presence is far less visible than the canonical gospels.[74]

Conclusion

The acceptance of only four gospels can be seen to take place gradually over time throughout history. Rather than being a decision made by a few powerful people, the setting apart of Matthew, Mark, Luke, and John can be seen following the first century in the writings of the Apostolic Fathers. The superiority of these four gospels is then stated more clearly in Justin Martyr's writing, and then finally in the writing of Irenaeus. Armies and powerful people were not the decision-makers. The testimony of faithful, suffering Christians from the time immediately following the writing of the New Testament is expressed in the writings of the Apostolic Fathers, Justin Martyr, and then Irenaeus.

In contrast, the non-canonical gospels are generally not well-attested in second-century Christian literature. While more study could be accomplished in this area, when the non-canonical gospels are present, they are often criticized rather than endorsed.

The testimony of these early church documents should not be undervalued. These were the sentiments of J. B. Lightfoot, the influential nineteenth century New Testament scholar. He urged readers in his day to value the traditions immediately following the New Testament to a greater extent. In an introduction to his comments on the Apostolic

---

72. Pilhofer, "Justin und das Petrusevangelium," 60–78.

73. For the argument that it refers to Jesus' memoirs, see Foster, "The relationship between Justin Martyr and the So-called *Gospel of Peter*," 104–12. For the argument that his memoirs refer to Peter's memoirs as found within the Gospel of Mark, see Stanton, *The Gospels and Jesus*, 100–101.

74. There may be some possibility that the *Gospel of the Hebrews* can be found within some of the Apostolic Fathers. Beatrice, "The '*Gospel according to the Hebrews*,'" 147–95.

Fathers, he had this to say about the importance of these early Christian documents:

> If you are familiar with Scripture, you owe it largely to these primitive witnesses to its Canon and its spirit. By their testimony we detect what is spurious, and we identify what is real. Is it nothing to find that your Bible is their Bible, your faith, their faith, your Saviour their Saviour, your God their God? Let us reflect also, that, when copies of the entire Scriptures were rare and costly, these citations were "words fitly spoken, apples of gold in pictures of silver." We are taught by them also that they obeyed the apostle's precept, "Let the word of Christ dwell in you richly in all wisdom; teaching and admonishing," etc.[75]

If reflection is given to canonical and non-canonical gospels in light of this, the canonical gospels are of greater value than the non-canonical ones.

---

75. Lightfoot, "Apostolic Fathers," 1:vii.

CHAPTER FOUR

Other Gospels

WHAT PICTURE OF JESUS is found in these non-canonical gospels? Some would appeal to these books to claim that early Christians did not view Jesus as both human and divine. For example, Dan Brown's novel, *The Da Vinci Code*, would assert that Jesus' divinity was not assured until Constantine stated so in AD 325.[1] At that time, the church selected those gospels that it wanted to support its position, but there were non-canonical gospels that would present a more human picture of Jesus, according to Brown.[2] Elaine Pagels would also encourage considering a diversity of gospels, particularly the *Gospel of Thomas*. Gospels like *Thomas* provide a more human picture of Jesus, according to her, and should not be distinguished from the canonical gospels.[3] Similarly, Bart Ehrman asserts that the non-canonical gospels present a different picture of Jesus than the canonical ones. Most notably, he claims that these were unfairly excluded. He writes,

> Someone decided that four of these early Gospels, and no others, should be accepted as part of the canon—the collection of sacred books of Scripture. But how did they make their decisions? When? How can we be sure they were right? And whatever happened to the other books?[4]

---

1. While Constantine attended this conference, he did not declare this ruling.
2. Brown, *The Da Vinci Code*, 232–34.
3. Pagels, *Beyond Belief*, 38.
4. Ehrman, *Lost Christianities*, 3.

Some scholars will appeal to non-canonical gospels to imply that the church has gotten Jesus wrong or unfairly limited him, but few take time to look at these other gospels even though they are readily accessible. There are nearly forty of them, and they can be read in books and over the internet.[5]

This chapter will provide a brief description of some of the most referenced non-canonical gospels.[6] In these explanations, there will be a short introduction, samples of texts, and some commentary.[7] Each one will draw conclusions about the picture of Jesus that is presented, and then determine whether the non-canonical gospel has been unjustly excluded.

The Gospel of Thomas

The most noteworthy of the noncanonical gospels is the *Gospel of Thomas*. It was written in the Coptic language, a language native to Egypt from the time of the first century. The current version of the *Gospel of Thomas* dates to the fourth century, although there may be parts of it that date much earlier.[8]

The *Gospel of Thomas* was found in the desert of Egypt just outside of Nag Hammadi in 1945. It is generally known to have Gnostic influence and is part of what is considered the Nag Hammadi Library. *Thomas* does not include any miracles, stories, or anything about the crucifixion. Instead, it contains a collection of 114 secret teachings of Jesus which claim to be recorded by Didymos Judas Thomas, the half-brother of Jesus.

Most of the statements in this *Gospel* open with the phrase, "Jesus said." What matters most in the picture of Jesus given in the *Gospel of Thomas* is not his death and resurrection, but the secret teachings that

---

5. See http://www.earlychristianwritings.com/index.html. For the Nag Hammadi Gospels see: http://www.gnosis.org/naghamm/nhl.html. In printed form, see Ehrman, *Lost Scriptures*. See also Cameron, *The Other Gospels*, and Meyer, *Nag Hammadi Scriptures*.

6. Those who want a fuller description of non-canonical gospels should consider other works with greater descriptions, such as Schneemelcher and Wilson, *New Testament Apocrypha*.

7. All texts from the non-canonical gospels, unless otherwise stated, are taken from Ehrman, *Lost Scriptures*.

8. See discussion in Chapter One.

he gave. Secret knowledge is front and center in the introduction to the *Gospel of Thomas*. The first two *Logions* read as follows.

> These are the secret teachings which the living Jesus spoke and which Didymos Judas Thomas wrote down. And he said, "Whoever finds the interpretation of these sayings will not experience death."
> Jesus said, "Let him who seeks continue seeking until he finds. When he finds he will become troubled. When he becomes troubled, he will be astonished, and he will rule over the all."[9]

The concern for hidden knowledge continues in other places within the book. In *Logion* 37, there is a statement as to how the disciples will finally appreciate Jesus.

> His disciples said, "When will you become revealed to us and when shall we see you?"
> Jesus said, "When you disrobe without being ashamed and take up your garments and place them under your feet like little children and tread on them, then [will you see] the son of the living one, and you will not be afraid."

The importance of new mysterious knowledge can be read in *Logion* 62. "Jesus said, 'It is to those [who are worthy of my] mysteries that I tell my mysteries. Do not let your (sg.) left hand know what your (sg.) right hand is doing.'" *Logion* 108 continues this trend. "Jesus said, 'He who will drink from my mouth will become like me. I myself shall become he, and the things that are hidden will be revealed to him.'"

The importance of hidden knowledge is also found in *Logion* 113.

> His disciples said to him, "When will the kingdom come?"
> [Jesus said,] "It will not come by waiting for it. It will not be a matter of saying 'here it is' or 'there it is.' Rather, the kingdom of the father is spread out upon the earth, and men do not see it."

These statements reveal a mystical and elitist version of Christian understanding based on secret interpretations and higher realities.

Some of the sayings within the *Gospel of Thomas* appear to resemble the New Testament Gospels, while others are clearly different from anything in the Bible. Several of these sayings seem as if they could come

---

9. The translation for the *Gospel of Thomas* is taken from Lambdin, "Gospel of Thomas," 126–38.

Other Gospels

from the Synoptic Gospels. Something that resembles the Parable of the Sower can be seen in *Logion 9*:

> Jesus said, "Now the sower went out, took a handful (of seeds), and scattered them. Some fell on the road; the birds came and gathered them up. Others fell on rock, and did not take root in the soil, and did not produce ears. And others fell on thorns; they choked the seed(s) and worms ate them. And others fell on the good soil and it produced good fruit: it bore sixty per measure and a hundred and twenty per measure."

Another parable that is similar to the New Testament can be found in *Logion* 20. In this *Logion*, something very similar to the Parable of the Mustard Seed can be found.

A number of the sayings in the *Gospel of Thomas* will seem similar to the New Testament. For example, the encouragement to love one's brother can be found in *Logion* 25–26.

> Jesus said, "Love your (sg.) brother like your soul, guard him like the pupil of your eye."
>
> Jesus said, "You (sg.) see the mote in your brother's eye, but you do not see the beam in your own eye. When you cast the beam out of your own eye, then you will see clearly to cast the mote from your brother's eye."

At times, the *Gospel of Thomas* will make additions to what Jesus is purported to say in the canonical gospels. For example, the *Gospel of Thomas* continues Jesus' care for children as in Mark 9:36–37, but then it makes significant additions to Jesus' care for the young in *Logion 22*.

> Jesus saw infants being suckled. He said to His disciples, "The infants being suckled are like those who enter the kingdom."
>
> They said to him, "Shall we then, as children, enter the kingdom?"
>
> Jesus said to them, "When you make the two one, and when you make the inside like the outside and the outside like the inside, and the above like the below, and when you make the male and female one and the same, so that the male not be male nor the female female; and when you fashion eyes in place of an eye, and a hand in place of a foot, and a likeness in place of a likeness; then will you enter [the kingdom]."

There are a number of other sayings, however, that are quite different from the canonical gospels. There is a substantial difference between the declarations that the disciples make about who Jesus is in Mark 8:27–30 and what they are recorded to say in *Logion* 13. Mark 8:27–30 reads:

> And Jesus went on with his disciples to the villages of Caesarea Philippi. And on the way he asked his disciples, "Who do people say that I am?" And they told him, "John the Baptist; and others say, Elijah; and others, one of the prophets." And he asked them, "But who do you say that I am?" Peter answered him, "You are the Christ." And he strictly charged them to tell no one about him.

When the disciples are asked about who Jesus is within *Logion* 13, they give a substantially different answer.

> Jesus said to his disciples, "Compare me to someone and tell me whom I am like."
> Simon Peter said to him, "You are like a righteous angel."
> Matthew said to him, "You are like a wise philosopher."
> Thomas said to him, "Master, my mouth is wholly incapable of saying whom you are like."
> Jesus said, "I am not your (sg.) master. Because you (sg.) have drunk, you (sg.) have become intoxicated from the bubbling spring which I have measured out."
> And he took him and withdrew and told him three things. When Thomas returned to his companions, they asked him, "What did Jesus say to you?"
> Thomas said to them, "If I tell you one of the things which he told me, you will pick up stones and throw them at me; a fire will come out of the stones and burn you up."

The *Gospel of Thomas*, also, judges the human body to be negative. *Logion* 87 reads, "Wretched is the body that is dependent upon a body, and wretched is the soul that is dependent upon these two." The idea is repeated then in *Logion* 112, which says, "Jesus said, 'Woe to the flesh that depends on the soul; woe to the soul that depends on the flesh.'" It then ends with a statement about gender transformation that devalues the body in *Logion* 114.

> Simon Peter said to them, "Let Mary leave us, for women are not worthy of life."
> Jesus said, "I myself shall lead her in order to make her male, so that she too may become a living spirit resembling you males. For every woman who will make herself male will enter the kingdom of heaven."

While this may sound out of place to modern ears, it is possible that it reflects ascetic trends from the second century.[10] Whether ancient or modern, the physical body is an inhibitor to true spiritual life, according to Gnostic teachings.

When the *Gospel of Thomas* provides comment about what type of person Jesus is, it may also present him as divine. This can be seen in *Logion* 77.

> Jesus said, "It is I who am the light which is above them all. It is I who am the all. From me did the all come forth, and unto me did the all extend. Split a piece of wood, and I am there. Lift up the stone, and you will find me there.

Jesus affirms that he is the light and the unique one who is above all which may point to his divinity (cf. *Logion*, 13, 61).[11]

The *Gospel of Thomas*, also, gives a mystical picture of faith. It focuses on a secret and higher knowledge that can be attained by the elite. Instead of conclusively presenting a Jesus who is human, it may also present a view of Jesus as divine.[12] It also suggests that, by imitating Jesus, one could have the hope of paradise in this life.[13] Scholars are still exploring whether individual statements within the *Gospel of Thomas* could provide further information about who Jesus is. With the dependence of the *Gospel of Thomas* on canonical gospels as presented earlier, its later date, and uncertain authorship, it is unlikely that *Thomas* will provide substantially new material about Jesus.

The Gospel of Mary

The *Gospel of Mary* is the only gospel that is purported to be written by a woman. It portrays a dialogue about the afterlife between Mary Magdalene and Jesus following his resurrection. This distinguishes it from the canonical gospels, where extended dialogues are not found. The form of this *Gospel* shows its interest in passing along secret knowledge.

The *Gospel of Mary* survives in three manuscripts, which are all fragmentary. The earliest of these dates to the early third century. The

---

10. Foster, *Apocryphal Gospels*, 40.
11. Bock, *Missing Gospels*, 98–99; cf. G. Ludemann, et. al., *Jesus after 2000 Years*, 620.
12. Contra Elaine Pagels' viewpoint. See Pagels, *Beyond Belief*, 68.
13. Perrin, *Thomas*, 136.

fullest manuscript that we possess for the *Gospel of Mary* dates to the fifth century. This is substantially later than the canonical gospels, which were recognized as a collection from the times of the church fathers, such as Irenaeus and Clement of Alexandria, if not Justin Martyr.[14]

The *Gospel of Mary* contains a dialogue between Jesus and the disciples following his resurrection. In this conversation, Jesus gives a revelation to the apostles about the nature of sin. He then gives a final blessing and command to preach the gospel. After his departure, the disciples are distraught, but Mary comforts them. Following this, Peter asks her about the vision that Mary saw. At this point, unfortunately, the text breaks for several pages. The *Gospel* continues by describing Mary Magdalene's account of the vision she had with the Lord. Its final section contains a debate between Mary and Andrew, Peter, and Levi about her vision and whether she is favored over them. The *Gospel* concludes with Levi urging them to go preach as Jesus encouraged them to do.

As with the *Gospel of Thomas*, the *Gospel of Mary* promotes secret knowledge. Note the interest of the disciples in her special revelation in *Gospel of Mary* 9.21–24.

> But they were grieved. They wept greatly, saying, "How shall we go to the gentiles and preach the gospel of the kingdom of the Son of Man? If they did not spare him, how will they spare us?" Then Mary stood up, greeted them all, and said to her brethren, "Do not weep and do not grieve nor be irresolute, for his grace will be entirely with you and will protect you. But rather let us praise his greatness, for he has prepared us and made us into men." When Mary said this she turned their hearts to the Good, and they began to discuss the words of the [Savior].
>
> Peter said to Mary, "Sister, we know that the Savior loved you more than the rest of women. Tell us the words of the Savior which you remember—which you know (but) we do not, nor have we heard them." Mary answered and said, "What is hidden from you I will proclaim to you." And she began to speak to them these words: "I," she said, "I saw the Lord in a vision and I said to him, 'Lord I saw you today in a vision.' He answered and said to me, 'Blessed are you, that you did not waver at the sight of me. For where the mind is, there is the treasure.' I said to him, 'Lord, now does he who sees the vision see it [through] the soul [or] through the spirit?' The Savior answered and said, 'He does not see through

---

14. See chapter three.

the soul nor through the spirit, but the mind which [is] between the two—that is [what] sees the vision and it is [. . .]."

Later on in the *Gospel of Mary*, there is a clash between Mary and Peter in 17.18–20. This may illustrate a struggle between gender roles within the early church, but it is more likely to represent a clash between "Gnostic" and "orthodox" adherents of the faith.[15]

> When Mary had said this, she fell silent, since it was to this point that the Savior had spoken with her. But Andrew answered and said to the brethren, "Say what you (wish to) say about what she has said. I at least do not believe that the Savior said this. For certainly these teachings are strange ideas." Peter answered and spoke concerning these same things. He questioned them about the Savior: "Did he really speak with a woman without our knowledge (and) not openly? Are we to turn about and all listen to her? Did he prefer her to us?"

The *Gospel of Mary* is a Gnostic text. It provides a window into the second century church and its struggles. Due to its late dating, it is right to conclude with C. M. Tuckett that "the *Gospel of Mary* almost certainly gives us little information about the historical Jesus or the historical Mary."[16] It is proper for a gospel with these characteristics to be separated from the canonical gospels.

The Gospel of Philip

The *Gospel of Philip* is a Gnostic gospel from Nag Hammadi. We possess only one copy of it, and this is not complete. It is not a narrative and, like the *Gospel of Thomas*, there are no miracle or passion accounts. It is not a "sayings" gospel, however, but instead is a group of mystical reflections that are linked together by common words. The train of thought has been noted to be difficult to follow.[17]

The *Gospel of Philip* has received a great amount of attention due to its provocative statement about Jesus and Mary Magdalene. In the *Da*

---

15. For a conflict between gender roles, see King, *Gospel of Mary of Magdala*, 3–12. For a clash between Gnostic and orthodox adherents of the faith, see Tuckett, "The Gospel of Mary," 51.

16. Tuckett, "*Gospel of Mary*," 52.

17. See this discussion in Turner, "On the coherence of the *Gospel according to Philip*," 223–50.

Vinci Code, author Dan Brown puts words from this gospel in the mouth of character Sir Leigh Teabing. He quotes this section from the *Gospel* and relates doubts about the way that the church has represented Jesus Christ.[18] Note the large number of ellipses, which show the breaks within the text, and the words in brackets, which give a suggested but not definitive reading. *Gospel of Philip* 63.30–64.5 reads:

> The [Lord loved Mary] more than all the disciples, and he kissed her on the [mouth many times]. The other [women/disciples] saw . . . him. They said to him, "Why do you [love her] more than all of us?" The Savior answered and said to them, "Why do not I love you as I do her?"

From this reading of the *Gospel of Philip*, Jesus and Mary appear to be lovers. Brown uses this statement within *The Da Vinci Code* to insinuate that the church has been keeping this from its followers. While some type of romantic relationship between Jesus and Mary Magdalene might make tantalizing reading, this interpretation of the *Gospel of Philip* should not be trusted. First, there are a significant number of missing words, making it unclear exactly what is being said.[19] Furthermore, reading the kiss found in this section of the *Gospel of Philip* in context with other ancient documents, likely does not indicate a romantic relationship. The kiss at that time illustrated a bond of loyalty and relationship between believers rather than a romantic relationship (cf. *Gos. Phil.* 58.30–59.6; Rom 16:16; cf. 1 Thess 5:26).[20] Thus, while Brown's use of this quotation has drawn attention to the *Gospel of Philip*, one should not conclude that this quotation reveals a romantic relationship between Jesus and Mary Magdalene.

Scholars do recognize that the *Gospel of Philip* has five sacraments within it: baptism, anointing, Eucharist, salvation, and bridal chamber (cf. *Gos. Phil.* 70.34–73.8). Scholars have particularly debated what is meant by bridal chamber. It is likely that it refers to a ritual practiced within the community that was reading *Philip*. A sample text about the bridal chamber is as follows from *Gospel of Philip* 70.9–22.

---

18. See further Brown, *Da Vinci Code*, 245–46.

19. All of the bracketed portions indicate supposed readings. They are not represented in the *Gospel of Philip*.

20. Foster, "*Gospel of Philip*," 74–75.

> If the woman had not separated from the man, she should not die with the man. His separation became the beginning of death. Because of this, Christ came to repair the separation, which was from the beginning, and again, unite the two, and to give life to those who died as a result of the separation, and unite them. But the woman is united to her husband in the bridal chamber. Indeed, those who have been united in the bridal chamber will no longer be separated. Thus, Eve separated from Adam because it was not in the bridal chamber that she united with him.

This passage also illustrates the importance of reunification of being, a key point for salvation from the *Gospel of Philip*'s perspective.[21]

Several points within the *Gospel of Philip* contradict Christian teaching. The *Gospel of Philip* attacks the virgin birth in 55.23–36.

> Some said, "Mary conceived by the Holy Spirit." They are in error. They do not know what they are saying. When did a woman ever conceive by a woman? Mary is the virgin whom no power defiled. She is a great anathema to the Hebrews, who are the apostles and the apostolic men. This virgin whom no power defiled [. . .] the powers defile themselves. And the Lord would not have said, "My Father who is in Heaven," unless he had another father, but he would have said simply "My father."

Besides contradicting the virgin birth, *Philip* also suggests that Joseph is the one who made the cross of Christ. He even grew the tree that was turned into the cross (*Gos. Phil.* 73.8–19). This *Gospel* also presents resurrection as something that someone must experience before death. The *Gospel of Philip* 73.1–8 says, "Those who say they will die first and then rise are in error. If they do not first receive the resurrection while they live, when they die they will receive nothing."[22]

While Jesus is found within the *Gospel of Philip*, the book rarely presents a citation from him. In his brief introduction to the *Gospel of Philip*, Paul Foster identifies seventeen sayings from Jesus within the entire book. Nine of these are quotations from the canonical gospels that are modifications of his words found within the canonical gospels. There are no additional statements that are derived from the historical Jesus. Foster finds the other eight sayings of Jesus within the *Gospel of Philip* to be

---

21. Foster, "*Gospel of Philip*," 68.
22. Foster, "*Gospel of Philip*," 76–80. Note how Paul counters this in 1 Corinthians 15:21–28.

influenced by Valentinian Gnosticism, which emerges from the second century.[23]

One example of these Gnostic statements can be found in *Gospel of Philip* 63.29–30: "The Lord went into the dye works of Levi. He took seventy-two different colors and threw them into the vat. He took them out all white. And he said, 'Even so has the Son of Man come as a dyer.'" This allusion to a dyer resembles Valentinian baptism procedure. Another example is found in *Gospel of Philip* 64.10–12: "Blessed is he who is before he came into being. For he who is, has been and shall be." This statement resembles Valentinian Gnosticism, in which the true Gnostic believer has the prospect of existing again in a reunited state.[24]

The view of Jesus presented within the *Gospel of Philip* appears to be greatly influenced by Valentinian Gnosticism. Due to the influence of Gnosticism that developed in the second century and the late dating of the *Gospel of Philip*, there is nothing that can be taken from it for understanding the person of Jesus.[25] It is not on par with the canonical gospels.

The Gospel of Truth

One other gospel that emerges from the Nag Hammadi discovery is the *Gospel of Truth*.[26] Unlike the previous three gospels, *Truth* is not written by a named individual. It is a description of a Gnostic at the time of his enlightenment. It displays Gnostic thought from the Valentinian school, from either Valentinus or a disciple of his.[27]

This book does not present us with any new historical material on Jesus. In the *Gospel of Truth*, Jesus does not speak, and he does not perform any miracles. The good news for this author is that he has been freed from error. The *Gospel* begins with these words:

---

23. Foster, *Apocryphal Gospels*, 48. This Gnosticism is considered to be Valentinian. Cf. Isenberg, "Gospel According to Philip," 130–41.

24. Foster, *Apocryphal Gospels*, 49.

25. Foster calls it worthless for understanding the historical Jesus. Foster, *Apocryphal Gospels*, 49.

26. Other gospels discovered at Nag Hammadi include the *Apocryhphon of John* or the *Sophia of Jesus Christ*. Due to space consideration, these as well as other gospel texts are not discussed within this chapter.

27. Irenaeus attributed this work to the disciples of Valentinus. Cf. *Haer.* 3.11.9. For discussion on authorship, see Robinson, *Coptic Gnostic Library*, 1:76–81.

> The gospel of truth is joy for those who have received from the Father of truth the grace of knowing him, through the power of the Word that came forth from the *pleroma*,[28] the one who is in the thought and the mind of the Father, that is, the one who is addressed as the Savior, (that) being the name of the work he is to perform for the redemption of those who were ignorant of the Father, while in the name [of] the gospel is the proclamation of hope, being discovery for those who search for him.

While historical acts about Jesus are not found, the author of the *Gospel of Truth* does interpret Jesus. Such an instance is found in 20.24–21.2.

> For this reason, the compassionate, faithful Jesus was patient in his sufferings until he took that book, since he knew that his death meant life for many. Just as in the case of a will which has not yet been opened, for the fortune of the deceased master of the house is hidden, so also in the case of the All which had been hidden as long as the Father of the All was invisible and unique in himself, in whom every space has its source. For this reason Jesus appeared. He took that book as his own. He was nailed to a cross. He affixed the edict of the Father to the cross.
>
> Oh, such great teaching! He abases himself even unto death, though he is clothed in eternal life. Having divested himself of these perishable rags, he clothed himself in incorruptibility, which no one could possibly take from him. Having entered into the empty territory of fears, he passed before those who were stripped by forgetfulness, being both knowledge and perfection, proclaiming the things that are in the heart of the Father, so that he became the wisdom of those who have received instruction. But those who are to be taught, the living who are inscribed in the book of the living, learn for themselves, receiving instructions from the Father, turning to him again.

This passage exhibits Gnostic thought. Salvation occurs through the reception of hidden knowledge. Jesus is the one who enlightens people, revealing what was hidden.

Knowledge and discovery is found throughout the *Gospel of Truth*. This is evident in 35.8–14.

> The deficiency of matter, however, is not because of the limitlessness of the Father who comes at the time of the deficiency. And yet no one is able to say that the incorruptible One will come in this

---

28. *Pleroma* means "fullness."

manner. But the depth of the Father is increasing, and the thought of error is not with him. It is a matter of falling down and a matter of being readily set upright at the finding of that one who has come to him who will turn back.

Other Gnostic ideas found within the *Gospel of Truth* include parables, rest, and anointing ideas.

The picture of Jesus within the *Gospel of Truth* is of a Gnostic redeemer. Humanity is in error, and the Gnostic Redeemer, interpreted in this case as Jesus, must come and reveal truth. In him is knowledge which will conquer ignorance and forgetfulness so that people might know the Father. Jesus Christ reveals truth to the enlightened who are able to read it in the book. Since the *Gospel of Truth* contains Gnostic thoughts like these which are dated second century or later, it offers an inferior picture of Jesus when compared with the canonical gospels.

The Gospel of Peter

The *Gospel of Peter* was a forgotten text until a portion of it was discovered at the end of the nineteenth century at a grave site in Akhmîm, Egypt. Early church historian Eusebius had likely made mention of the text earlier (*Hist. eccl.* 3.3.2; 6.12.1–6). In his *Ecclesiastical History*, Eusebius records the decision of early church leader Serapion of Antioch, who deemed it to be heretical (*Hist. eccl.* 6.12.3–6).

Unlike the previous non-canonical gospels that have been considered, the *Gospel of Peter* does not promote secret mysteries or higher knowledge. Instead, it describes the events of Jesus' crucifixion and resurrection and elaborates on them.[29] It begins with Pilate washing his hands at Jesus' trial. As the narrative continues, it follows the canonical gospels closely, particularly the Gospel of Matthew. There are some notable differences between it and Matthew, however. For example, verse 10 describes Jesus' death on the cross "as if he had no pain." Then, when Jesus emerges from the tomb, the cross that he was on actually speaks in *Gospel of Peter* 38–42:

---

29. Another non-canonical gospel that refers to the crucifixion of Jesus is the *Gospel of Nicodemus*, also called the *Acts of Pilate*. This is dated to the fourth century AD. Due to considerations of space, it will not be treated here.

> When the solders saw these things, they woke up the centurion and the elders—for they were also there on guard. As they were explaining what they had seen, they saw three men emerge from the tomb, two of them supporting the other, with a cross following behind them. The heads of the two reached up to the sky, but the head of the one they were leading went up above the skies. And they heard a voice from the skies, "Have you preached to those who are asleep?" And a reply came from the cross, "Yes."

The *Gospel of Peter* concludes with several events that also show similarity with the Gospel of Matthew. The centurions are found as in Matthew, and they declare that Jesus was the Son of God. Instead of returning to the chief priests following the resurrection of Jesus, they return to Pilate and not the chief priests in the *Gospel of Peter*. As in Matthew, Mary Magdalene and the other Mary visit Jesus' tomb where they meet an angel. After speaking with him, however, they flee in terror, which is more like the Gospel of Mark than the Gospel of Matthew. Unlike any of the four canonical gospels, the disciples grieve Jesus' death, followed by Simon Peter, Andrew, and Levi going off to fish.

The *Gospel of Peter* contains several ideas that are not in agreement with Christian teaching over the centuries. For example, Docetism, the belief that Jesus did not have real human flesh, may be found in the *Gospel of Peter*. Jesus does not feel pain in *Gospel of Peter* 10 as he undergoes what would be considered a horrific death on the cross. Only a Jesus without authentic human flesh, as Docetism claims, could go through such a death painlessly.[30]

Besides Docetism, the *Gospel of Peter* is known for its anti-Semitic feelings. The blame for the crucifixion of Jesus is not placed on Pilate; he is absolved (*Gos. Pet.* 46). Instead, culpability is placed squarely upon the Jewish people. The *Gospel of Peter* records this in 25, 28–30 following the death of Jesus.

> Then the Jews, the elders, and the priests realized how much evil they had done to themselves and began beating their breasts, saying, "Woe to us because of our sins. The judgment and the end of Jerusalem is near." . . . The scribes, Pharisees, and elders gathered together and heard all the people murmuring and beating their

---

30. Others see further Docetic influence in *Gospel of Peter* 18 when Jesus utters on the cross, "My power, O power, you have left me behind!" Cf. Harris, *A Popular Account of the Newly Recovered Gospel of St. Peter*, 35.

breasts, saying, "If such great signs happened when he died, you can see how righteous he was!" The elders became fearful and went to Pilate and asked him, "Give us some soldiers to guard his crypt for three days to keep his disciples from coming to steal him. Otherwise the people may assume he has been raised from the dead and then harm us."

As stated previously, the *Gospel of Peter* shows dependence upon the canonical gospels.[31] It maintains in part Pilate's decision, the crown of thorns, the mocking of Jesus, darkness coming over the land, the offer for Jesus to drink vinegar and gall, and the rending of the Temple curtain in two. At Jesus' tomb, the *Gospel of Peter* preserves the presence of the guard, the stone being rolled away, and the visit of Mary Magdalene and the other Mary.

While the *Gospel of Peter* maintains many of the details that would be found within the passion accounts of the canonical gospels, it should not be viewed as being equal to the canonical gospels for several reasons. First, it supplies several details that would be associated with second century ideas like anti-Semitism. The conflict between Christendom and Judaism was a second century phenomenon in comparison to the time of Christ's crucifixion. Second, the picture of Jesus that is preserved within the *Gospel of Peter* promotes his deity but much less his humanity. This image reflects Docetic influences, a second century phenomenon. Finally, several of the details within the *Gospel of Peter* are unrealistic and interpretive, such as a speaking cross and the heads of people reaching to the skies.

The *Gospel of Peter* represents a creative recounting of one segment of Jesus' life, the passion events.[32] It is inferior to the canonical gospels and in error in several places, however.

The Infancy Gospel of Thomas

The *Gospel of Peter* is not the only non-canonical gospel to elaborate on segments of the life of Jesus that are not represented in Matthew, Mark, Luke, and John. The *Infancy Gospel of Thomas* develops Jesus' life before his ministry. Only a few incidents of Jesus' early life are found in the canonical gospels. The Gospels of Matthew and Luke are the only canonical ones to record the birth of Jesus. Mark and John omit any reference to the

31. See chapter one.
32. Foster, "*Gospel of Peter*," 41.

birth of Jesus. Details about Jesus' childhood are confined to Jesus' trip with his parents to the Temple as a twelve year old in Luke 2:41–52. The *Infancy Gospel of Thomas* records several stories from Jesus' early years.

The *Infancy Gospel of Thomas* claims to have been written by Didymos Thomas. It covers approximately seven years, beginning with a story when Jesus was five and then concluding with Jesus' trip to the Temple when he was twelve. It should not to be confused with the *Gospel of Thomas*. The latter is a collection of sayings, while the former involves stories about Jesus as young boy.

The first story of this gospel relates an incident that occurred when Jesus was five years old. The *Infancy Gospel of Thomas* 2:1–5 reads:

> When this child Jesus was five years old, he was playing by the ford of a stream; and he gathered the flowing waters into pools and made them immediately pure. These things he ordered simply by speaking a word. He then made some soft mud and fashioned twelve sparrows from it. It was the Sabbath when he did this. A number of other children were also playing with him. But when a certain Jew saw what Jesus had done while playing on the Sabbath, he left right away and reported this to his father, Joseph, "Look, your child at the stream has taken mud and formed twelve sparrows. He has profaned the Sabbath!" When Joseph came to the place and saw what had happened, he cried out to him, "Why are you doing what is forbidden on the Sabbath?" But Jesus clapped his hands and cried to the sparrows, "Be gone!" And the sparrows took flight and went off, chirping. When the Jews saw this they were amazed; and they went away and reported to their leaders what they had seen Jesus do.

Supernatural events continue throughout this book. In chapters 6 through 8, Jesus prophesies of his upcoming death upon the cross during an interaction with Zacchaeus. In subsequent chapters, Jesus raises a dead child, carries water in a cloak, conducts a miraculous harvest, and miraculously repairs a bed. Later, he heals his brother James after he is bitten by a snake.

> Now Joseph sent his son James to bundle some wood and bring it to the house. The child Jesus also followed him. While James was gathering the firewood, a snake bit his hand. When he was stretched out on the ground dying, Jesus came up to him and breathed on the bite. The pain immediately stopped, the animal burst, and straight away James was returned to health. (*Inf. Gos. Thom.* 12)

Jesus Tried and True

The *Infancy Gospel of Thomas* concludes by retelling the story of Jesus going to Jerusalem with his parents (*Inf. Gos. Thom.* 19). Instead of having Jesus listening to the teachers, as he does in Luke 2:41–52, Jesus is the one who teaches the scribes about the Law. *Infancy Gospel of Thomas* 19:3–4 says:

> When his mother Mary came up to him she said, "Why have you done this to us, child? See, we have been distressed, looking for you." Jesus replied to them, "Why are you looking for me? Don't you know that I must be with those who are my Father's?" The scribes and Pharisees said, "Are you the mother of this child?" She replied, "I am." They said to her, "You are most fortunate among women, because God has blessed the fruit of your womb. For we have never seen or heard of such glory, such virtue and wisdom."

In this chapter, the *Infancy Gospel of Thomas* is dependent upon the Gospel of Luke. The outstanding wisdom of the young Jesus is prominently on display.[33]

This non-canonical gospel has been considered to be influenced by Gnosticism. Recently, some have noticed the connection that the *Infancy Gospel of Thomas* may have with other Greco-Roman accounts that praise a god or noteworthy individual such as Hermes, Hercules, Alexander the Great, Plato, and Apollonius during their childhood. Other examples of praising a notable person can also be found in Jewish literature, such as infancy stories about Abraham, Moses, and Elijah. These embellished infancy stories foreshadow the greatness of an individual in his adulthood. Such a practice fits with the concept of childhood within the ancient world, in which an esteemed figure was understood to have special skills and abilities from a young age.[34] Childhood then became an opportune time to present propaganda on a person's life. It is possible that these embellished accounts about Jesus within the *Infancy Gospel of Thomas* followed this pattern. Rather than being influenced by Gnosticism, this non-canonical gospel may have been composed in order to draw attention to Jesus during his childhood well before his remarkable ministry.[35]

---

33. Other features within this non-canonical gospel may show a dependence upon Luke, as well. In the Gospel of Luke, Elijah is recognized as a cursing wonder-worker, which may overlap with the presentation of Jesus in this non-canonical gospel as Jesus is presented here; e.g., *Inf. Gos. Thom.* 8, 14. Cf. Fitzmeyer, "More about Elijah coming first," 295–96.

34. Cf. Pelling, "Childhood and Personality in Greek Literature," 217, 235–40.

35. Chartrand-Burke, "The *Infancy Gospel of Thomas*," 134–37.

The picture of Jesus within the *Infancy Gospel of Thomas* resembles the canonical gospels somewhat. Jesus is portrayed as human and divine, although in this work his divine abilities are displayed in his childhood. He does appear selfish, however. He maims playmates, confounds teachers, and performs miracles for his own advantage. He is not the compassionate Jesus that is presented within the canonical gospels. Its presentation of Jesus is not greater or even supplemental to Matthew, Mark, Luke, and John, however. The *Infancy Gospel of Thomas* embellishes portions of the Gospel of Luke, showing its dependence. It is inferior to the canonical gospels and has been rightly excluded from the canon.

The Protevangelium of James

The *Infancy Gospel of Thomas* is not the only non-canonical gospel that concerns the beginnings of Jesus' early life. The *Protevangelium of James* presents the beginnings of Jesus' life as well as the birth of his mother Mary. It claims to have been written by James, the half-brother of Jesus (cf. *Prot. Jas.* 25.1–2; Mark 6:3), but this is not possible due to the late dating of the work. The book includes portions of Matthew and Luke which were composed following the death of James, and thus it is impossible for James to have written it.

Most of the non-canonical gospels that are being considered in this chapter are known by one or two manuscripts. Some are even known by fragments of a manuscript. By comparison, the *Protevangelium of James* is well represented and circulated widely.[36] There are over 140 Greek manuscripts of this work which have been catalogued in five different textual families.[37] Besides these many copies, it is mentioned within the third century by church fathers such as Origen and Clement of Alexandria.[38]

The *Protevangelium of James* did not always have this name. In the Orthodox tradition, the book is called *Birth of Mary* with the added explanation *Revelation of James*. It was first called *Protevangelium of James*

---

36. Another non-canonical gospel which circulated widely was the *Epistle of the Apostles*. It is a second century document and in agreement with much of church tradition. It criticizes Gnosticism. The conclusions that could be drawn about this document are similar to what can be drawn by the *Protevangelium of James* in this chapter.

37. de Strycker, "Die grieschischen Handschriften des Protevangeliums Iacobi," 577–612.

38. Cf. Origen, *Comm. Matt.* 10.17; Clement of Alexandria, *Strom.* 7.16.93.

in the sixteenth century by French scholar Guillaume Postel. It is considered a gospel because it contains narratives related to Jesus' birth. It is a *proto-* or first gospel because the book's first half focuses on Mary. The *Protevangelium of James* includes much about Mary: her conception, birth, adolescence, marriage to Joseph, pregnancy, and the safeguarding of her virginity. Most of the book, however, focuses on her and then the events leading up to Jesus' birth. Less than half concerns the birth of Jesus. It eventually concludes with the death of Herod the Great.

Although the *Protevangelium of James* tells of events before the time of Jesus' birth, the book shows considerable dependence upon Matthew and Luke. This can be especially seen in the sections that describe the birth of Jesus which agree with these canonical gospels. The order for a census from Augustus leads to Mary and Joseph traveling towards Bethlehem, as in Luke. Wise men from the east come to visit Jesus after following a star. They ask scribes where the Messiah is to be born, and they reply by saying, "In Bethlehem of Judea. For that is what is found in the Scripture." Herod then encourages the wise men to go look for Jesus and then to let him know when they find him. The wise men are led to Jesus' birthplace and give their gifts of gold, frankincense, and myrrh. They are then warned not to return to Judea. Herod then orders the killing of the infants less than two years of age (*Prot. Jas.* 21.1–22.1; cf. Matt 2:1–16). There are a few embellishments in this story, such as Jesus being born in a cave rather than a manger, and dialogue between Mary and Joseph in their travel to Bethlehem. Despite these additions, there are many aspects that sound as if they have been borrowed from the Gospels of Matthew and Luke.[39]

Besides this dependence, the *Protevangelium of James* also exhibits reliance upon later theological tradition. It promotes the perpetual virginity of Mary. For example, it contains a scene in which Mary's virginity is examined following the birth of Jesus. After his birth, the midwife Salome expresses doubt that Mary as a virgin has given birth. She says in 19.3, "As the Lord my God lives, if I do not insert my finger and examine her condition, I will not believe that the virgin has given birth." Salome then investigates Mary in 20.1–2:

> The midwife went in and said to Mary, "Brace yourself, for there is no small controversy concerning you." Then Salome inserted her finger in order to examine her condition, and she cried out, "Woe

---

39. Cameron, *Other Gospels*, 107–8.

to me for my sin and faithlessness. For I have put the living God to the test, and see, my hand is burning, falling away from me." She kneeled before the Master and said, "O God of my fathers, remember that I am a descendent of Abraham, Isaac, and Jacob. Do not make me an example to the sons of Israel, but deliver me over to the poor. For you know, O Master, that I have performed my services in your name and have received my wages from you."

She then holds out her hand to Jesus for healing and is healed (*Prot. Jas.* 20.3–4).[40]

Another influence from theological tradition can also be found. Mary's birth is patterned after the birth of Samuel. Her mother's name is Anna, the Greek form of the name Hannah. Anna is barren as Hannah was, but she prays to the Lord that her barrenness may be removed. After the birth of the child, she praises God like Hannah (cf. 1 Sam 1–2:10; *Prot. Jas.* 2–6). This Old Testament picture of Mary's birth contributes to the honor that the author wants to ascribe to her.

The picture of Jesus that the *Protevangelium of James* provides is very much in agreement with the canonical gospels; Jesus is fully human and divine. It is not in contradiction with them. The *Protevangelium of James* is dependent upon the canonical gospel accounts and expands upon them to support its main theme, a high regard for Mary.[41] Its inclusion among the canonical gospels would add little to the picture of Jesus, although it could alter the viewpoint of Mary for some. It is an inferior gospel.

The Gospel of Judas

The most recently discovered non-canonical gospel is the *Gospel of Judas*. While it was known that there was such a work from second century writer Irenaeus, it was not found until 1978 in the village of Ambar, which is north of Al Minya, Egypt.[42] After its discovery, it took several decades for it to be published. During this time, the *Gospel* was stolen, hidden,

---

40. Cf. Num 5:11–28. Bruce, *Jesus and Christian Traditions outside the New Testament*, 86–87. Another addition from later theological tradition can be seen in Mary's offspring. The children that are a part of her family are ascribed to Joseph, who is declared to be married prior to being with Mary (*Prot. Jas.* 9.2).

41. Foster, "*Protevangelium of James*," 123–24.

42. Irenaeus criticizes this text in *Against Heresies* 1.31.1. For further on this intriguing story of publication, see Foster, *Apocryphal Gospels*, 120–21.

frozen, and sold for a large price. All of this caused the codex containing the *Gospel of Judas* to deteriorate. In 2001, the task of reconstruction began. Great effort was invested, and the manuscript was published in 2006. When it was released to the public, there was a great stir as if this document could reverse the understanding of Christianity.[43]

The *Gospel of Judas* is about a secret discourse that Judas had with Jesus three days before Jesus' final Passover. It concerns secret knowledge like other Gnostic Gospels. Its introduction states this plainly in 1.1: "This is the hidden word of the pronouncement, containing the account about wh[en Je]sus spoke with Judas [I]scari[ot] for eight days, three days before he observed Passover."[44] Thus, with its interest in secret knowledge, it is similar to the *Gospel of Thomas*, the *Gospel of Mary*, the *Gospel of Philip*, and the *Gospel of Truth*, as opposed to other gospels that contain narratives about Jesus' life.

The *Gospel of Judas* is composed of two parts. The first section is a dialogue between Jesus and his disciples after he encounters them taking the Eucharist. Rather than commending them, he laughs at them. While the disciples were thinking that partaking of the Eucharist was an act of piety, Jesus in the *Gospel of Judas* considers this to be an act of idolatry. By taking the Eucharist, they are demonstrating that they do not really know him. This can be found in 2.6–11.

> He replied, telling them, "It is not you I am laughing at—you are not even doing this by [yo]ur own will—but (I'm laughing because) in this (offering of thanks), your 'God' will receive praise."
> "Teacher, *you* are [. . .] the Son of our God," they said.
> Jesus said to them, "Do you (really think you) know me—how? Truly I say to you, no race from the people among you will ever know me."

As the *Gospel* continues, it will only be Judas who has the strength within himself to respond appropriately to face Jesus. In 2.22–26, the following confrontation takes place.

> Judas said to him, "I know who you are and which place you came from—you came from the realm of the immortal Barbelo—but I am not worthy to proclaim the name of the one who sent you."

---

43. See the article "Greatest Archaeological Discovery of All Time."

44. The translation of the *Gospel of Judas* is from Karen King in Pagels and King, *Gospel of Judas and the Shaping of Christianity*.

Then Jesus, recognizing that he perceived even more of such exalted matters, said to him, "Separate from them. I will tell you the mysteries of the kingdom."

Judas recognizes that secret insights are needed into Jesus' life which distinguishes him from others. He claims that Jesus is from the aeon of Barbelo.[45] Jesus realizes that Judas is then to be distinguished from the other disciples, and he begins to tell Judas secret revelation.

The secret revelation that Judas receives is about creation. Unlike the way Genesis describes creation, the *Gospel of Judas* presents creation like a genealogy. In other words, entity A creates B. Then B creates C, and C creates D, and so on (*Gos. Jud.* 10–12). This is unlike the Genesis account in which God speaks things into existence, creating things out of nothing (cf. Gen 1:1–2:3).

Things unfortunately turn sour in the creation process in the *Gospel of Judas*. Instead of a fall as is found in the Genesis account (cf. Gen 3), there is a weakening of the light that emanates from the first creation. As the sequence of creation progresses, the rulers of the underworld are created (*Gos. Jud.* 12.5–21). Then after these corrupt beings are created, eventually Adam and Eve are created. They are told that they will not live long. They are the dregs of creation.

Following this secret revelation, Judas is then set apart as being special.[46] Jesus explains this role of Judas as the betrayer saying in 15.3–16:

> As for you, you will surpass them all. For you will sacrifice the human being who bears me. Already your horn is raised up, your anger is full, your star has passed by, and your heart has [preva]iled.
> "Tr[uly I say to you,] 'your end . . .'"
> [*about five and a half lines are untranslatable*]
> . . . the ru[ler] who is destroyed. [An]d then the place of the great race of Adam will be exalted, because prior to heaven and earth and the angels, through the realms that race exists.
> "Behold, everything has been told to you. Lift up your eyes and see the cloud and the light which is in it and the stars which surround it. And the star that leads the way, that is your star."

---

45. Barbelo is a deity in the Gnostic hierarchy.

46. There is controversy as to whether Judas is exonerated, denigrated, or placed somewhere in between. See further Gathercole, "*Gospel of Judas*," 90-91; DeConick, "*Gospel of Judas*," 96-102.

Following this, Judas receives a special revelation in a cloud. He then betrays Jesus and receives money from the chief priests. The secret message of revelation has been the key component for Judas as this *Gospel* presents it.[47]

The picture of Jesus that is found within the *Gospel of Judas* is quite different from other recognized perspectives of Jesus. He is not an appealing figure. He is not connected with the love of humanity or of God within the entire book. There is nothing said about the purpose of his death upon the cross. He also is separated from Judaism and identified with Gnostic figures such as Barbelo. In the words of N. T. Wright, "[the *Gospel of Judas*] tells nothing about the real Jesus or for that matter the real Judas."[48]

It is clearly inferior to the canonical gospels. It contains the presence of Gnostic figures such as Barbelo, Autogenes, and Adamas which are all recognized as second century Gnostic ideas. Furthermore, the *Gospel of Judas* appears to add these Gnostic ideas on top of the canonical gospel perspective. There is also the likely dependence of *Judas* upon the Gospel of Matthew (e.g., Matt 21:46 and *Gos. Jud.* 16.1–3; Matt 21:32; cf. *Gos. Jud.* 1.4). Thus, the ideas within the *Gospel of Judas* are best seen as late additions, supplementing the canonical Gospel of Matthew with Gnostic ideas.[49]

The Jewish-Christian Gospels

There are several named gospels that are Jewish and Christian in origin: *Gospel of the Hebrews*, *Gospel of the Nazareans*, and *Gospel of Ebionites*. Some believe, however, that these three are in fact two—the *Gospel of the Hebrews* and *Gospel of Ebionites*, with the *Gospel of the Nazareans* as part of the *Gospel of the Hebrews*. It is open for debate whether there are two or three of these Jewish-Christian Gospels.

Each of the Jewish-Christian gospels is influenced by a substantial amount of Judaism that is mixed into their Christian perspective. Jesus lived and conducted his ministry within a Jewish environment. He was crucified in Jerusalem. It was in this city that his early followers gathered after his resurrection (cf. Acts 1). A number remained in Jerusalem after

---

47. Gathercole, "The *Gospel of Judas*," 91.
48. Wright, *Judas and the Gospel of Jesus*, 13.
49. Gathercole, *The Gospel of Judas*, 134–38.

the persecution of Stephen (Acts 7). These stayed and followed Jewish laws of circumcision, diet, and Sabbath observance.

At Pentecost and especially following the persecution that came about due to the death of Stephen, the early Christians shared the gospel message with those who were outside of Judaism. As a result, many believed in Jesus Christ (cf. Acts 14:27). This led to confusion within the broader Christian community that needed to be resolved. At the Apostolic Council in Acts 15, it was decided that Gentiles could indeed be a part of the Christian community without following Jewish laws such as circumcision. Faith in Jesus Christ was the only requisite, although the Gentiles were also to abstain from food sacrificed to idols, from sexual immorality, and from the meat of strangled animals and from blood (Acts 15:20, 29).

There were some, however, who were less comfortable with these decisions. While they acknowledged Jesus as Messiah, they practiced greater adherence to the Law and functioned as Law-observant Jews. It is from this group that the Jewish-Christian gospels emerge. The martyrdom of James and the destruction of Jerusalem in AD 70 led to the loss of the strength of this group and their dispersion. Only a few fragments of their literary works remain.

No independent manuscript has been found for any of these. The early church fathers mention their existence and record small portions of these gospels in some places. Writing from the latter half of the second century, Irenaeus is the first witness of a Jewish-Christian gospel. He identifies a group called the Ebionites who were using an adapted version of the Gospel of Matthew (*Haer.* 1.26.2; 3.11.7) but who deny the virgin birth (*Haer.* 5.1.3; cf. 3.21.3). This could lead one to believe that this group was using the Gospel of Matthew with only the portions of the virgin birth removed.[50] Later church fathers such as Clement of Alexandria, Origen, Epiphanius, and Jerome record small fragments of these Jewish-Christian gospels.

The titles of these works are not found in many places either. Only the title of the *Gospel of the Hebrews* exists in quotations from early Christian writers such as Clement of Alexandria, Origen, and Didymus the Blind. The last two titles—*Gospel of the Nazareans* and *Gospel of the Ebionites*—are modern constructs. We know of their existence from church fathers

---

50. Gregory, "Jewish-Christian Gospels," 57.

Epiphanius and Jerome, who refer to a gospel that the Nazareans used. Epiphanius is the only one who refers to a gospel that the Ebionites used.

The earliest appearance of a passage from the Jewish-Christian Gospel is recorded within the writings of Clement of Alexandria, who lived in the late second century and early third century. The passage he cites is from the *Gospel of the Hebrews*. In *Miscellanies* 2.9.45, he writes, "As it is also written in the Gospel according to the Hebrews, 'The one who is amazed will rule, and the one who rules will find rest.'" Scholars have noted a resemblance to *Logion* 2 in the *Gospel of Thomas* but also Matthew 7:7.[51]

The second earliest passage from the *Gospel of the Hebrews* is found in Origen's commentary on John. It reads, "If anyone accepts the Gospel according to the Hebrews, there the Savior himself says, 'Just now my mother, the Holy Spirit, took me by one of my hairs and carried me up to the great mountain, Tabor.'" Such a statement could have Jewish and Christian thought found within it. The idea of a prophet being lifted by his hair overlaps with Jewish Scripture (cf. Ezek 8:6; Dan 14:36). Mount Tabor could also refer to Jesus' temptation or transfiguration. Thus, this text may also fit alongside the synoptic gospels.[52]

The *Gospel of the Nazareans* is recognized to be an expanded version of the Gospel of Matthew. It is largely preserved in the writings of Jerome which date from the late fourth to early fifth century AD. There are also marginal annotations to this *Gospel* in several ancient manuscripts from Origen's commentary on the Gospel of Matthew.

The fifth fragment of this *Gospel* is found in Jerome, *Commentary on Matthew* 12:13.

> In the Gospel that the Nazareans and Ebionites use, which I recently translated from Hebrew into Greek, and which most people consider the authentic version of Matthew, the man with a withered hand is described as a mason, who sought for help in words like these: "I was a mason who made a living with my hands; I

---

51. The *Gospel of Thomas* in *Logion* 2 reads, "Jesus said, 'Let him who seeks continue seeking until he finds. When he finds, he will become troubled. When he becomes troubled, he will be astonished, and he will rule over all.'" It also may agree with Synoptic Gospel tradition, such as Matthew 7:7, which says, "Ask and it will be given to you; seek and you will find; knock and the door will be opened to you" (cf. Luke 11:9). Gregory, "Jewish-Christian Gospels," 59.

52. Gregory, "Jewish-Christian Gospels," 60.

beseech you, Jesus, restore my health so I do not have to beg for food shamefully."

Later in this same commentary in 27:51, this fragment from the *Gospel of the Nazareans* is found. "In the Gospel we have often referred to, we read that 'the enormous lintel of the temple was broken and split apart.'" These passages and others from the *Gospel of the Nazareans* are known to be closely related to the Gospel of Matthew.[53]

Church father Epiphanius of Salamis of the fourth century is the sole witness to the last of the Jewish-Christian Gospels—the *Gospel of the Ebionites*. He preserved small portions of the *Gospel of the Ebionites* within his writing *Panarion* (which translated means "medicine chest"). This *Gospel* is recognized to be a harmony of Matthew and Luke and likely Mark.[54] It does not contain anything about Jesus' birth. The theology of the Ebionites has crept in at places, as can be seen by the fact that both John the Baptist and Jesus are presented as vegetarians.[55]

It is important to understand who Epiphanius was in order to interpret what we have received of this *Gospel*. Epiphanius was a heresy hunter who wanted to root out false teaching and preserve the message of the early church as found in the Nicene Creed. He was opposed to the Ebionites and used the *Gospel of the Ebionites* within his writing to attack them. The topics that Epiphanius represents from this *Gospel* include the ministry and lineage of John, the ministry and diet of John, John's baptism of Jesus, and Jesus' call of the Twelve. There are three sayings also represented concerning family, the abolition of sacrifices, and the Passover.

In *Refutation of All Heresies* 30.13.7–8, he quotes the following from the *Gospel of the Ebionites*.

> And after much has been recorded it proceeds:
> When the people were baptized, Jesus also came and was baptized by John. And as he came up from the water, the heavens were opened and he saw the Holy Spirit in the form of a dove that descended and entered into him. And a voice (sounded) from heaven that said: Thou art my beloved Son, in thee I am well pleased. And again: I have this day begotten thee. And immediately a great light shone round about the place. When John saw this, it saith, he saith unto him:

53. Cameron, *Other Gospels*, 98.
54. See further Gregory, "Prior or Posterior?" 344–60.
55. Cameron, *Other Gospels*, 103.

> Who art thou, Lord? And again a voice from heaven (rang out) to him: This is my beloved Son in whom I am well pleased. And then, it saith, John fell down before him and said: I beseech thee, Lord, baptize thou me. But he prevented him and said: Suffer it; for thus it is fitting that everything should be fulfilled.[56]

This section displays a knowledge of the Synoptic Gospels (Matt 3:13–17; Mark 1:9–11; Luke 3:21–23). Other places within the *Gospel of the Ebionites* also display knowledge particularly of the Synoptic Gospels.[57]

Due to the fragmentary nature, a complete picture of Jesus within these gospels cannot be definitively concluded. What seems striking is the great agreement between these Jewish-Christian pictures and Jesus of the canonical gospels. The *Gospel of the Ebionites* may show uneasiness with parts of the synoptic gospel tradition, but it draws on this tradition rather than refuting it when it portrays Jesus. It only contradicts the canonical gospels directly concerning John's diet and its denial that Jesus participated in the Passover meal.[58]

While the Jewish-Christian Gospels support keeping the Jewish Law, much of their contents are in agreement with the canonical gospels. Church leaders such as Clement, Origen, and Didymus the Blind drew on the *Gospel of the Hebrews* for support, and Jerome used the *Gospel of the Nazareans*. While the *Gospel of the Ebionites* contradicts the canonical gospels in places, it claims to build upon the Gospel of Matthew. With the support that these draw from the canonical gospel tradition, these Jewish-Christian gospels are inferior to the canonical ones.

Papyrus Egerton 2, also known as the Unknown Gospel

Papyrus Egerton 2 is one of the earliest preserved witnesses of the gospel tradition and is dated around AD 200. Until its publication in 1935, the world did not know about this work, since it was not mentioned in any

---

56. The translation is taken from Vielhauer and Strecker, "Gospel of the Ebionites," 169. While Epiphanius will criticize the *Gospel of the Ebionites* and its misguided theology (*Pan.* 30.13.2–3), the fragments that we have display a dependence upon the Synoptic Gospels.

57. Cf. Vielhauer and Strecker, "Gospel of the Ebionites," 169–71.

58. Gregory, "Jewish-Christian Gospels," 66.

ancient source. Its publication drew a great deal of attention in the early half of the twentieth century.[59]

There are three leaves of a codex for *Papyrus Egerton 2*. These contain five narratives which are a confrontation between Jesus and the Jewish leaders similar to John 5:39–47 and 10:31–39, a healing of a leper similar to Synoptic accounts (Matt 8:1–4; Mark 1:40–45; Luke 5:12–16; 17:11–14), a controversy about paying taxes to Caesar also similar to the Synoptic Gospels (cf. Matt 22:15–22; Mark 12:13–17; Luke 20:20–26), a miracle that Jesus performed by the Jordan river with no Synoptic parallels, and a few words that may resemble a confrontation between the Jews and Jesus like John 10:30–32. The author is unknown.

The first narrative reads as follows.

> [And Jesus said] to the lawyers: "[Punish] every wrong-doer and [transgressor], but not me. [For that one does not consider] how he does what he does."
>
> Then he turned to the rulers of the people and spoke this word: "Search the Scriptures, for you think that in them you have life. They are the ones that testify concerning me. Do not think that I came to accuse you to my Father. The one who accuses you is Moses, in whom you have hoped."
> They replied, "We know full well that God spoke to Moses. But we do not know where you have come from."
> Jesus answered them, "Now what stands accused is your failure to believe his testimonies. For if you had believed Moses, you would have believed me. For that one wrote to your fathers concerning me . . ."

In this confrontation between Jesus and the lawyers and rulers of the people, Jesus seems to answer that he is not transgressing the Scriptures. He fulfills the Scripture, and thus the Scripture should be read in light of him. The wording from this fragment closely resembles John's Gospel.

While some have asserted that *Papyrus Egerton 2* presents independent tradition,[60] the vast majority believe that the author seems to know and has reused the Gospel of John.[61] While it does have some indepen-

---

59. See Bell and Skeat, *Fragments of an Unknown Gospel*.
60. Cf. Koester, *Ancient Christian Gospels*, 205–15; Cameron, *The Other Gospels*, 73.
61. Nicklas, "*Papyrus Egerton 2*," 148–49; Foster, *The Apocryphal Gospels*, 111; Nierynck, "*Papyrus Egerton 2* and the Healing of the Leper," 773–83; Jeremias and Schneemelcher, "Papyrus Egerton 2," 96–99.

dent material, *Papyrus Egerton 2*, like many non-canonical gospels, uses material from the canonical gospels. There is also indication that *Papyrus Egerton 2* contains material that supports Jesus as Son of God, since he is called "Lord" and "Son of God."[62] Its picture of Jesus is similar to the canonical gospels and builds upon them. As with other non-canonical gospels, it supports the superiority of the canonical ones.[63]

Papyrus Oxyrhynchus 840

Many papyrus manuscripts were discovered in Oxyrhynchus, but one of the most significant is *Papyrus Oxyrhynchus 840*. On this small leaf of what was a parchment book (8.8 x 7.4 cm) is tiny writing of two stories about Jesus that we do not have recorded in any other place. The size of this fragment may indicate that it was used as an amulet in the fourth or fifth century, or it may be a miniature codex. It is considered to be "an unknown gospel of Synoptic type."[64] Some have thought that it contains some original material about Jesus.[65]

Papyrus Oxyrhynchus records parts of two stories. The first seven lines record the end of a discussion that Jesus had in Jerusalem. It tells of an apocalyptic judgment that will befall the evildoers of humanity. Following this is a sharp confrontation between Jesus and a chief Pharisaic priest named Levi about purification rules in the temple. A translation of the entire fragment is reproduced below.

> ... he who intends beforehand to strike first deviously plans out everything.
>
> But take care lest you also suffer the same things as them, for not only among the living do the evil-doers among men receive judgment, but they also will endure eternal punishment and great torment in the life to come.
>
> And he took them and led them into the place of purification itself and was walking in the temple. A certain Pharisee, a chief priest named Levi, came along and met them and said to the Savior, "Who allowed you to trample this place of purification

---

62. Nicklas, "*Papyrus Egerton 2*," 149.

63. Other fragmentary gospels such as *Papyrus Oxyrhynchus* 840 and the *Fayum Gospel* also show some dependence upon canonical gospel material.

64. Jeremias and Schneemelcher, "Oxyrhyncus Papyrus 840," 94.

65. E.g., Jeremias, *Unknown Sayings of Jesus*, 47–60, 104–5.

and to see these holy vessels, when you have not bathed yourself nor have your disciples washed their feet? But, being defiled, you trampled this temple place which is clean, where not one walks or dares to view these holy vessels except he who has bathed himself and changed his clothes."

And then the Savior stood with the disciples and answered, "Are you therefore, being here in this temple, clean?

He said to him, "I am clean. For I bathed in the Pool of David, and went down by one staircase and came up by another, and put on white and clean garments, and then I came and looked upon these holy vessels."

The Savior answered him and said, "Woe to you blind men who do not see! You have bathed in only these natural waters in which dogs and pigs lay night and day. And having washed, you have wiped the outer skin, which also prostitutes and pipe-girls anoint and wash and wipe and beautify for the lust of men, but the inside of them is full of scorpions and wickedness. But, I and my disciples, who you say have not bathed, have been bathed in living waters [from heaven] which come from [the Father above]. But woe to . . .[66]

The picture of Jesus in this gospel is that he is Savior. The word is used three times of Jesus in this brief narrative. Nothing heretical has been noted within it.

Papyrus Oxyrhynchus 840 shows a number of overlaps with the Synoptic Gospels and is indirectly dependent upon them. Recent research has noted that this fragment has clear verbal and structural agreements with the canonical gospels: Matthew 23:1–39; Mark 7:1–23; Luke 11:37–52; John 7:1–52 and 13:1–30. Furthermore, these passages from the canonical gospels evidence the same themes and wording as this fragmentary gospel: ceremonial washing, inner and outer cleanliness, and conflict with Jewish leaders.[67] It was likely a later production than the canonical gospels and influenced by them.

Due to its influence from the canonical gospels, *Papyrus Oxyrhynchus* 840 does not deserve the same standing as the canonical gospels. It could have been produced by a second century Jewish Christian group which was reacting against Pharisaic Judaism of the day. Other scholars

---

66. Kruger, *Gospel of the Savior*, 68.
67. Kruger, "Papyrus Oxyrhynchus 840," 167.

have suggested that it emerged from Manichean or Gnostic influence.[68] With its interest in ritual purity, further study of this papyrus would likely help bring clarity to branches of Jewish Christianity within the second century.

Conclusion

This chapter has considered a sampling of non-canonical gospels. A survey of these illustrates several things. The non-canonical gospels are not all uniform in their picture of Jesus. When Jesus is presented, the way he is presented is oftentimes in agreement with a number of the canonical gospels. These present Jesus as fully God and fully man as the tradition of the church states (e.g., *Protevangelium of James*, *Infancy Gospel of Thomas*, *Papyrus Egerton 2*). A number of the non-canonical gospels present a Jesus who is more divine than human. At times, he is presented from a Docetic perspective, only *appearing* to have human flesh (*Gospel of Peter*). In other non-canonical gospels, he is more Gnostic and functions as the secret revealer of heavenly mysteries (*Gospel of Thomas*, *Gospel of Philip*, *Gospel of Mary*, *Gospel of Truth*, *Gospel of Judas*). In these cases, they have focused more on Jesus' divine nature rather than human, unlike the claims of Brown.[69] Even the *Gospel of Thomas* may display a high view of Jesus (i.e., as divine) in places, according to some (*contra* Pagels).

In considering the claim raised by Ehrman that the non-canonical gospels were unfairly excluded, several things can be said. Most of the non-canonical gospels surveyed build upon the picture of the canonical ones (*Gospel of Peter*, *Gospel of Judas*, *Protevangelium of James*, *Infancy Gospel of Thomas*, the Jewish-Christian gospels, *Papyrus Egerton 2*). By doing so, they imply that the canonical ones are superior. Several of these non-canonical works also incorporate second century ideas such as Gnosticism into their writings (*Gospel of Philip*, *Gospel of Mary*, *Gospel of Truth*, *Gospel of Judas*). Others incorporate ideas derived from church tradition, such as the perpetual virginity of Mary or second century viewpoints of childhood (*Protevangelium of James*, *Infancy Gospel of Thomas*).

68. For a second century Jewish Christian origin, see Kruger, "Papyrus Oxyrhynchus," 168–69. For a Manichean origin, see Bovon, "Fragment Oxyrhynchus 840," 705–28. For a Gnostic origin, see Tripp, "Meanings of the Foot-Washing," 237–39.

69. I am thankful to my colleague Jordan Scheetz for drawing my attention to this point.

These later ideas that have infused these non-canonical works make them inferior to the canonical gospels. These non-canonical gospels, therefore, are inferior to the canonical gospels.

Chapter Five

Conclusion

JESUS TRIED AND TRUE has argued for the superiority of the canonical gospels over the non-canonical ones for understanding the person of Jesus. It has done so by evaluating these works in relation to three categories: date, source, and reception. In all three, the canonical gospels receive much better support than the non-canonical ones. With the possible exception of some small portions of the *Gospel of Thomas*, the canonical gospels are much earlier than the non-canonical ones. The source of the canonical gospels rests on eyewitness testimony which encourages trust. The reception of the canonical gospels by those within the early church is substantially greater in the Apostolic Fathers, Justin Martyr, Irenaeus, and others than the non-canonical gospels can claim. Furthermore, much of the content of the non-canonical gospels can be traced to the gospels that compose the New Testament, also supporting the superiority of the canonical gospels. With these factors in mind, it is understandable why the early Christians selected Matthew, Mark, Luke, and John to be part of the New Testament canon, while excluding the others.

If the non-canonical gospels were excluded years ago from the New Testament, some further questions should be asked. Do the non-canonical gospels have any value today? Are they artifacts from history that ought to be disregarded, or should they be treasured? Should they be censored, or should they be studied? While this volume has argued definitively for the superiority of the canonical gospels, it recognizes that there is value in possessing, reading, and studying other gospels. While the non-canonical gospels should not be included in the Bible, these other gospels should not be censored or destroyed.

Conclusion

Historical value for Non-Canonical Gospels

The non-canonical gospels are of historical value, and thus can help in the study of the period of history in which they were written. They are primary texts that illustrate the opinions of some and illuminate the varied currents that flowed throughout the second and third centuries. While it cannot be determined how many were persuaded by their ideas, some inevitably were influenced.[1] The Christian movement was struggling with other ideas in the second and third century. Many of these non-canonical gospels (e.g., *Gospel of Thomas*, *Gospel of Philip*, *Gospel of Mary*, *Gospel of Truth*, *Gospel of Judas*) do express different ideas about Jesus. Since we possess these, it allows the opportunity to study these differing views in their own words.

Many of these non-canonical gospels can be helpful for understanding Gnosticism. While each of the gnostic gospels is different in format, they display a similarity in outlook. They all promote hidden knowledge and a denial of worldly pursuits. They aim for the salvation of the individual by a particular experience and offer keys to reach that experience by knowledge. Without these texts, primary material for understanding gnosis or Gnosticism would be missing. Scholars would be left to rely on ancient authors who were critical of gnosis or Gnosticism, rather than upon materials that promote these ideas.[2] A number of non-canonical gospels then become critical primary source material for studying Gnosticism.

Without the non-canonical gospels, it would be difficult to appreciate the ideas that have influenced some aspects of Christian teaching for generations. Within the New Testament gospels, Mary's role is minimal, but her role is greatly expanded within the *Protevangelium of James*, in which her family, upbringing, childhood, and the selection of Joseph are all related. Her presentation at the Temple, which is derived from the *Protevangelium of James*, became the basis for many paintings, too. The teaching of the perpetual virginity of Mary emerges from this document, as well. This gospel provides early documentary evidence for the reverence of Mary. Without it, there would be a loss of important historical value.

---

1. Foster, *The Non-Canonical Gospels*, xvii.
2. See further Markschies, *Gnosis*, 48–58.

A number of the non-canonical gospels are important for understanding artwork, particularly from medieval times. Many of the icons of the Greek and Slavonic churches could not be understood without appreciating the non-canonical gospels. Scholars have noted that, without the apocryphal motifs, eastern icons and western paintings would be "inconceivable."[3]

The non-canonical gospels are also valuable for understanding ideas that arose and challenged the early church. A rising anti-Jewish sentiment can be found within the *Gospel of Peter*. Within this non-canonical gospel, the Jews are plainly responsible for the crucifixion of Jesus. This gospel also prolongs the death of Jesus, due to malevolence that is blamed on the Jewish people.[4] The same document also reveals early influences of Docetism, as Jesus appears not to suffer pain in his death. The *Gospel of Peter* provides primary evidence for these ideas.

Rather than discarding gospels like these, efforts should be made to find and study all ancient texts. Attempts should be made to recover more complete versions of fragmentary gospels, such as the *Gospel of the Hebrews*, *Gospel of the Nazareans*, and *Gospel of Ebionites*. Discovery of these Jewish-Christian gospels would be a great help for understanding the Jewish elements within early Christianity. A more complete version of the many fragmentary gospels, such as the *Gospel of Peter, Papyrus Egerton 2*, the *Fayum Fragment,* and *Papyrus Oxyrhnchus 840*, would also benefit our understanding of the second century.[5] These provide primary source material for understanding the forces affecting second- and third-century Christianity.

Non-Canonical Gospels and Lost Christianities

While greater study of the non-canonical gospels will aid the understanding of the second and third century, it should not be concluded that these texts are equal voices within the Christian movement and are lost Christianities. To claim, as Pagels and Ehrman do, that the non-canonical

---

3. Santos Otero, *Die handschrifliche Überlieferung* 1:22; Schneemelcher, ed., *New Testament Apocrypha*, 65.

4. Elliott, "Non-Canonical Gospels and the New Testament Apocrypha," 3–6.

5. While not a gospel, recovering Papias' *Exposition of the Sayings of the Lord* should also be pursued.

gospels were alternative Christianities that were unfairly excluded by intolerant early Christians is to go beyond the evidence.

Early church history indicates that there was a clear preference for eyewitness testimony, as was seen in chapter two in the statements of Papias. The earliest Christian witnesses in the second century also show a decided preference for the canonical sources. While there is not hostility evident within the documents that come from the early second century, there was nonetheless preference for the canonical over the non-canonical gospels, as was seen in chapter three. The Apostolic Fathers, Justin Martyr, the Muratorian Canon, and the *Diatesseron* show a clear preference for the canonical gospels without being antagonistic to other non-canonical gospels. To claim that that there was a "proto-orthodox" group that became hostile to other Christianities is to put too much value in power relationships within the early (and persecuted) Christian community. It seems better to conclude that the canonical gospels were preferred because their information about Jesus was deemed to be of higher quality.

Besides the evidence for the reception of the canonical gospels within the early Christian church, early church history supports the viewpoint of Jesus as fully human *and* fully divine. This is evident from one of the earliest extant works of Christian literature apart from the New Testament writings, *1 Clement* (AD 95–97). The deity and humanity of Jesus is found in several places within this book.[6] The reading of *1 Clement* 42.1–3 especially connects the succession of the idea that Jesus is human and divine, and that this idea comes from the apostles.

> The apostles have preached the Gospel to us from the Lord Jesus Christ; Jesus Christ [has done so] from God. Christ therefore was sent forth by God, and the apostles by Christ. Both these appointments, then, were made in an orderly way, according to the will of God. Having therefore received their orders, and being fully assured by the resurrection of our Lord Jesus Christ, and established in the word of God with full assurance of the Holy Ghost, they went forth proclaiming that the kingdom of God was at hand.[7]

Other early witnesses within the Apostolic Fathers stress the humanity and deity of Christ which emerges from the apostles. The letters of Ignatius (AD 107–110) connect the humanity and deity of Christ with

---

6. See *1 Clement* Prologue, 21.6; 24.1–2; 32.2; 49.6; 58.2; 59.2–4.
7. Translation is from *ANF* 1:16.

the gospel in his letter to the Philadelphians. Perhaps most telling is the viewpoint of Jesus that Ignatius defends at a controversy with the church in Philadelphia in his *Letter to the Philadelphians* 8.2.

> I exhort you to do nothing from partisanship but in accordance with Christ's teaching. For I heard some say, "If I do not find it in the archives, I do not believe it to be in the gospel." And when I said, "It is written," they answered me, "That is just the question." But for me the archives are Jesus Christ, the inviolable archives are his death and resurrection and faith through him—in which, through your prayers, I want to be justified.[8]

The gospel is the death and resurrection of Jesus and is connected with Scriptural authority (cf. Ign. *Phld.* 5.1–2; 9.1–2).[9] Polycarp also affirms the divinity and humanity of Jesus (cf. Pol. *Phil.* 6.3; 9; 12).

The writings of Clement of Rome, Ignatius, and Polycarp of Smyrna are recognized to be the most influential documents within the Apostolic Fathers. They support a Jesus as he is presented within the canonical gospels. These men were not power brokers in the Roman Empire who excluded one expression over another. Instead, these men were persecuted, and two of them were martyred. In their writings, they preserve the apostolic line of the church from the previous generation which wrote the canonical gospels. There is no comparable influence of the non-canonical gospels upon these documents.[10]

This, therefore, further contradicts the viewpoints of those who want to see every gospel as an equal expression of Christianity, as Pagels or Ehrman do. The ideas within the canonical gospels show themselves to be distinguished from an early time.

Superiority, Apocryphal, and an Example

How superior are the canonical gospels? To this point, this volume has categorized the gospels as either inside or outside of the canon. Is it worth using the word *apocryphal* to distinguish these gospels, a term which can

---

8. Schoedel, *Ignatius of Antioch*, 209.

9. Hill, "Ignatius, 'the Gospel,' and the Gospels," 271–77. See other references in Ignatius' writings that support the humanity and deity of Jesus: Ign. *Eph.* 1; Ign. *Mag.* 6; Ign. *Trall.* 9; Ign. *Rom.* 1; Ign. *Phld.* 1.

10. Bock, *Missing Gospels*, 204.

mean "esoteric," "hidden," or "spurious?" Is such a description worthy for gospels outside of the canon?

From the evidence presented within this work, it is worth returning to the word *apocryphal* to designate gospels outside of the canon. Many of the non-canonical gospels present differing views of Jesus that would not be in agreement with the canonical gospels. The picture of Jesus in many of these non-canonical gospels is that he is divine instead of human *and* divine.[11] One of these pictures must yield: either the picture of Jesus within the canonical gospels, or those which are in the non-canonical gospels. This volume has presented the superiority of the canonical gospels over the non-canonical ones. When a decision must be made concerning which information to accept about Jesus, the material within the non-canonical gospels must yield; and thus, the word *apocryphal* is appropriate for them.[12]

In our world which continues to recover works of antiquity, a return to the understanding of early church history is necessary. It has been the goal of this study to present this history and evaluate it. As the public continues to evaluate new findings about Jesus, the stance that Origen took toward other gospels would be a helpful guide.

Origen was born in the late second century in Alexandria, Egypt, the second greatest city in the Roman world. He grew up in a city known for its intellectualism in the ancient world, since it had the preeminent library. Alexandria also received fresh ideas from the many merchants that would enter the city, and great ancient intellectuals such as Plato, Euclid, Menelaos, Ktisibios, Philo, and Clement influenced the city. Origen also received individual training from his father in the Scriptures and in Greek liberal arts. Origen inherited the valued tradition of intellectualism. He earned respect among the secular philosophers of Alexandria. Intellectuals from around the ancient world debated with him. The early church leader Ephiphanius believes that Origen wrote six thousand volumes.

While he was raised with this intellectual tradition, he was no mere ivory tower figure. His family experienced persecution when he was in his late teenage years. This even took the life of his father. After this

---

11. Contra Brown and Pagels.

12. Note the differentiation of gospels that are read and those which are considered heretical from within early Christian literature, as seen in the listing of books. Scheetz, "Books of the Bible in early Christianity," 2–5. *Hist. eccl.* 3.3, 3.25, Muratorian canon, and Athanasius' 39th Pascal Letter.

significant event, Origen took up the honorable profession of teaching. Despite persecution, he would instruct Christians within the church, even while others had fled Alexandria. At great personal risk, Origen visited imprisoned Christians. Roman authorities even placed soldiers around his house. During the persecution of AD 250, Origen was thrown into prison and was tortured.[13] While this did not take his life at that moment, the result of this persecution led to his death.

As an ancient intellectual who suffered for his beliefs, Origen's voice is worth hearing afresh in this age. Origen knew of other gospels in his day, such as the *Gospel of Peter* and the *Gospel of the Hebrews*, yet he did not give them the same status as the canonical gospels. Instead, he writes this in his Homily on Luke 1:1 (c. AD 245), addressing the complication of so many gospels.

> Matthew to be sure, and Mark and John, as well as Luke did not "take in hand" to write, but filled with the Holy Ghost have written the Gospels. "Many have taken in hand to write, but only four Gospels are recognized." From these only the doctrines concerning the person of our Lord and Savior are to be derived. I know a certain gospel which is called *The Gospel according to Thomas* and *A Gospel according to Matthias*, and many others we have read. We do not in any way want to be considered ignorant because of those who imagine that they possess some knowledge if they are acquainted with these. Nevertheless, among all these we have approved solely what the church has recognized, which is that only the four Gospels should be accepted.[14]

Origen knew and understood non-canonical gospels. He did not give them all equal weight, however. It was good for him to learn novel views, but he remained steadfast to the picture of Jesus tried and true as presented in the Gospels of Matthew, Mark, Luke, and John. His model is a worthy one for today.

---

13. *Hist. eccl.* 6.3.4; 6.39.5. Cf. Litfin, *Getting to Know the Church Fathers*, 144–57.

14. This is taken from the Homily on Luke 1:1, according to the Latin translation of Jerome. Williams, *Tradition, Scripture, and Interpretation*, 169.

Appendix 1

Secret Gospel of Mark

ONE OF THE MOST controversial of all of the non-canonical gospels is the *Secret Gospel of Mark*. Morton Smith, one of the most provocative biblical scholars of the twentieth century, discovered the *Secret Gospel of Mark* in a seventeenth century book in an Orthodox monastery in the Holy Land. At the back of this book were several blank pages that had been used by an eighteenth century scribe, who supposedly copied part of a letter from Clement of Alexandria (AD 182–202) to one named Theodore. The contents of this letter indicate that Mark had produced two different versions of the Gospel of Mark—one for church members, and an expanded edition for the spiritually elite. This expanded edition of Mark's Gospel had been entrusted to Christians in Alexandria, but it had become misused by a group called the Carpocratians, a group of Gnotics known for their unlawful sexual behavior.[1]

Clement provides two accounts from the *Secret Gospel of Mark* within this letter. This citation follows Mark 10:34 and reads:

> They came to Bethany, and a woman was there whose brother had died. She came and prostrated herself before Jesus, saying to him, "Son of David, have mercy on me." But his disciples rebuked her. Jesus became angry and went off with her to the garden where the tomb was.
>
> Immediately a loud voice was heard from the tomb. Jesus approached and rolled the stone away from the entrance to the tomb. Immediately he went in where the young man was, stretched out his hand.

---

1. For Smith's side of this discovery, see M. Smith, *The Secret Gospel*.

Appendix 1

> The young man looked at him intently and loved him; and he began pleading with him that he might be with him. When they came out of the tomb they went to the young man's house, for he was wealthy.
> And after six days Jesus gave him a command. And when it was evening the young man came to him, wearing a linen cloth over his naked body. He stayed with him that night, for Jesus was teaching him the mystery of the Kingdom of God. When he got up from there, he returned to the other side of the Jordan.

Major questions remain about the reliability of this document. Did Clement write the letter? Could this letter be an ancient or modern forgery? While Smith published photographs of the document, why is it inaccessible?[2] Why did this letter disappear after thirty years? If it was indeed written by Clement, could he have been mistaken about Mark's authorship of an alternative gospel to the Gospel of Mark? Were the contents of this letter known by the end of the second century? Did the church delete portions of the *Secret Gospel of Mark* in order to form the canonical Gospel of Mark? Why is the *Secret Gospel of Mark* not mentioned in any other ancient source?

There have been several scholars who have reacted negatively to Morton Smith's discovery.[3] Some have stated that the *Secret Gospel of Mark* is dependent upon canonical material.[4] Others have doubted its historical reliability.[5] Still others have called it a forgery.[6] Jacob Neusner, a former student of Morton Smith, called the work "the forgery of the century."[7]

While this non-canonical gospel has received a great deal of attention, the *Secret Gospel of Mark* has largely been omitted within discussions

---

2. For a copy of the letter by Clement, see http://www-user.uni-bremen.de/~wie/Secret/letter-engl.html (Accessed: January 9, 2012).

3. Carlson, *Gospel Hoax*; Jeffrey, *Secret Gospel of Mark Unveiled*. In contrast, see Brown, *Mark's Other Gospel*, which argues for the validity of *Secret Mark*.

4. Cf. Brown, "The Relation of 'The Secret Gospel of Mark' to the Fourth Gospel," 466–85; Grant, "Morton Smith's Two Books," 58–64; Neirynck, "La fuite du jeune home en Mc 14,51–52," 43–66; Gundry, "Excursus on the Secret Gospel of Mark," 612.

5. Brown, *Mark's Other Gospel*. Cf. Ehrman, "Response to Charles Hedrick's Stalemate,"155–63.

6. For questions about the authenticity of the letter, see Quesnell, "The Mar Saba Clementine," 48–67.

7 Neusner and Neusner, *Price of Excellence*, 78.

Appendix 1

about the historical Jesus. The controversy about this book will continue for quite some time. Until it resolves itself, it is best not to include novel views from this work into the discussion about who Jesus is.[8]

---

8. Foster, "*Secret Mark*," 180–81. Note especially how Ehrman refuses to bring the *Secret Gospel of Mark* into discussions about gospel accounts, even though the contents of *Secret Gospel of Mark* could propel his own views. Ehrman, "Response to Charles Hedrick's Stalemate," 162–63.

Appendix 2

Early Christian Creeds

The Apostles' Creed[9]

I BELIEVE IN GOD, the Father Almighty, Creator of heaven and earth.

And in Jesus Christ, his only Son, our Lord, who was conceived of the Holy Spirit, born of the Virgin Mary, suffered under Pontius Pilate, was crucified, died, and was buried; he descended into hell. On the third day he rose from the dead; he ascended into heaven, sits at the right hand of God the Father Almighty. Thence he shall come to judge the living and the dead.

I believe in the Holy Spirit, the holy catholic church, the communion of saints, the forgiveness of sins, the resurrection of the body, and the life everlasting. Amen.

The Nicene Creed[10]

We believe in one God, the Father, the Almighty, Maker of heaven and earth, of all that is seen and unseen. We believe in one Lord, Jesus Christ, the only Son of God, eternally begotten of the Father, God from God, light from light, true God from true God, begotten, not made, one in being with the Father. Through him all things were made. For us humans and our salvation, he came down from heaven: by the power of the Holy

---

9. Pelikan and Hotchkiss, *Creeds and Confessions of Faith in the Christian Tradition*, 669.

10. Pelikan and Hotchkiss, *Creeds and Confessions of Faith in the Christian Tradition*, 672. This is the Western Recension of the Niceno-Constantinopolitan Creed.

Spirit, he was born of the Virgin Mary, and became man. For our sake he was crucified under Pontius Pilate, he suffered, died and was buried. On the third day he rose again in fulfillment of the Scriptures; he ascended into heaven and is seated at the right hand of the Father. He will come again in glory to judge the living and the dead, and his kingdom will have no end. We believe in the Holy Spirit, the Lord, the giver of life, who proceeds from the Father and the Son. With the Father and the Son he is worshipped and glorified. He has spoken through the prophets. We believe in one holy, catholic, and apostolic church. We acknowledge one baptism for the forgiveness of sins. We look for the resurrection of the dead, and the life of the world to come. Amen.

The Chalcedonian Statement[11]

So, following the saintly fathers, we all with one voice teach the confession of one and the same Son, our Lord Jesus Christ: the same perfect in divinity and perfect in humanity, the same truly God and truly man, of a rational soul and a body; consubstantial with the Father as regards his divinity, and the same consubstantial with us as regards his humanity; like us in all respects except for sin; begotten before the ages from the Father as regards his divinity, and in the last days the same for us and for our salvation, from Mary the Virgin God-bearer as regards his humanity; one and the same Christ, Son, Lord, Only-begotten, acknowledged in two natures which undergo no confusion, no change, no division, no separation; at no point was the difference between the natures taken away through the union, but rather the property of both natures is preserved and comes together into a single person and a single subsistent being; he is not parted or divided into two persons, but is one and the same only-begotten Son, God, Word, Lord Jesus Christ, just as the prophets taught from the beginning about him, and as the Lord Jesus Christ himself instructed us, and as the creed of the fathers handed it down to us.

---

11. Pelikan and Hotchkiss, *Creeds and Confessions of Faith in the Christian Tradition*, 181.

Bibliography

Abramowski, L. "Die Erinnerungen der Apostel bei Justin." In *Das Evangelium und die Evangelien*, edited by P. Stuhlmacher, 341–53. Tübingen: Mohr, 1983.

Aland, K. *Synopsis Quattuor Evangeliorum*. 10th edition. Stuttgart: Biblia-Druck, 1993.

Alexander, L. A. "The Living Voice: Skepticism towards the Written Word in Early Christian and in Graeco-Roman Texts." In *The Bible in Three Dimensions*, edited by D. J. Clines et al., 221–48. JSOTSup 87. Sheffield: Sheffield Academic, 1990.

Augustine, *The Harmony of the Gospels* in NPNF2. Volume 6, 77-236.

Ballard, F. *The Miracles of Unbelief*. Edinburgh: T & T Clark, 1908.

Bartlet, V. "Papias' Exposition: Its Date and Contents." In *Amicitiae Corolla: a volume of essays presented to J. R. Harris on the occasion of his eightieth birthday*, edited by H. G. Wood, 15–44. London: University of London, 1933.

Bauckham, R. *Gospel Women: Studies of the Named Women in the Gospels*. Grand Rapids: Eerdmans, 2002.

———. *Jesus and the Eyewitnesses: The Gospels as Eyewitness Testimony*. Grand Rapids: Eerdmans, 2006.

———. "The Study of Gospel Traditions outside the Canonical Gospels: Problems and Prospects." In *Gospel Perspectives: The Jesus Tradition outside the Gospels*, edited by D. Wenham, 383–86. Sheffield: JSOT Press, 1984.

Baur, F. C. *Kritische Untersuchungen über die kanonischen Evangelien: ihr Verhältnis zu einander, ihren Charakter und Ursprung*. 2nd edition. Hildesheim: Georg Olms, 1999.

Beatrice, P. F. "The '*Gospel according to the Hebrews*' in the Apostolic Fathers." *NovT* 48 (2006) 147–95.

Bell, H. I. and T. C. Skeat, *Fragments of an Unknown Gospel and Other Early Christian Papyri*. London: British Museum, 1935.

Bellinzoni, A. J. "The Gospel of Luke in the Apostolic Fathers: An Overview." In *Trajectories through the New Testament and the Apostolic Fathers*, edited by A. Gregory and C. M. Tuckett, 45–68. Oxford: OUP, 2005.

———. *The Sayings of Jesus in the Writings of Justin Martyr*. SNT 17. Leiden: Brill, 1967.

Black, D. A. *Why Four Gospels? The Historical Origins of the Gospels*. 2nd edition. Gonzalez: Energion, 2010.

Blomberg, C. "Tradition and Redaction in the Parables of the Gospel of Thomas." In *The Jesus Tradition outside the Gospels: Gospel Perspectives*, edited by D. Wenham, 177–205. Sheffield: JSOT Press, 1985.

Bock, D. L. *Jesus according to Scripture: Restoring the Portrait from the Gospels*. Grand Rapids: Baker, 2002.

———. *Luke 1:1–9:50*. BECNT. Grand Rapids: Baker, 1994.

———. *The Missing Gospels: Unearthing the Truth behind Alternative Christianities*. Nashville: Nelson, 2008.

Bibliography

Bockmuehl, M. *The Mission of James, Peter, and Paul.* NovTSup 115. Leiden: Brill, 2004.
———. *Seeing the Word: Refocusing New Testament Study.* Grand Rapids: Baker, 2006.
Borg, M., editor. *The Lost Gospel Q: The Original Sayings of Jesus.* Berkeley: Ulysses, 1996.
Bovon, F. "Fragment Oxyrhynchus 840, Fragment of a Lost Gospel, Witness of an Early Christian Controversy over Purity." *JBL* 119 (2000) 705–28.
Brent, A. "Ignatius and Polycarp: The Transformation of New Testament Traditions in the Context of Mystery Cults." In *Trajectories through the New Testament and the Apostolic Fathers*, edited by A. Gregory and C. M. Tuckett, 325–50. Oxford: OUP, 2005.
Brown, D. *The Da Vinci Code.* New York: Doubleday, 2003.
Brown, R. E. *The Death of the Messiah.* 2 vols. New York: Doubleday, 1994.
———. *The Gospel According to John XIII–XXI.* Garden City: Doubleday, 1966.
———. "The *Gospel of Peter* and Canonical Gospel Priority." *NTS* 33 (1987) 321–43.
———. "The Relation of 'The Secret Gospel of Mark' to the Fourth Gospel." *CBQ* 36 (1974) 466–85.
Brown, S. *Apostasy and Perseverance in the Theology of Luke.* AnBib 36. Rome: Pontifical Biblical Institute, 1969.
———. *Mark's Other Gospel: Rethinking Smith's Controversial Discovery.* Studies in Christianity and Judaism 15. Waterloo: Wilfrid Laurier University Press, 2005.
Bruce, F. F. *Jesus and Christian Traditions outside the New Testament.* Grand Rapids: Eerdmans, 1974.
Byrskog, S. *Story as History – History as Story.* WUNT 123. Tübingen: Mohr, 2000.
Cameron, R. "On Comparing Q and the *Gospel of Thomas*." In *Early Christian Voices in Texts, Traditions, and Symbols*, edited by D. H. Warren, et al., 59–70. Leiden: Brill, 2003.
———. *The Other Gospels: Noncanonical Gospel Texts.* Philadelphia: Westminster, 1982.
Carlson, S. C. *The Gospel Hoax: Morton Smith's invention of the Secret Gospel of Mark.* Waco: Baylor, 2005.
Carlyle, M. "First Clement." In *The New Testament in the Apostolic Fathers*, edited by the Oxford Society of Historical Theology, 37–62. Oxford: Clarendon, 1905.
Carson, D. A. *The Gospel According to John.* PNTC. Grand Rapids: Eerdmans, 1991.
——— and D. J. Moo. *An Introduction to the New Testament.* 2nd edition. Grand Rapids: Zondervan, 2005.
———. "Matthew." In *The Expositor's Bible Commentary. Volume 8 Matthew, Mark, Luke*, edited by F. E. Gaebelein. Grand Rapids: Zondervan, 1984.
Casey, M. *Sacred Reading: The Ancient Art of Lectio Divia.* Ligouri, MO: Triumph, 1995.
Charlesworth, J. H. "Tatian's Dependence upon Apocryphal Traditions," *HeyJ* 15 (1974) 5–17.
Chartrand-Burke, T. "The *Infancy Gospel of Thomas*." In *The Non-Canonical Gospels*, edited by P. Foster, 126–38. London: T & T Clark, 2008.
Cohen, S. D. J. *Josephus in Galilee and Rome.* Leiden: Brill, 1979.
Colson, F. H. "*Taxei* in Papias: The Gospels and the Rhetorical Schools." *JTS* 14 (1912) 62–69.
Cotelier, Jean-Baptiste. *Sanctorum Patrum qui temporibus apostolicus floruerunt, Barnabae, Clementis, Hermae, Ignatii, Polycarpi, opera edita et inedita, vera et suppositicia.* Paris, 1672.
Cranfield, C. E. B. *The Gospel according to Saint Mark.* CGTC. Cambridge: CUP, 1966.
Creed, J. M. *The Gospel according to St. Luke.* London: Macmillan, 1930.

Bibliography

Crossan, J. D. *The Birth of Christianity: Discovering What Happened in the Years Immediately After the Execution of Jesus*. San Francisco: HarperOne, 1998.
———. *The Cross that Spoke*. San Francisco: Harper and Row, 1988.
———. *Four Other Gospels*. Minneapolis: Winston, 1985.
Davies, S. L. *The Gospel of Thomas and Christian Wisdom*. New York: Seabury, 1983.
———. "Thomas the Fourth Synoptic Gospel." *BA* 46 (1983) 6–14.
Davies, W. D. and D. C. Allison. *A critical and exegetical commentary on the gospel according to Saint Matthew*. ICC. 3vols. Edinburgh: T & T Clark, 1987–1997.
DeConick, A. D. "The *Gospel of Thomas*." In *The Non-Canonical Gospels*, edited by P. Foster, 13–29. London: T & T Clark, 2008.
———. "The *Gospel of Judas*: A Parody of Apostolic Christianity." In *The Non-Canonical Gospels*, edited by P. Foster, 96–109. London: T & T Clark, 2008.
———. *The Original Gospel of Thomas in Translation, with a Commentary and New English Translation of the Complete Gospel*. LNTS 287. London: T & T Clark, 2006.
———. *Recovering the Original Gospel of Thomas: A History of the Gospel and its Growth*. LNTS 286. London: T & T Clark, 2005.
———. *Seek to See Him: Ascent and Vision Mysticism in the Gospel of Thomas*. VCSup 33. Leiden: Brill, 1996.
de Strycker, E. "Die griechischen Handschriften des Protevangeliums Iacobi." In *Griechische Kodikologie und Textüberlieferung*, edited by D. Harlfinger, 577–612. Darmstadt: Wissenschaftliche Buchgesellschaft, 1980.
Dillon, E. J. "The Primitive Gospel." *Contemporary Review* (1983) 857–70.
Drobner, H. R. *The Fathers of the Church: A Comprehensive Introduction*. Peabody, MA: Hendrickson, 2007.
Dunn, J. D. G. *Christology in the Making: A New Testament Inquiry into the Origins of the Doctrine of the Incarnation*. 2nd edition. Grand Rapids: Eerdmans, 1996.
Edwards, J. R. *The Gospel according to Mark*. Grand Rapids: Eerdmans, 2002.
Ehrman, B. D. *The Apostolic Fathers*. LCL. 2 vols. Cambridge, MA: Harvard, 2003.
———."Christianity Turned on its Head: The Alternative Vision of the Gospel of Judas." In *The Gospel of Judas*, edited by R. Kasser, et al., 77–120. Washington: National Geographic, 2006.
———. *Jesus, Interrupted: Revealing the Hidden Contradictions in the Bible (and Why We Don't Know About Them*. New York: HarperOne, 2009.
———. *Lost Christianities: The Battles for Scripture and the Faiths we never knew*. New York: OUP, 2005.
———. *Lost Scriptures: Books that did not make it into the New Testament*. Oxford: OUP, 2003.
———. *The New Testament: A Historical Introduction to the Early Christian Writings*. 4th ed. Oxford: OUP, 2008.
———. "Response to Charles Hedrick's Stalemate." *JECS* 11 (2003) 155–63.
Eichorn, J. G. *Einleitung in das Neue Testament*. 3 Volumes. Leipzig: Beidmannischen, 1804.
Elliott, J. K. "Christian Apocrypha in Art and Texts." In *Early Christian Voices in Texts, Traditions, and Symbols*, edited by D. H. Warren, et al., 283–92. Leiden: Brill, 2003.
Ellis, E. E. *The Gospel of Luke*. NCB. 2nd edition. Grand Rapids: Eerdmans, 1974.
Eusebius. *The Ecclesiastical History*. LCL. Translated by J. E. L. Oulton. Cambridge: Harvard, 2001.

Bibliography

Evans, C. A. *Fabricating Jesus: How Modern Scholars Distort the Gospels*. Downers Grove: IVP, 2006.

———, et al. *Nag Hammadi Texts and the Bible*. NTTS 18. Leiden: Brill, 1993.

Fitzmeyer, J. A. *The Gospel according to Luke (I–IX)*. AB 28. Garden City, NY: Doubleday, 1981.

———. "More about Elijah coming first." *JBL* 104 (1985) 295–96.

Foster, P. *The Apocryphal Gospels: A Very Short Introduction*. Oxford: OUP, 2009.

———. "The *Gospel of Peter*." In *The Non-Canonical Gospels*, edited by P. Foster, 30–42. London: T & T Clark, 2008.

———. *The Gospel of Peter: Introduction, Critical Edition and Commentary*. TENT 4. Leiden/Boston: Brill, 2010.

———. "The *Gospel of Philip*." In *The Non-Canonical Gospels*, edited by P. Foster, 68–83. London: T & T Clark, 2008.

———. *The Non-Canonical Gospels*. London: T & T Clark, 2010.

———. "The *Protevangelium of James*." In *The Non-Canonical Gospels*, edited by P. Foster, 110–25. London: T & T Clark, 2008.

———. "The relationship between Justin Martyr and the so-called *Gospel of Peter*." In *Justin Martyr and his Worlds*, edited by S. Parvo and P. Foster, 104–12. Minneapolis: Fortress, 2007.

———. "Secret Mark." In *The Non-Canonical Gospels*, edited by P. Foster, 171–82. London: T & T Clark, 2008.

France, R. T. *The Gospel of Mark*. NIGTC. Grand Rapids: Eerdmans, 2002.

———. *The Gospel of Matthew*. NICNT. Grand Rapids: Eerdmans, 2007.

———. *Matthew*. TNTC. Grand Rapids: Eerdmans, 1985.

———. *Matthew—Evangelist and Teacher*. Eugene, OR: Wipf & Stock, 2004.

Funk, R. W. *The Five Gospels: What Did Jesus Really Say? The Search for the Authentic Words of Jesus*. San Francisco: HarperOne, 1996.

Gamble, H. Y. *Books and Readers in the Early Church*. New Haven: Yale, 1995.

Gathercole, S. "The *Gospel of Judas*." In *The Non-Canonical Gospels*, edited by P. Foster, 84–95. London: T & T Clark, 2008.

———. *The Gospel of Judas*. Oxford: OUP, 2007.

Gerhardsson, B. *The Reliability of the Gospel Tradition*. Peabody, MA: Hendrickson, 2001.

———. "Mark and the Female Witnesses." In *Dumu-E2-Dub-Ba-A: Studies in Honor of Ake W. Sjoberg*, edited by H. Behrens et al., 217–26. Philadelphia: University Museum, 1989.

Gnilka, J. *Das Evangelium nach Markus*. EKKNT. 2 vols. Zürich: Neukirchen-Vluyn, 1978.

"The Gospel of Judas Iscariot: World Exclusive 'Greatest Archaeological Discovery of all Time' Threat to 2000 years of Christian teaching." *The Mail on Sunday* March 12, 2006.

Grant, R. M. "The Apostolic Fathers' First Thousand Years." *Church History: Studies in Christianity and Culture* 57 (1988) 20–28.

———. "Morton Smith's Two Books," *AThR* 56 (1974) 58–64.

——— and D. N. Freedman. *The Secret Sayings of Jesus*. Garden City, N.Y.: Doubleday & Company, 1960.

"The Greatest Archaelogical Discovery of All Time." *The Mail* 12 March 2006.

Green, J. B. "Death of Jesus" in *DJG* 146–63.

———. "The Gospel of Peter: Source for a Pre-canonical Passion Narrative." *ZNW* 78 (1987) 293–301.

Gregory, A. C. and C. M. Tuckett, eds. *The Reception of the New Testament in the Apostolic Fathers*. Oxford: Oxford University Press, 2005.

Gregory, A. C. and C. M. Tuckett, "*2 Clement* and the Writings that later formed the New Testament." In *The Reception of the New Testament in the Apostolic Fathers*, edited by A. C. Gregory and C. M. Tuckett, 251–92. Oxford: Oxford University Press, 2005.

———. "Jewish Christian Gospels." In *The Non-Canonical Gospels*, edited by P. Foster, 54–67. London: T & T Clark, 2008.

———. "Prior or Posterior? The *Gospel of the Ebionites* and the Gospel of Luke." *NTS* 51.3 (2005) 344–60.

Guelich, R. A. *Mark 1–8:26*. WBC 34A. Dallas: Word, 1989.

Gundry, R. H. *Matthew: A Commentary on His Handbook for a Mixed Church under Persecution*. 2nd edition. Grand Rapids: Eerdmans, 1994.

———. *Mark: A Commentary on His Apology for the Cross*. 2 vols. Grand Rapids: Eerdmans, 2009–2010.

———. *Matthew: A Commentary on His Literary and Theological Art*. Grand Rapids: Eerdmans, 1982.

Hagner, D. A. *Matthew 1–13*. WBC 33A. Dallas: Word, 1993.

Hahneman, G. M. *The Muratorian Fragment and the Development of the Canon*. OTM. Oxford: Clarendon, 1992.

Hall, C. A. *Learning Theology with the Church Fathers*. Downers Grove: IVP, 2002.

———. *Reading Scripture with the Church Fathers*. Downers Grove: IVP, 1998.

Harris, J. R. *A Popular Account of the Newly Recovered Gospel of St. Peter*. London: Hodder and Stoughton, 1883.

Hays, R. B. "The Corrected Jesus." *First Things* 43 (May 1994) 43–48.

Hengel, M. *The Four Gospels and the One Gospel of Jesus Christ*. Harrisburg: Trinity, 2000.

———. *The Johannine Question*. Philadelphia: Trinity, 1989.

———. *Studies in the Gospel of Mark*. London: SCM, 1985.

——— and A. M. Schwemer, *Paul between Damascus and Antioch: the unknown years* Louisville: Westminster, 1997.

Hill, C. E. "The Debate over the Muratorian Fragment and the Development of the Canon." *WTJ* 57 (1995) 437–52.

———. "Ignatius, 'the Gospel,' and the Gospels." In *Trajectories through the New Testament and the Apostolic Fathers*, edited by A. C. Gregory and C. M. Tuckett, 267–86. Oxford: OUP, 2005.

———. *The Johannine Corpus in the Early Church*. Oxford: OUP, 2004.

———. "Justin and the New Testament Writings." *Studia Patristica* 30, edited by E. A. Livingstone, 42–48. Leuven: Peeters, 1997.

Hill, D. *The Gospel of Matthew*. NCB. Grand Rapids: Eerdmans, 1972.

Hofius, O. "Isolated Sayings of Jesus." In *New Testament Apocrypha: Volume 1 Gospels and Related Writings*, edited by W. Schneemelcher and R. McL. Wilson, 88–91. Louisville: Westminster, 1991.

Holmes, M. W. *The Apostolic Fathers: Greek Texts and English Translations*. Grand Rapids: Baker, 1999.

Holtzmann, H. J. *Die synoptische Evangelien: ihr Ursprung und ihr geschichtlicher Charakter*. Leipzig: Engelmann, 1863.

Hurtado, L. *Lord Jesus Christ: Devotion to Jesus in Earliest Christianity*. Grand Rapids: Eerdmans, 2003.

Bibliography

Inge, W. R. "Ignatius." In *The New Testament in the Apostolic Fathers*, edited by the Oxford Society of Historical Theology, 63–83. Oxford: Clarendon, 1905.

Inowlicki, S. "'Neither Adding nor Omitting Anything': Josephus' Promise not to Modify the Scriptures in Greek and Latin Context." *JJS* 56 (2005) 48–65.

Isenberg, W. W. "Gospel According to Philip." In *The Nag Hammadi Library*, edited by J. M. Robinson, 130–41. San Francisco: Harper and Row, 1988.

Jeffrey, P. *The Secret Gospel of Mark Unveiled: Imagined Rituals of Sex, Death, and Madness in a Biblical Forgery*. New Haven: Yale University Press, 2007.

Jenkins, P. *Hidden Gospels: How the Search for Jesus Lost its Way*. Oxford: Clarendon, 2001.

Jeremias, J. and W. Schneemelcher, "Papyrus Egerton 2." In *New Testament Apocrypha: Volume 1 Gospels and Related Writings*, edited by W. Schneemelcher and R. McL. Wilson, 96–99. Louisville: Westminster, 1991.

———. *Unknown Sayings of Jesus*. London: SPCK, 1964.

Josephus, F. *The Jewish War*. LCL. Translated by H. St. J. Thackeray. Cambridge: Harvard University Press, 1997.

Keener, C. *A Commentary on the Gospel of Matthew*. Grand Rapids: Eerdmans, 1999.

Kennedy, G. "Classical and Christian Source Criticism." In *The Relationships among the Gospels: An Interdisciplinary Dialogue*, edited by W. O. Walker, 125–55. San Antonio: Trinity University Press, 1978.

King, K. L. *The Gospel of Mary of Magdala: Jesus and the First Woman Apostle*. Santa Rosa, CA: Polebridge Press, 2003.

———. "Hearing, Seeing, and Knowing God: *Allogenes* and the *Gospel of Mary*." In *Early Christian Voices in Texts, Traditions, and Symbols*, edited by D. H. Warren, et al., 319–32. Leiden: Brill, 2003.

Kloppenborg, J. Q. *The Earliest Gospel: An Introduction to the Original Stories and Sayings of Jesus*. Louisville: Westminster, 2008.

Köstenberger, A. *John*. BECNT. Grand Rapids: Baker, 2001.

Koester, H. *Ancient Christian Gospels: Their History and Development*. Harrisburg: Trinity Press International, 1990.

———. "Gospels and Gospel Traditions in the Second Century." In *Trajectories through the New Testament and the Apostolic Fathers*, edited by A. C. Gregory and C. M. Tuckett, 27–44. Oxford: OUP, 2005.

———. *Introduction to the New Testament*. 2 vols. New York: De Gruyter, 1982.

———. "The Synoptic Sayings Gospel Q in the Early Communities of Jesus' Followers." In *Early Christian Voices in Texts, Traditions, and Symbols*, edited by D. H. Warren, et al., 45–58. Leiden: Brill, 2003.

Köhler, W. D. *Die Rezeption des Matthäusevangeliums in der Zeit vor Irenäus*. WUNT 2.24. Tübingen: Mohr, 1987.

Krosney, H. *The Lost Gospel: The Quest for the Gospel of Judas*. Washington: National Geographic, 2007.

Kruger, M. *The Gospel of the Savior: An Analysis of P.Oxy. 840 and Its Place in the Gospel Traditions of Early Christianity*. Leiden: Brill, 2005.

———. "Papyrus Oxyrhynchus 840." In *The Non-Canonical Gospels*, edited by P. Foster, 157–70. London: T & T Clark, 2008.

Kümmel, W. G. *The New Testament: The History of the Investigation of Its Problems*. New York: Abingdon, 1970.

Kürzinger, J. *Papias von Hierapolis und die Evangelien des Neuen Testaments*. Regensburg: Pustet, 1983.

Bibliography

Lake, K. "The *Didache.*" In *The New Testament in the Apostolic Fathers*, edited by the Oxford Society of Historical Theology, 24–36. Oxford: Clarendon, 1905.
Lambdin, T. O. "Gospel of Thomas." In *The Nag Hammadi Library in English*, edited by J. Robinson, 126–38. Leiden: Brill, 1988.
Lane, W. L. *The Gospel of Mark*. Grand Rapids: Eerdmans, 1974.
Latourette, K. "The Christian Understanding of History." *AHR* 54:2 (January 1949) 259–76.
Lessing, G. E. *Neue Hypothese über die Evangelisten als blos menschichliche Geschichtschreiber betracht* in *Theologischer Nachlass*. Berlin: 1778.
Lightfoot, J. B. *The Apostolic Fathers*. Grand Rapids: Baker, 1956.
———. "Apostolic Fathers." In *ANF* 1:3–5.
Litfin, B. *Getting to Know the Church Fathers: An Evangelical Introduction*. Grand Rapids: Brazos, 2007.
Loisy, A. *Le quatrième évangile: les épitres dites de Jean*. Paris: Émile Nourry, 1921.
Lüdemann, G. et al. *Jesus after 2000 Years*. Amherst, NY: Prometheus, 2001.
Luz, U. *Matthew: A commentary*. 3 vols. Minneapolis: Augsburg, 1989.
Mack, B. L. *The Lost Gospel: The Book of Q and Christian Origins*. San Francisco: HarperOne, 1993.
Markschies, *Gnosis: An Introduction*. Translated by J. Bowden. London: T & T Clark, 2003.
McDonald, L. M. *The Biblical Canon: Its Origin, Transmission, and Authority*. Peabody, MA: Hendrickson, 2007.
McKnight, S. "Matthew, Gospel of" in *DJG* 526–41.
Marshall, I. H. *The Gospel of Luke: a commentary on the Greek text*. NIGTC. Grand Rapids: Eerdmans, 1978.
Martyn, J. L. *History and Theology in the Fourth Gospel*. NTL. 3rd edition. Louisville: Westminster, 2003.
Massaux, E. *Influence de l' Évangile de saint Matthiew sûr la littérature chrétienne avant saint Irénée*. Louvain: Publications Universitaires, 1950.
May, J. D. "The Four Pillars: The Fourfold Gospel before the time of Irenaeus." *TrinJ* 30 (2009) 72–75.
Meier, J. P. *A Marginal Jew*. 2 vols. New York: Doubleday, 1994.
———. *The Vision of Matthew: Christ, Church and Morality in the First Gospel*. New York: Paulist, 1979.
Ménard, J. *L' Évangelie de Vérité*. Leiden: Brill, 1972.
Metzger, B. M. *The Canon of the New Testament: Its Origin, Development, and Significance* 4th ed. Oxford: OUP, 2009.
Meyer, M. *The Gnostic Gospels of Jesus: The Definitive Collection of Mystical Gospels and Secret Books about Jesus of Nazareth*. San Francisco: HarperOne, 2005.
Meyer, M. W. ed., *The Nag Hammadi Scriptures: The Revised and Updated Translation of Sacred Gnostic Texts*. New York: Harper Collins, 2007.
Miller, R. J. *The Complete Gospels: Annotated Scholars Version*. San Francisco: HarperOne, 1994.
Mirecki, P. A. "Peter, Gospel of." In *ABD* 5:278–81.
Morris, L. *The Gospel according to John*. Grand Rapids: Eerdmans, 1971.
Naveh, J. "Nameless People." *IEJ* 40 (1990) 108–23.
Neirynck, F. "La fuite du jeune home en Mc 14,51–52." *ETL* 55 (1979) 43–66.
Neusner, J. and N. Neusner, *The Price of Excellence: Universities in Conflict during the Cold War Era*. New York: Continuum, 1995.

Bibliography

Nicklas, T. "*Papyrus Egerton 2.*" In *The Non-Canonical Gospels*, edited by P. Foster, 139–49. London: T & T Clark, 2008.

Nierynck, F. "*Papyrus Egerton 2* and the Healing of the Leper." In *Evangelica II Collected Essays 1982-1991*, edited by F. Nierynck, 773–83. BETL 99. Leuven: Peeters, 1991.

Oden, T. C. *Ancient Christian Commentary on Scripture*. Downers Grove: IVP, 1998–2011.

Osborn, E. F. *Justin Martyr*. Tübingen: Mohr, 1973.

Santos Otero, A. de *Die handschriftliche Überlieferung der altslavischen Apokryphen*. 2 vols. Berlin: de Gruyter, 1978, 1981.

Pagels, E. *Beyond Belief: The Secret Gospel of Thomas*. New York: Random House, 2003.

———. *The Gnostic Gospels*. New York: Random House, 2004.

——— and K. King, *The Gospel of Judas and the Shaping of Christianity*. New York: Penguin, 2008.

Paget, J. C. *The Epistle of Barnabas: Outlook and Background*. Tubingen: Mohr, 1994.

Paget, J. C. "The *Epistle of Barnabas* and the Writings that later formed the New Testament." In *The Reception of the New Testament in the Apostolic Fathers*, edited by A. C. Gregory and C. M. Tuckett, 229–50. Oxford: OUP, 2005.

Pelikan, J. and V. Hotchkiss, *Creeds and Confessions of Faith in the Christian Tradition: Volume 1 Rules of Faith in the Early Church*. New Haven: Yale University, 2003.

Pelling, C. "Childhood and Personality in Greek Literature," in *Characterization and Individuality in Greek Literature*, edited by C. Pelling, 217–40. Oxford: Clarendon, 1990.

Perrin, N. *Thomas: the Other Gospel*. Louisville: Westminster, 2007.

Pesch, R. *Das Markusevangelium*. 2 vols. HTKNT. Freiburg: Herder, 1976–80.

Patterson, S. J. *The Gospel of Thomas and Jesus*. Sonoma: Polebridge Press, 1993.

Petersen, W. L. *Tatian's Diatesseron: Its Creation, Dissemination, Significance, and History in Scholarship*. VCSup 25. Leiden: Brill, 1994.

Pilhofer, P. "Justin und das Petrusevangelium." *ZNW* 81 (1990) 60–78.

Porter, S. and G. L. Heath, *The Lost Gospel of Judas: Separating Fact from Fiction*. Grand Rapids: Eerdmans, 2007.

Quesnell, Q. "The Mar Saba Clementine: A Question of Evidence." *CBQ* 37 (1975) 48–67.

Quispel, G. *Tatian and the Gospel of Thomas: Studies in the History of the Western Diatesseron*. Leiden: Brill, 1975.

———. "The Gospel of Thomas and the New Testament." *VC* 11 (1957) 189–207.

Ramsey Michaels, J. *John: A Good News Commentary*. NIBC. San Francisco: Harper & Row, 1984.

Reicke, B. "Synoptic Prophecies of the Destruction of Jerusalem." In *Studies in New Testament and Early Christian Literature*, edited by D. Aune, 121–34. NovTSup 3. Leiden: Brill, 1972.

Richardson, C. C. "An Anonymous Sermon, Commonly Called Clement's Second Letter." In *Early Christian Fathers*, edited by C. C. Richardson, 183–202. Reprinted. Philadelphia: Westminster, 1970.

Riley, G. J. *Resurrection Reconsidered*. Minneapolis: Fortress, 1995.

Riesner, R. *Paul's Early Period: Chronology, Mission Strategy, Theology*. Grand Rapids: Eerdmans, 1998.

Roberts, A. and J. Donaldson. *The Ante-Nicene Fathers: translations of the writings of the Fathers down to 325 AD*. Reprinted. Grand Rapids: Eerdmans, 1951.

Robinson, J. A. T. *Redating the New Testament*. London: SCM, 1976.

Bibliography

Robinson, J. M. *The Coptic Gnostic Library: A Complete Edition of the Nag Hammadi Codices*. 5 vols. Leiden: Brill, 2000.

———. *The Critical Edition of Q: Synopsis Including the Gospels of Matthew and Luke, Mark and Thomas with English, German, and French Translations of Q and Thomas*. Hermeneia. Leuven: Peeters, 2000.

———. "On Bridging the Gulf from Q to the *Gospel of Thomas*." In *Nag Hammadi, Gnosticism, and Early Christianity*, edited by C. W. Hedrick and R. Hodgson, 127–76. Peabody, MA: Hendrickson, 1986.

Schaff, P. *The Apostolic Fathers with Justin Martyr and Irenaeus*. Grand Rapids: Eerdmans, 2001.

Scheetz, J. "The books of the Bibles in early Christianity." *HTS Teologiese Studies/Theological Studies* 68 (2012) 1–8.

Schleiermacher, F. "Über die Zeugnisse des Papias von unseren ersten beiden Evangelien." *TSK* 5 (1832) 335–68.

Schneemelcher, W. and R. McL. Wilson. *New Testament Apocrypha: Volume 1 Gospels and Related Writings*. Louisville: Westminster, 1991–92.

Schoedel, W. R. *The Apostolic Fathers: Polycarp, Martyrdom of Polycarp, Fragments of Papias* Camden: Nelson, 1967.

———. *Ignatius of Antioch: a commentary on the letters of Ignatius of Antioch*. Philadelphia: Fortress, 1985.

Smith, M. *The Secret Gospel: the Discovery and Interpretation of the Secret Gospel*. New York: Harper and Row, 1973.

Snodgrass, K. R. "The Gospel of Thomas: A Secondary Gospel." *Second Century: A Journal of Early Christian Studies* 7 (1989–1990) 19–38.

Stanton, G. N. "Jesus Traditions and Gospels in Justin Martyr and Irenaeus." In *The Biblical Canons*, edited by J. M. Auwers and H. J. De Jonge, 353–70. BETL CLXIII. Leuven: Leuven University Press, 2003.

———. *The Gospels and Jesus*. Oxford: OUP, 1989.

Stein, R. H. *Mark*. ECNT. Grand Rapids: Baker, 2008.

———. *Studying the Synoptic Gospels: Origin and Interpretation*. 2nd ed. Grand Rapids: Baker Academic, 2001.

Stillman, M. "The Gospel of Peter: A Case for Oral-Only Dependency?" *ETL* 73 (1997) 114–20.

Strobel, A. " Textgeschichtliches zum Thomas-Logion 86 (Mt 8,20/Lk 9,58)." *VC* 17 (1963) 211–24.

Sundberg, A. C. "Canon Muratori: A Fourth Century List" *HTR* 66 (1973) 1–41.

Tacitus, *The Annals of Imperial Rome*. Translated by M. Grant. London: Penguin, 1996.

Tasker, R. V. G. *The Gospel according to St. Matthew*. TNTC. Grand Rapids: Eerdmans, 1961.

Thiessen, G. *The Gospels in Context: Social and Political History in the Synoptic Tradition*. Translated by L. M. Maloney. Minneapolis: Fortress, 1991.

Torrey, C. C. *The Four Gospels: a New Translation*. New York: Harper, 1933.

Tripp, D. "Meanings of the Foot-Washing: John 13 and Papyrus Oxyrhynchus 840." *ExpTim* 103 (1992) 237–39.

Tuckett, C. M. *Nag Hammadi and the Gospel Tradition*. Edinburgh: T & T Clark, 1986.

———. "The *Didache*." In *The Reception of the New Testament in the Apostolic Fathers*, edited by A. F. Gregory and C.M. Tuckett, 83–128. Oxford: OUP, 2005.

Bibliography

———. "The *Gospel of Mary*." In *The Non-Canonical Gospels*, edited by P. Foster, 43–53. London: T & T Clark, 2008.

———. *The Gospel of Mary*. Oxford: OUP, 2007.

———. "Thomas and the Synoptics." *NovT* 30 (1988) 132–57.

Turner, M. L. "On the coherence of the *Gospel according to Philip*." In *The Nag Hammadi Library after 50 years: Proceedings of the Society of Biblical Literature Commemoration*, edited by J. D. Turner and A. McGuire, 223–50. Leiden: Brill, 2007.

Verheyden, J. "The *Shepherd of Hermas* and the Writings that later formed the New Testament." In *The Reception of the New Testament in the Apostolic Fathers*, edited by A. C. Gregory and C. M. Tuckett, 293–330. Oxford: OUP, 2005.

Vielhauer, P. and G. Strecker, "The Gospel of the Ebionites." In *New Testament Apocrypha: Volume 1 Gospels and Related Writings*, edited by W. Schneemelcher and R. McL. Wilson, 166–71. Louisville: Westminster, 1991.

von Harnack, A. *The Date of Acts and of the Synoptic Gospels*. New York: Putnam, 1911.

von Soden, H. *Die Schriften des Neuen Testaments*. Göttingen: Vandenhoeck, 1911, 1913.

Vööbus, A., *Early Versions of the New Testament*. PETSE 6. Stockholm: Estonian Theological Society, 1954.

Walker, P. "A Place for Hebrews? Contexts for a First-Century Sermon." In *The New Testament in Its First Century Setting: Essays on Context and Background in Honour of B.W. Winter on His 65th Birthday*, edited by P. J. Williams, et al., 231–49. Grand Rapids: Eerdmans, 2004.

Webber, R. *Ancient-Future Faith: Rethinking Evangelicalism for a Postmodern World*. Grand Rapids: Baker, 1999.

Wiarda, T. "Peter as Peter in the Gospel of Mark," *NTS* 45 (1999) 19–37.

Williams, D. H. *Retrieving the Tradition and Renewing Evangelicalism*. Grand Rapids: Eerdmans, 1999.

———. *Tradition, Scripture, and Interpretation. A Sourcebook of the Ancient Church*. Grand Rapids: Baker, 2006.

Williams, J. F. *Other Follwers of Jesus: Minor Characters as Major Figures in Mark's Gospel*. JSNTSup 102. Sheffield: Sheffield Academic Press, 1994.

Witherington, B. "Birth of Jesus." In *DJG* 66–69.

———. *The Gospel of Mark: A Socio-Rhetorical Commentary*. Grand Rapids: Eerdmans, 2001.

———. *The Jesus Quest: The Third Search for the Jew of Nazareth*. Carlisle: Paternoster, 1995.

Wright, N. T. *Judas and the Gospel of Jesus: Have we missed the truth about Christianity?* Grand Rapids: Eerdmans, 2006.

Yarborough, R. W. "The Date of Papias: a Reassessment" *JETS* 26 (1983) 181–91.

Index of Scripture, Ancient Texts, and Ancient Authors

OLD TESTAMENT

Genesis
1:1–2:3	121
3	121

Exodus
3:6	84

Numbers
1:1–16	40
5:11–28	119

Deuteronomy
6:5	7

1 Samuel
1–2:10	119

Isaiah
1:16–20	83–84
29:13	81
40:3	7
54:1	95

Ezekiel
8:6	124

Daniel
14:36	124

Zechariah
13:7	80

OLD TESTAMENT APOCRYPHA

4 Ezra
8:3	79
9:15	79

NEW TESTAMENT

Matthew
1:22	8
2:1–16	118
2:2	77
2:15	8
3:3	7
3:13–17	34, 126
3:15	8, 73, 75
3:17	85
4:18	38
4:23	3
4:24–25	3
5:3	81
5:5	69
5:7	80
5:10	25, 81
5:14	25
5:17	8
5:23–24	11

Matthew–continued

Reference	Page
5:26	72
5:28	83
5:29	83
5:32	83
5:39–41	72
5:44	83
5:46–47	71
5:46	83
6	70
6:2–4	25
6:3	25
6:5	70
6:16	69
6:9–13	70
6:9–10	85
6:12	81
6:13	81
6:14	80
6:19–20	83
6:24	22
7:2	80
7:6	25, 69
7:7–11	22
7:7	124
7:12	69, 80
7:13–14	69
7:21	81
7:23	81
8:1–4	3, 127
8:14–15	3
8:16–17	3
8:17	8
9:1–8	3
9:6	7
9:9	37
9:13	80, 83
9:14–17	3
9:20	63
10:1–4	3
10:1	40
10:2–4	40
10:3	37
10:16	25, 73, 81
10:28	81, 96
10:32	81
10:40–41	69
11:4	81
11:25–27	22
11:27	84
11:30	25
12:1–8	3
12:9–14	3
12:15–16	3
12:17	8
12:46–13:58	5
13:20–21	81
13:24–30	25
13:30	81
13:35	8
13:38	81
13:40	81
13:44	25
13:45–46	25
13:47–50	25
15:8	81
15:13	25, 73, 75
16:13–20	4
16:21–23	4
16:24–28	4
16:26	83
17:1–9	4
17:10–13	4
17:14–21	4
17:22–23	4
17:24–27	4, 11, 37
18:1–5	4
18:2	73
18:6–9	4
18:6	81
18:10–14	4
18:15–18	4
18:19–20	4, 73
18:20	25
18:21–22	4
18:23–35	5
18:23–25	37

Index of Scripture, Ancient Texts, and Ancient Authors 157

19:1–2	5
19:3–12	5
19:12	73, 83
19:13–15	5
19:16–22	5
19:18–19	69
19:23–30	5
19:28	40
20:1–16	5, 37
20:17–19	5
20:20–28	5
20:20	45
20:29–34	5
21:32	122
21:46	122
22	10
22:6–7	10
22:14	79
22:15–22	127
22:36–39	69
22:37	7
23:1–39	129
23:13	25
23:16–22	11
23:37–39	22
24	10, 11
24:1–29	10
24:4	69
24:14	79
24:15–18	6
25:14–30	37
26:24	81
26:31	80
26:41	81
27:3–10	37
27:18	6
27:34	80
27:55–56	44
28:1	44
28:11–15	37
28:19	69

Mark

1:3	7
1:9–11	34, 126
1:14–15	38
1:16–17	38
1:21–22	3
1:23–28	3
1:29–31	3
1:32–34	3
1:35–38	3
1:36	39
1:39	3
1:40–45	3, 127
2:1–12	3
2:10	7
2:13–17	3, 37
2:17	81
2:18–22	3
2:23–28	3
3:1–6	3
3:7–12	3
3:13–19	3
3:14	41
3:16–19	40
3:16	38
3:17	8, 86
3:18	37
3:31–6:6	5
4:18–19	81
5:8	6
5:22	43
5:25	63
5:41	8
6:3	117
6:7	40
7:1–23	129
7:6	81
7:11	8
7:13	32
7:15	67
7:34	8
8:2–3	45
8:3	45

Mark–continued

8:27–30	4, 104
8:29	39
8:29–32	39
8:31–33	4
8:34–9:1	4
8:34	9
9:1–8	40
9:2–10	4
9:5	39
9:6	39, 40
9:11–13	4
9:14–29	4
9:30–32	4
9:33–37	4
9:36–37	103
9:38–41	4
9:42–50	4
9:42	81
9:50	67
10:1	5
10:2–12	5
10:11–12	67
10:13–16	5
10:17–22	5
10:19	69
10:23–31	5
10:28	39
10:32–34	5
10:34	139
10:35–45	5
10:46–52	5
12:13–17	67, 127
12:28	43
12:28–31	69
12:30	7
13	8, 9
13:5	69
13:14–16	6
13:14	13
14:21	81
14:22–25	67
14:22	40
14:27–31	40
14:27	80
14:36	8
14:50–54	40
14:66–72	40
15:10	6
15:22	8
15:34	8
15:40	44
15:47	44
16:4	44
16:7	38
16:8	39

Luke

1:1–4	30, 32, 57, 60, 62
1:1–2	30
1:1	138
1:2	32
1:3–4	12, 31, 33
2:41–52	115, 116
3:4	7
3:21–23	126
3:21–22	34
3:23	31
4:31–32	3
4:33–37	3
4:38–39	3
4:40–41	3
4:42–43	3
4:44	3
5:1–11	3
5:12–16	3, 127
5:17–26	3
5:24	7
5:27–32	3, 37
5:32	81
5:33–39	3
6:1–5	3
6:6–11	3
6:12–16	3
6:13–16	40
6:15	37

Index of Scripture, Ancient Texts, and Ancient Authors 159

6:17–19	3	12:8	81
6:20	81	12:13–14	25
6:27	67	12:16–21	25
6:28	83	12:39	67
6:29	67	12:49	25
6:30	83	13:24	69
6:31	69, 80	13:27	81
6:32	71	13:34–35	22
6:34	83	13:35a	13
6:35	71, 80	14:34–35	4
6:36	80	15:3–7	4
6:37	67, 80	16:13	22
6:38	80	17:1–2	4
6:46	81	17:2	81
7:36	43	17:4	4
8:1–3	41	17:11–14	127
8:19–56	5	17:12–19	42
8:29	6	17:20–21	25
8:43	63	18:14	5
9:1	40	18:15	5
9:18–21	4	18:15–17	5
9:22	4	18:18–23	5
9:23–27	4	18:24–30	5
9:28–36	4	18:28–30	40
9:37–43a	4	18:31–34	5
9:43b–45	4	18:35–43	5
9:46–48	4	19:10	81
9:49–50	4	19:20	69
9:51	5	19:33–34	13
9:51–18:14	5	20:20–26	127
10:3	81	21:13	31
10:7	67	21:20–22	6
10:16	84	21:20	13
10:21–22	22	22:19	84
10:27	7	23:5	31
11	70	23:29	25
11:2–4	70	23:39	43
11:4	81	23:49	44
11:9–13	22	23:55	44
11:9	124	24:44–48	31
11:27–28	25		
11:37–52	129		
11:45	43		
12:4–5	81, 96		

John

1:1	35, 86
1:7–8	34
1:7	33
1:9	26, 86
1:14–16	36
1:14	26
1:15	33
1:19	34
1:20	86
1:32–37	33–34
1:32	34
1:34	34
1:40–41	59
1:43	59
1:45–49	59
3:5	83, 86
3:8	77
3:10–13	36
3:26	34
4	76
4:10–14	76
4:13–15	26
5:21	81
5:25	81
5:33	34
5:36	34
5:39–47	127
6:1	14
6:13	76
6:44	81
7:1–52	129
7:32–36	26
8:12	26
8:28	76
8:29	76
9:5	26
10:9	76, 77
10:30–32	127
10:31–39	127
11:16	21, 59
12:1–8	76
13:1–30	129
13:20	76
13:23	60
14:1–6	21
15:26–27	41
18:22	43
18:26	34
18:31–33	13
19:25–27	34
19:34–35	34
19:34	43
20	35
20:19–24	21
20:24–31	21
20:27–28	14
20:30–31	34
21	35
21:1	14
21:2	59
21:19	14
21:21–23	35
21:23	35
21:24–25	35
21:24	35

Acts

1	122
1:1–2	12, 31
1:1	31
1:8	31
1:21–22	31, 41
1:22	31
2:32	31
3:1–4:31	41
3:12–26	95
3:15	31
4:33	31
6:14	32
7	123
8:14–25	41
10:36–42	31–32
10:39	31, 41
10:41	31
13:31	31
14:27	123
15	123

15:20	123
15:29	123
20:18–35	95
27	12
28	12

Romans

1:1	46
12:14	67
12:17	67
12:18	67
13:7	67
14:10	67
14:13	67
14:14	67
16:16	108

1 Corinthians

7:10–11	67
9:14	67
11:2	32
11:23–26	67
11:23	32
15:3	32
15:21–28	109

Galatians

2:13–14	78

Colossians

4:13	48
4:14	61

1 Thessalonians

5:2	67
5:13	67
5:15	67
5:26	108

1 Peter

1:1	46
5:13	48

2 Peter

2:21	32

1 John

1:1–5	36
4:11–16	36

3 John

9–12	36

Jude

3	32

APOSTOLIC FATHERS
49, 67–81, 84, 87, 98, 132, 135, 136

1 Clement
68, 80, 81, 95, 135

Prologue	135
13.2	80
15.2	81
21.6	135
24.1–2	135
32.2	135
42.1–3	135
46.7–8	80
46.8	80
49.6	135
58.2	135
59.2–4	135

2 Clement
49, 67, 68, 81, 95, 96

2.4	81, 96
2.7	81
3.2	81
4.2	81
4.5	81
5.2–4	81, 95, 96
12.2	95
17.3	95

Didache
64, 67, 68, 69–72, 80, 81

1.1	69
1.2	69
1.3–5	71
1.3	71
1.4	71–72
1.5	72
2.2–3	69
3.7	69
5.2–4	81, 95, 96
6.1	69
7.1	69
8.1	69
8.2–3	69–70
9.5	69
11.2–4	69
11.3	70
15.3	70
15.4	70

Epistle of Barnabas
49, 64, 67, 68, 78–80, 81

4.14	79
5.8–9	80
5.12	80
16.3–4	79

Ignatius of Antioch
10, 16, 27, 49, 50, 51, 67, 68, 73–78, 80, 81, 135, 136

Letter to the Ephesians
67, 73, 76

1	136
3.1	73
5.2	73, 76
6.1	76
9.2	50
15.1–2	50
17.1	76
19.1	77

Letter to the Magnesians
67, 73, 76,

2.1	50
6	136
7.1	76
8.2	76
13.1	50

Letter to the Philadelphians
67, 73, 136

1	136
3.1	74
5.1–2	77, 136
7.1	76, 77
7.8	77
8.2	78, 136
9.1	76, 77
9.1–2	78, 136

Letter to Polycarp
67, 73

2.2	73

Letter to the Romans
67, 73

1	136
2.2	73
7.2	76
7.3	76

Letter to the Smyrnaeans
67, 73

1.1	73
1.1b	75
5.1	78
6.1	73
7.2	78

Letter to the Trallians
67, 73

1.1	73
9	136
11.1	74

Index of Scripture, Ancient Texts, and Ancient Authors

Polycarp's Letter to the Philippians
60, 67, 68, 73, 74, 80, 81, 136

2.3	80, 81
5.2	81
6.1–2	81
6.3	136
7.2	81
9	74, 136
12	136

Shepherd of Hermas
49, 64, 67, 68, 81, 89

SIMILITUDES

3.3	81
4.2	81
5.2	81
9.20.1–2	81

VISIONS

3.6.5	81

OTHER EARLY NON-CANONICAL CHRISTIAN WRITINGS

Anti-Marcionite Prologue to Luke
61

Apocryphon of James
18

Athanasius Thirty-Ninth Festal Letter
94, 137

Clement of Alexandria
xix, 9, 14, 47, 60, 95, 96, 106, 117, 123, 124, 137, 139

STROMATA

2.9.45	124
3.19.32	95
7.16.93	117

Didymus the Blind
96, 123, 126

Eusebius
9, 14, 49, 50, 51, 52, 53, 55, 58, 59, 60, 61, 62, 64, 73, 91, 94, 112

ECCLESIASTICAL HISTORY

2.14.6	9
2.15.2	9
3.3	137
3.3.2	112
3.22.1	74
3.22.36	73
3.24.7	14
3.24.15	61–62
3.25	64, 137
3.25.1	64
3.25.1–7	94
3.25.3–5	64
3.25.6–7	64
3.36.1–2	50
3.36.2	74
3.39.1	51
3.39.3–4	51–52, 58
3.39.13	51
3.39.15	53
3.39.16	55
5.8.2	55
5.20.5–6	59–60
6.3.4	138
6.12.1–6	112
6.12.3–6	112
6.14.5–7	60
6.14.6–7	9
6.14.7	14, 60
6.25.3–14	94
6.25.4	55
6.39.5	138

Epiphanius
55, 96, 123, 124, 125, 126

Epiphanius-continued
REFUTATION OF ALL HERESIES
30.3	55
30.13.7–8	125–126

Fayum Fragment
   16, 18, 128, 134

Gospel of the Ebionites
   xvii, 16, 17, 18, 63, 88, 96, 122–126, 134

Gospel of the Egyptians
   18

Gospel of the Hebrews
   xvii, 16, 17, 18, 57, 63, 64, 98, 122–126, 134, 138

Gospel of Judas
   xvii, xviii, xxi, 16, 18, 62, 96, 97, 119–122, 130, 133

1.1	120
1.4	122
2.6–11	120
2.22–26	120–121
10–12	121
12.5–21	121
15.3–16	121
16.1–3	122

Gospel of Mary
   xvii, 16, 17, 18, 62, 63, 105–107, 120, 130, 133

9.21–24	106–7
17.18–20	107

Gospel of Matthias
   138

Gospel of the Nazareans
   16, 17, 62–63, 122–126, 134

Gospel of Peter
   xvii, 1, 16, 17, 18, 20, 27, 28, 62, 64, 95, 97, 98, 112–114, 130, 134, 138

10	112, 113
18	113
25	113–114
28–30	113–114
38–42	112–113
46	113

Gospel of Philip
   xvi, 16, 17, 18, 62, 63, 107–110, 120, 130, 133

55.23–36	109
58.30–59.6	108
63.30–64.5	108
63.29–30	110
64.10–12	110
70.9–22	108–9
70.34–73.8	108
73.1–8	109
73.8–19	109

Gospel of Thomas
   xvi xvii, xix, xx, xxi, 1, 16, 17, 18, 19, 20–28, 62, 63, 64, 95, 96, 100–5, 106, 107, 115, 120, 124, 130, 132, 133, 138

1–2	102
1.1	63
2	124
3	25
5	24
6	25
8	25
9	24, 103
10	25
13	26, 104, 105
14	25
20	25, 103
22	95, 103
24	26
25–26	103
28	26
30	25
32	25

Index of Scripture, Ancient Texts, and Ancient Authors   165

34	25
37	102
38	26
39	25
40	25
50	23
57	25
61	105
62	25
63	25
69a	25
72	25
76	25
77	23, 25, 105
79	25
87	104
90	25
93	25
102	25
109	25
112	104
113	102
114	104

Gospel of Truth
xvi, xix, 16, 17, 18, 62, 97, 110–112, 120, 130, 133

1	110–111
20.24–21.2	111
35.8–14	111–112

Hippolytus
xix

Infancy Gospel of Thomas
xvii, 16, 17, 62, 96, 114–117, 130

2:1–5	115
6	115
8	115, 116
12	115
14	97, 116
19	116
19:3–4	116

Irenaeus
xix, 14, 21, 49, 50, 51, 55, 59, 60, 61, 67, 82, 91–94, 96, 97, 98, 106, 110, 119, 123, 132

AGAINST HERESIES

1.9.4	92
1.20.1	96–97
1.25.1	61
1.26.2	96, 123
1.31.1	96, 119
2	92
2.26.1–2	92
2.27.2	92
3	92
3.1.1–3.1.2	92–93
3.1.1	13, 55, 60
3.1.2	9
3.10.1	92
3.10.5	92
3.11.1	92
3.11.7	96, 123
3.11.8	93–94
3.11.9	94, 97, 110
3.21.3	96, 123
5.1.3	96, 123
5.33.4	51

Jerome
52, 55, 73, 123, 124, 126, 138

COMMENTARY ON MATTHEW

12:13	124–125
27:51	125

ON ILLUSTRIOUS MEN

3	56
18	52

PROLOGUE IN MATTHEW
55–56

PREFACE IN THE FOUR GOSPELS
56

Jewish Christian Gospels
xvii, 122–126, 130, 134

For further references see *Gospel of the Hebrews, Gospel of the Nazareans,* and *Gospel of the Ebionites*

Justin Martyr
xix, 27, 67, 81–87, 88, 91, 97, 98, 106, 132, 135

First Apology
1–29	82
14.1	85
14.4–5	83
15–17	83
15.1	83
15.3	83
26.8	85
30–60	82
42.1	85
44.12	85
44.13	85
45.6	85
46	86
61–68	82
61.3	83, 86
66.3	84, 85
67.3	85

Second Apology
3.6	85
3.8	85
15.3	85

Dialogue with Trypho
2–8	82
9–47	82
17–18.1	84
48–108	82
63	84
88	86, 88
88.3	85
103.8	85, 86

105	87
106.3	97–98
106.4	86
108–142	82

Muratorian Fragment
67, 89–91, 135, 137

Lines 1–32	90

Origen
xix, 47, 55, 73, 94, 96, 117, 123, 124, 126, 137, 138

Commentary on Matt.
10.17	117

Homily on Luke
1:1	138
6	73

Oxyrhynchus Papyrus 840
16, 128–130, 134

1.5	25
1.7	25
1.28	26
654.3	25
654.6	25
655.2	25
655.24	26
655.38	26

Papias' Exposition of the Sayings of the Lord
9, 36, 48–60, 63, 65, 67, 134, 135

Papias Fragments as referenced in Ehrman, The Apostolic Fathers
1	49
3	49
15	49
16	49

Papyrus Egerton 2
　　xvii, 16, 17, 18, 63, 126–128, 130, 134

Philip of Side
　　50, 51

　　FRAGMENTS
　　4.6　　　　　　　　　　　50

Protevangelium of James
　　16, 62, 63, 117–119, 130, 133
　　2–6　　　　　　　　　　119
　　9.2　　　　　　　　　　119
　　19.3　　　　　　　　　118
　　20.1–2　　　　　　118–119
　　20:3–4　　　　　　　　119
　　21.1–22.1　　　　　　118
　　25.1–2　　　　　　　　117

Q
　　xx, 21, 22, 23

Quadratus
　　51

Secret Gospel of Mark
　　16, 17, 139–141

Tatian
　　26, 87–89

　　DIATESSERON 87–89, 135

Tertullian
　　xix, 47, 55, 60, 94

　　AGAINST MARCION
　　4.2　　　　　　　　　47, 55
　　4.3　　　　　　　　　　60

EARLY JEWISH SOURCES

Josephus 31, 33, 47, 53

　　AGAINST APION
　　1.47　　　　　　　　　　33
　　1.55　　　　　　　　　　31

　　JEWISH ANTIQUITIES
　　1.17　　　　　　　　　　53
　　6.196　　　　　　　　　53
　　10.218　　　　　　　　　53
　　14.1　　　　　　　　　　53
　　18.342　　　　　　　　31
　　19.125　　　　　　　　31
　　20.260–63　　　　　　53

　　JEWISH WAR
　　1.18　　　　　　　　　　33
　　7ff　　　　　　　　　　　47

　　LIFE
　　1.47　　　　　　　　　　33

Mishnah

　　M. SHEQALIM
　　5:1　　　　　　　　　　42

Philo
　　53, 137

　　ON MOSES
　　2.34　　　　　　　　　　53

OTHER ANCIENT GREEK AND ROMAN LITERATURE

Apollonius
　　116

Euclid
　　137

Ktisibios
   137

Lucian
   39

Menelaos
   137

Quintilian
   52

Plato
   116, 137

Pliny
   52

Polybius
   52
1.3.1–5	33
1.5.1	33
1.12.5–7	33

Porphyry
   39

Seneca
   52

Tacitus
   9

   ANNALS
15.44	9

www.ingramcontent.com/pod-product-compliance
Lightning Source LLC
Chambersburg PA
CBHW071515150426
43191CB00009B/1535